advertising cultures

Culture, Representation and Identities is dedicated to a particular understanding of 'cultural studies' as an inherently interdisciplinary project critically concerned with the analysis of meaning. The series focuses attention on the importance of the contemporary 'cultural turn' in forging a radical re-think of the centrality of 'the cultural' and the articulation between the material and the symbolic in social analysis. One aspect of this shift is the expansion of 'culture' to a much wider, more inclusive range of institutions and practices, including those conventionally termed 'economic' and 'political'.

Books in the series:

Representing Black Britain
Black and Asian Images on Television
Sarita Malik

Cultural Economy
Cultural Analysis and Commercial Life
Edited by Paul du Gay and Michael Pryke

advertising cultures
gender, commerce, creativity
sean nixon

SAGE Publications

London • Thousand Oaks • New Delhi

First published 2003

 SAGE Publications Ltd
6 Bonhill Street
London EC2A 4PU

SAGE Publications Inc
2455 Teller Road
Thousand Oaks, California 91320

SAGE Publications India Pvt Ltd
B-42, Panchsheel Enclave
Post Box 4109
New Delhi – 100 017

British Library Cataloguing in Publication data

A catalogue record for this book is available from the British
Library

ISBN 0 7619 6197 6
ISBN 0 7619 6198 4 (pbk)

Library of Congress Control Number: 2002109621

Typeset by Mayhew Typesetting, Rhayader, Powys
Printed and bound in Great Britain by Athenaeum Press, Gateshead

contents

acknowledgements

Academic researchers often depend upon the good grace of others in pursuing their research and I am grateful to the advertising people who generously put time aside in their busy schedules to see me and who shared their experience of working in advertising with me. While I cannot thank them by name because of the importance of anonymising their testimonies, they know who they are and I hope they feel that I have done justice to their accounts. Ann Murray Chatterton at the IPA can be thanked by name and was especially generous with her time. The AHRB provided me with support to enable me to complete the book and I thank them for this. I am also grateful to the University of Essex for continuing to believe in the value of academic research and for supporting this through its system of research leave and the Research Promotion Fund.

Versions of chapters of the book were presented at numerous conferences and seminars and I am particularly grateful to audiences at the Department of Sociology and Cultural Studies, University of Birmingham, the MA in History of Design group at the Royal College of Art, the Department of Sociology, London School of Economics, the Centre for Metropolitan History, University of East London, and The Social History Society Annual Conference in York.

Advertising Cultures continues a journey I began with my first book, *Hard Looks*, and many people have accompanied me along the way and helped to share and give direction to my thinking and to the contours of the book. Friends and colleagues in particular have provided wise counsel and intellectual support during the writing of this book and I am especially grateful to Chris Breward, Ben Crewe, Paul du Gay, Stuart Hall, Angela McRobbie, Frank Mort, Keith Negus, Mike Roper and Bill Schwarz. David Rose provided helpful guidance on occupational classifications and self-completion questionnaires. Frank Mort and Angela McRobbie took on the task of reading the final manuscript and both deserve a special mention for their acuity and intellectual generosity and support.

Julia Hall and Jamilah Ahmed at Sage have both been excellent publishers to work with. My parents, Carole and John Nixon have been an important source of continuing support and I remain immensely grateful for that. A final special thank you is due to Claire Nixon. Her wisdom, humour and love have provided the backdrop for this book. It is dedicated to her.

introduction

In April 2000, in its regular end-piece feature 'A life in the day of', the *Sunday Times* magazine documented a typical day in the life of Mark Wnek, the 41 year-old executive creative director of London-based advertising agency Euro-RSCG Wnek Gosper, who had recently been awarded the job of promoting Ken Livingstone's bid to become London Mayor. Written in a punchy diary style, Wnek's account mixed together his views on advertising, creativity and agency life with details of the lifestyle that he pursued in and around work. His account went as follows:

My latest philosophy is that none of us learn enough or give enough. I've given up a lot lately: cigarettes, alcohol, caffeine, dairy products, salt and sugar. And I'm learning to play golf. I'm the most competitive person alive, which means that I apply myself thoroughly to the task, it's like meditation to me. So what if it's selfish? It's a start. Consequently I jump out of bed feeling great. . . . Getting dressed is bish, bash, bosh. Clothes are important to me, because they make a visual statement. I've got 300 shirts and ties at home and another 100 at the office. Every single pair of my underpants is Calvin Klein and my shoes are Gucci, but that's purely because they're comfortable. Giorgio Armani makes clothes for squat Italian blokes and they fit me. These are things that after 20 not-unsuccessful years in the business you get used too.

    I get my washing stuff together and drive to the Harbour Club in my big fat second-hand Mercedes. Then I run on a machine for half an hour. . . . I probably think too much when I'm running – but then I'm a copywriter. My clients pay me to think. I have a blast in the shower, then I drive into work. I like the process to hurt. A little pain and suffering is a good idea. Never mind that I work 300 hours a week – that's irrelevant. I think everyone should do something that hurts.

    The first thing I do is go through my lists, all hand-written from the night before. . . . I speed read all the papers. I'm like a life commando. I've learnt to extract information at breakneck speed. . . . I've got a creative department of 30 people. I assign a brief to a team, and if they don't come up with anything, they get fired. . . . There are two types of creative person: the one who draws upon a reservoir of life stuff, and the other who is simply brilliant. I'm a lot of the former and a touch of the latter. I have never, for one second, been afraid. The moment the fear gets you, you're out. Advertising is what gives society resonance and colour. Without it, we are nothing. That's why it's so important to put stuff out which is clever and witty and makes you think, instead of being blanket-bombed with mind-less crap. Working here is like playing for West Ham – we're a premiership team and there's huge expectation. If you can't cut it, take-up pig farming or something (*Sunday Times Magazines*, 14/4/00: 90).

Mark Wnek's short, but extraordinary, narrative was shot through with a mixture of the banality and self-aggrandisement that often characterised the *Sunday Times* magazine's 'A Life in the Day of' feature and the testimonies of those sections of the metropolitan elite typically represented on its pages. However, it was in other ways, a tantalising little text because of the glimpses that it offered into the personal and professional life of a creative advertising person like Wnek and the social scripts that gave direction to his life. Certainly in this latter regard, his narrative was revealing. In its detailing of his preoccupation with the latest fads in healthy living and lifestyle and his stylistic self-consciousness with regard to how he looked and dressed for work, Wnek's narrative confirmed certain ideas about the modernity of advertising practitioners and their proximity to the most contemporary signs of urban life and consumption not only in the work that they performed, but also in their own lifestyles. A competitive and combative view of the business in which he had made his name was also evident in his account, together with a mode of self-presentation in relation to work that played up the ideal of the workaholic and ruthless advertising manager.

Wnek's narrative was suggestive in other ways. It offered additional insights into his approach to the business of advertising. Notably, it presented him as someone motivated by a positive and optimistic view of the commercial practice in which he was engaged and driven by an ambition to produce advertising that added to the 'colour' of life through its cleverness and style. His account also suggested that this was a commercial practice that rested upon distinctive understandings of the creative people who performed this task and the sources of their creativity – 'reservoir of life stuff' individuals or those who were 'instinctively brilliant', as he put it. In fact, if we push further at this latter theme, we can see in Wnek's whole narrative a delineating of a particular model of the creative person in advertising and their distinctive habitus built around the cultivation of a flamboyant and assertive persona.

Mark Wnek's narrative is an appropriate place to start this book because creative people in advertising and their subjective dispositions and self-dramatisations are who *Advertising Cultures* sets out to examine. The book focuses on the work experiences and attributes of a group of young male art directors and copywriters working for London-based advertising agencies and a group of their female colleagues.[1] It details the identities and motivations that animated and gave direction to their working lives and also sets out to explore the informal cultures in which they worked, as well as tracking these individuals as they moved through the social networks that abutted to the advertising agencies in which they spent so much of their time. There are good reasons for wanting to document these creative cultures and the subjective identities of creative people. As a range of sociological commentators and cultural critics have argued, advertising and the wider commercial field have acquired a new centrality and salience to economic and cultural life in the last decade and a half or so. Certainly, developments within the commercial domain have been central to recent accounts of social and cultural change in Britain, together with much of Western Europe and North America. These changes have often been read in optimistic and epochal terms. Scott, for example, argued that 'the cultural economy ['those sectors that cater to consumers demands for amusement, ornamentation, self-affirmation, social display and so on'] was becoming one of the leading edges of contemporary capitalism' (Scott, 1997: 323, 1999; see also Wernick, 1991; Slater, 1997), while for Lash and Urry (1994) the commercial cultural industries were integral to a shift towards a new era of 'reflexive modernity'. For other commentators still, like Scase and Davis, these sectors of commercial endeavour were paradigmatic of wider developments in economic life that characterised a shift towards greater knowledge and information intensive forms of economic activity (Scase and Davis, 2000; see also Leadbeater, 1999). Less grandiose arguments from within cultural analysis have also confirmed the impact of the world of commercially produced goods and services upon particular social constituents and definitions of the good life through this period, and explored the interweaving of these developments with popular politics and governmental strategy (Hall, 1984; Mort, 1989; du Gay, 1996; Mort, 1996; Nixon, 1996).

Advertising has occupied an important place within these diverse accounts of economic and cultural change and represented a particularly visible marker of the dynamism of commercial society. For a sociologist like Andrew Wernick, it was central to a new phase in the rise of a 'promotional culture', in which more and more areas of life were dominated by the logic of promotion and associated processes of commodification, while for a more prosaic commentator like the business analyst and style watcher Peter York, advertising was an indispensable part of the matrix of metropolitan life, central to the intoxicating confluence of promotion, art, financial markets and government that characterised the recent period of commercial restructuring (Wernick, 1991; York, 1995: 136–64).

Recent policy initiatives have served to foreground the central role of the dynamic sectors of the commercial and associated media industries to processes of social and economic change and renewal. In policy statements, especially those emanating from the Department of Culture, Media and Sport (DCMS) in Britain, emphasis has particularly been upon the forms of creativity and cultural innovation that flow from these sectors and a concern to nurture these currents as part of a project of economic and cultural 'modernisation'. Advertising has figured strongly within this policy rhetoric as well. As the DCMS website proudly proclaimed 'Britain's creativity is flourishing as never before, whether in creative industries like advertising or film, or in the visual and performing arts. Our art, artistry and expertise is valued all over the world' (see also Smith, 1997). Here, then, was a sector (advertising) in which Britain was palpably a 'winner' in the global economy and one which – along with other industries like film, design, digital media, music and architecture – lay close to the beating heart of 'Britain's creativity', itself raised to an aspect of the national character.

Assessments of this order have contributed to a partial upturn in the social fortunes of advertising and specifically to the recognition conferred upon the advertising industry in Britain, with the views of advertising practitioners increasingly courted by the quality press and broadcasters[2] and some advertising people even being awarded high public honours. The cultural recognition evident in these developments is not without its historical precedents and contemporary accounts of the role of the creative and commercial industries have tended to occlude a longer history in which these sectors have been seen as pivotal to the restructuring of liberal western democracies (Mort, 2000). More significantly, the growing recognition conferred upon the industry and arguments about its new salience to economic and cultural life have proceeded with little sustained attention to the inner workings of these worlds of 'creative' work. While some attention has been given to the formal practices, institutional arrangements and types of expertise prevalent within this sector, little remains known about the social make-up of the advertising industry in Britain, its informal cultures or the subjective identities of its key practitioners (Schudson, 1993; Moeran, 1996; Nixon, 1996; McFall, 2002). In the few instances where these cultural intermediaries have been addressed by sociologists, studies have tended to foreground in a general way their role as taste shapers and to consider the social make-up of this group rather abstractly in class terms (Featherstone, 1991; Wynne, 1998; Wynne and O'Connor, 1995).

Cultural critics have also offered generally attenuated accounts of this field of commercial endeavour. Certainly the established approaches that have framed the study of consumption and commercial cultures within cultural studies have tended to privilege consumers and practices of consumption at the expense of a more expanded account of the commercial domain. More or less absent from these accounts has been attention to the work-based cultures of the commercial industries or the cultural resources that its practitioners draw on in living out particular social scripts within this field of commercial activity. The account that I develop over the next seven chapters places these substantive issues at the heart of its concerns and, in so doing, sets out to render more specific the over-general claims about commercial society that contemporary sociologists and cultural critics have been prone to advance.

In working against these established traditions of cultural and socio-logical analysis, my account has been driven by the insistence that much can be gained from foregrounding these previously neglected aspects of the worlds of commercial endeavour. In fact, it is a central contention of the account that follows that opening up the informal cultures and subjective identities of advertising practitioners is an indispensable part of an adequate account of the commercial practices performed by advertising agencies. However, in insisting on this point, my intention is not to reduce the commercial practices of advertising to the subjectivity of its key practitioners or the cultures of agencies. The process of commercial cultural production in which advertising agencies are engaged is highly structured and involves a range of practitioners deploying different kinds of formal knowledge and expertise, as well as the mobilisation of a set of economic and cultural resources, in order to generate promotional materials and associated services for clients. This process, however, is clearly also shaped by more informal factors and judgments, including those bound up with the particular social make-up and subjectivities of key practitioners. It is clear, for example, that informal knowledge possessed by practitioners about the target consumer but not itself present in the market research or planning documentation, can be important in helping agencies to manage the relationship between their clients and consumers. This is especially germane in those markets where the key advertising people – essentially the art directors and copywriters – are culturally close to the target consumer. Furthermore, the cultural identi-fications of practitioners and the wider occupational culture in which they move will both provide resources for and set certain limits to the process of cultural production in which they are engaged. Thus, the subjective dis-positions of key practitioners and the meanings, values and normative assumptions written into their occupational cultures will be important in mediating the process of reaching out to and connecting with consumers. It is this insistence, then, that has prompted me to ask: what is the social make-up of the core advertising jobs? What kind of values do these practitioners hold? What subjective dispositions and attributes animate their working lives? What kind of occupational culture do they work in?

In centre-staging these questions, *Advertising Cultures* is, as I have already indicated, strongly particularistic in its focus as it seeks to break with the problems of overgenerality that have dogged recent sociological and cultural studies accounts of advertising and commercial society. In focusing on a specific set of jobs in advertising and a particular group of advertising people, I further privilege a story about gender and, specifically, masculinity. In this sense it is evident, again, why Mark Wnek's narrative was a particularly appropriate and apposite place to start this book. His account was richly indicative of a certain kind of flamboyant, combative and self-conscious style of masculinity. This surfaced in not only the extravagant tone of his testimony and its choice of wildly gendered metaphors ('I'm a life commando', indeed), but was also present in his investment in a highly contemporary style of masculinity carried through the codes of dress and self-presentation. It is this link between masculinity and creative jobs dramatised in his account that the book centrally explores. Again, there are good reasons for narrowing the focus of the book in this way. One of the areas of commercial provision where advertising practitioners have played a more intensified role in recent years has been in relation to men's markets and the consumption identities of young men. In fact, the industry has been central to the dissemination of new popular representations of masculinity shaped through the repertoires of style and individual consumption from the mid-1980s through to the present. These advertising representations have been key to the consolidation of a new set of masculine identities shaped through the world of commercially produced goods and services. The most notable of these have been the figures of the 'new man' and 'new lad'. It is worth pausing to reflect on the cultural significance of these consumerist masculine scripts. Both the 'new man' and the 'new lad' were characterised by the way they opened up consumer pleasures previously marked as taboo or socially dubious for groups of men and each, in their own way, represented a distinct configuration of a more or less coherent form of post-permissive heterosexual masculinity shaped through this world of goods (see Mort, 1989; Mort, 1996; Nixon, 1996; Nixon, 1997; Nixon, 2001). As I have argued elsewhere, however, there were important differences between these social scripts, even if commentators within the commercial industries themselves typically overplayed them (Nixon, 1996; Nixon, 2001). At its most ruptural, the 'new man' embodied a partial loosening of the binary codes that regulated cultural relations between hetero- and homosexual masculinities. In so doing, it resignified these relations through a more inclusive form of homosociability carried through a blurring of the visual style of gay and straight-identified men (see also Mort, 1996). The 'new lad', on the other hand, represented a certain repositioning of these consumerist masculine scripts against the sexual ambiguities of its precursor and a more trenchant version of heterosexual masculinity shaped around the consumer pleasures of 'cars, girls, sport and booze'. In the case of the 'new lad', then, the predominant ordering of the social rituals of consumption was more exclusively heterosocial.

Both these cultural identities enjoyed a degree of popular legitimacy and recognition that suggested that they were connected with the felt movements of the culture of groups of young men over the last 15 years or so. Of the two identities, the figure and idea of the 'new lad' and its distinctive idioms have enjoyed the more prodigious currency from the mid-1990s through to the present. So-called 'loaded ladspeak', derived from the men's magazine, *Loaded*, that dominated the market for young men's magazines in the mid-late 1990s, was excitedly taken up – to be enjoyed as well as disparaged – by the broadsheet press and other parts of the media, including advertising agencies. Certainly, the idioms of 'ladspeak' and its ironic celebration of masculine juvenility provided an important shorthand for advertising agencies concerned with targeting these lucrative young male markets (see *Independent on Sunday*, 3/9/95: 10; *Guardian*, 26/2/96: 14–15; *Campaign*, 11/10/96: 40–1; 1/11/96: 27).

What is striking, given the extensive interest in these shifting masculine scripts from both popular and academic commentators from the mid-1980s through to the present, is that little remains known about the gender cultures within the commercial industries – including advertising – that have mediated the production and circulation of these new masculine identities. In fact, the gender cultures of the advertising industry and the gender identities of its key people have remained more or less invisible. Exploring these issues is especially pertinent in relation to the ad men central to *Advertising Cultures*. Art directors and copywriters occupy a pivotal place within the processes of cultural production that have underpinned the new representations of masculinity and it is clear, as I have already insisted, that their own cultural knowledge and dispositions can exert a particularly strong informal influence over the finished adverts. The art directors and copywriters whom I focus upon in the book were all aged between 25–38 years of age and had started, or were establishing their careers in the mid-1990s, at a point when advertising's interest in young male markets was at a particularly high level. As such, they were close in age to the male consumers subject to this sustained commercial interrogation and it is their relationship to these shifting codes of masculinity carried through the forms of gendered commerce in which they were involved that the book sets out to explore. In doing so, I do not detail the relationship between the advertising creatives whom I interviewed and the specific campaigns that they worked on. The book has been constrained by ethical considerations concerning the need to anonymize their testimonies and the concern to avoid including material that would make them easily identifiable. None the less, I do make some specific claims about the relationship between the subjective identities and informal cultures of these practitioners and the advertising and promotion they were engaged in producing. To this end, *Advertising Cultures* centrally asks the following questions: What were the informal gender cultures in which these advertising men worked? What cultural resources did they draw on in living out particular gender identities at work? What scope did this field of commercial endeavour offer for living out distinctive forms of masculinity? How, in short, was gender written into the creative cultures of advertising and into the subjective identities of its creative practitioners? In Part 3 of the book, I turn centrally to these questions and explore the informal cultures of the creative departments in which the practitioners worked and detail the kinds of gender identities privileged within these cultures. I push at the social scripts the men I interviewed drew upon and elucidate some of the tensions and inner conflicts that shaped these men's subjective investments in this world of creative work.

Advertising Cultures is not only a book about gender. The question of creativity also looms large. Much of the reason for advertising's improved cultural standing in Britain has been bound up with assessments – or perhaps better, reassessments – of the 'creativity' of British advertising and the emergence of London as a centre of 'creative excellence' within the global advertising and marketing industry.[3] In this regard, the configuring of advertising as a 'creative industry' within the DCMSs policy statements represents but one instance of a wider celebration, dominant within the industry itself since the late 1980s, of the 'creativity' of London-based agencies. Significantly, this configuring of the industry's identity was not unrelated to advertising agencies more expanded involvement in young male markets. Style and lifestyle products aimed at young men offered scope for the development of a more image-led form of advertising upon which the industry's reputation for 'creativity' often rested. And while other markets and product fields were also implicated in these developments, the public profile of campaigns aimed at young men was not inconsequential in informing the reputation for 'creativity' enjoyed by London-based agencies.[4] The practitioners central to this book were implicated in this valorizing of creativity in very particular ways. They were often seen as an agency's most prized assets and as being the key sources of creativity within the processes of cultural production that agencies performed. Moreover, it was their expertise and skill, together with the peculiarities of their training, which was seen to lay behind the reputation acquired by the London-based industry as a centre of 'creative excellence'. In Part 2 of the book, I explore the currency of ideas about creativity within the occupational cultures in which these practitioners worked and reflect on the place of the rubric of creativity within their own sense of themselves as creative people.

Central to these chapters and the account of the occupational ethos and identity of these young ad men that I develop is a sustained reflection on the idea of creativity itself. The word, as will already be evident, looms large throughout the story I tell. Clarifying its meanings is essential to my arguments. The term figures, firstly, as a noun, creative, to collectively describe the jobs of art director and copywriter. When I talk of creatives or creative jobs or creative people, then, I am simply referring to this functional distinction. But there are also broader and more slippery conceptual issues bound up with the idea of creativity. As has been well documented, the term has emerged as something of a cant word in recent years. Its appropriation within government policy and the statements of the DCMS that we have already encountered represent only one version of its expanded currency and field of application. Particularly important within this process has been the way ideas of creativity have figured within prescriptive management literature and accounts of organisational reform. Within this body of writing, the idea of creativity has typically been bound up with the broader 'cultural turn' within management thinking and it is the links between organisational cultures and worker's creativity that has often loomed large in programmes of organisational re-engineering (du Gay, 1996). This pre-scriptive literature has typically deployed the idea of creativity to denote a general human capacity or disposition for invention, novelty and newness. In this regard, it forms part of a more widespread cultural process by which the idea of creativity has moved away from what Raymond Williams defined as 'exclusivist' definitions in which it was associated with a capacity for 'originality' and 'innovation' among a small group of gifted individuals, towards 'inclusivist' accounts that attribute the quality to a whole host of activities and (working) practices (Williams, 1976: 82–4). For Williams, there were dangers evident in this broadening out of creativity's semantic reach. Preeminent among these was his concern that the expanded field of application of the idea of creativity had eroded the conceptual value of the term. As he noted, a term that was once meant to 'embody a high and serious claim' about the value of particular kinds of human practice, 'has become so conventional . . . that it is applied to practices for which, in the absence of the convention, nobody would think of making such claims. Thus, any imitative or stereotyped literary work can be called, by con-vention, 'creative writing' and advertising copywriters officially describe themselves as 'creative' (Williams, 1976: 84).

Williams' comments are instructive and prompt the kind of clearing of the ground regarding the conceptual reach of the idea of creativity, parti-cularly in relation to advertising, that I undertake in Part 2. Certainly, the term is rendered especially opaque within the occupational cultures of advertising and exploring its currency and multiple uses within these cultures necessities some definitional labour. In doing so, I draw upon Keith Negus' suggestive arguments about creativity developed in his work on popular music (Negus, 1995; 1998). At the heart of Negus' arguments is a concern to see claims about creativity (of a certain practice or cultural form) as highly context-dependent and shaped by value judgments in which recognition is conferred upon (or denied to) certain degrees of novelty or difference. Negus suggests that judgements about creativity are typically less to do with questions of absolute novelty or originality as with the way cultural practices or forms introduce some element of novelty or difference into a recognisable field of meaning. It is this mixture of familiarity and difference that discussions about creativity typically focus on and it is the small degrees of 'differentness' that are the subject of intense debate. This emphasis is also related to an insistence that debates about creativity are always local to specific fields of representation or domains of cultural practice and are not best thought of through the idea of creativity as the unfolding of a general human capacity that exists across all social fields or compartments of existence. More than that, debates about creativity are always informed by struggles over the authority of certain institutions or social actors to confer recognition upon a cultural practice or form and include the tensions between groups of protagonists to legitimate certain kinds of difference and novelty.

In Part 2, I explore how the practitioners I interviewed deployed the language of creativity and how it was bound up with their own attempts to legitimate the cultural practices they performed. Part 2 also explores the place of the rubric of creativity within the collective, institutional life of the industry and draws out the way the term was deployed by agencies and their corporate representatives to delineate the kinds of expertise offered by agencies to clients. Looming large here is an attention to the way a configuring of the identity of agencies as 'creative businesses', and the wider industry as a 'creative industry', was bound up with the moves by these businesses to consolidate a clearer sense of their commercial role. In developing this argument, I flesh out a picture of the London-based industry during the mid to late 1990s. This was a period of change and uncertainty for the agency sector shaped by both the legacy of the economic recession of the early 1990s and more deep-rooted changes in the commercial environment in which they worked. Creative people were caught up in the dislocations of agency life that flowed from these externals pressures on agencies in very particular ways and it is both the nature of these dislocations and their effects on the status and organisation of creative jobs that Part 2 – and specifically, Chapters 2 and 3 – explore.

At the heart of the account that I develop in *Advertising Cultures*, as will already be clear, are the testimonies of the group of young ad men whom I interviewed and their female colleagues. Weaving my account of the creative cultures of agencies around these narratives has raised a specific methodological question that is worth commenting on briefly. This concerns the status of their narratives and how I have read them. My primary concern throughout has been to pay close attention to the language and metaphors they used and the associated modes of expression that they deployed, as much as it has been to document the directly factual content of their statements.[5] These former dimensions were revealing in terms of their subjective identities. In many instances, then, the practitioners said more than they intended to when talking about colleagues, working partners and the mundane routines of the job. These dimensions of their accounts were especially important in offering ways into the kinds of masculinity lived by the men I interviewed. It was how their gender identities showed themselves when they were substantively talking about something else that interested me. I have also attempted to be attentive to those moments in their accounts where certain things were not said (could not be said), as much as what was said and it is the absences in their testimonies that I also read in terms of what this might tell us about their gender identities.

The interviews were not, however, only revealing in terms of the talking that took place. The non-verbal dimensions were also important and I have been attentive to how the practitioners interacted with me more broadly through ways of sitting and other corporeal dispositions. Their gender also showed itself in how they dressed and presented themselves in visual terms and I registered this aspect by keeping a photographic record of the men and women I interviewed.

There is a further dimension at stake here in the interpretation of the practitioners' narratives and associated forms of self-presentation. This derives from the social relations of the research process. What the practitioners said and how they presented themselves was palpably produced in part by my promptings and their relationship to me was inevitably a key part of the dynamic that shaped what they said and how they expressed themselves. As is clear from the testimonies that animate the arguments of the book, the conversations that I had with the practitioners were often the setting for a sustained process of self-reflection by them. In this sense, the interviews often exemplified Pierre Bourdieu's contention that 'respondents see interviews as opportunities to explain themselves, that is, to construct their own point of view both on themselves and on the world. Thus, we might speak of an induced and accompanied self-analysis' (Bourdieu, 1996: 24). A recurrent element of this self-analysis was a concern to defend themselves and their work (their jobs) from a denigrating view of advertising that they appeared to read off from my status as an academic researcher. In this sense, their perception of me as potentially hostile to, or at the very least condescending towards, advertising sharpened and prompted a particular set of self-reflections organised around the cultural standing of advertising. It is this question of the cultural standing of advertising, in fact, that looms large throughout this account. This had both occupational and gendered dimensions for the practitioners and how they handled these forms a central, recurring theme of the book. In this sense, it is the subjective consequences for these practitioners of working in this commercial field that connects Parts 2 and 3 of the book.

Before turning in detail to the occupational culture and the subjective identities of these creative people, however, it is appropriate to spell out further the conceptual arguments that have shaped the distinctiveness of the book and to delineate how its approach to advertising differs from other influential accounts of advertising and commercial society. It is to these arguments that I want to now turn.

advertising, cultural intermediaries and cultural analysis

part 1

advertising and commercial culture

Recent accounts of social and cultural change across the industrialised West generated from within the human and social sciences have made much of the increasing centrality of consumption and the consumer economy to the ordering of economic and cultural life. Within the sociological literature this process has often been characterised in epochal terms as variously marking the birth of a 'consumer society', 'postmodern culture' or the passage to an era of 'liquid modernity' (inter alia, Jameson, 1984; Baudrillard, 1988; Harvey, 1989; Featherstone, 1991; Wernick, 1991; Slater, 1997; Bauman, 2000). Other sociologists and sociologically-informed commentators have cast these processes in more prosaic terms, preferring to describe the emergence of more information and knowledge intensive forms of flexible accumulation and economic activity (Hirst and Zeitlin, 1991; Leadbeater, 1999; Scase and Davis, 2000). Whatever the formulation, commercial expertise and the world of commercially produced goods and services are seen to have acquired a new centrality and salience. At the same time, an extended attention within historical and cultural studies to the symbolic meanings of commodities and commercial texts, together with their place within the cultures of consumption of particular social groups, has served to draw attention to the worlds of commerce and to the institutions and social actors that constitute this area of cultural and economic endeavour.

In this chapter, I want to reflect quite selectively on some of these heterogeneous arguments. There is good reason for this. Taken as a whole, this body of work has provided a major impetus for the account of the informal workplace cultures of advertising developed in this book. At its best this range of work has furnished us with impressive accounts of the impact of commercial society and commercial players at both the level of societal organisation and at that of more intimate subjective desires. Significantly, however, my own account has been as strongly shaped by disagreements with some of the substantive foci and broader conceptual frameworks of much of this work, particularly as this has borne upon the analysis of advertising, as it has by more positive engagements. At the heart of this are two principle lines of disagreement. First, the over-general and epochal nature of the models of cultural change into which advertising (and commercial culture more broadly) have frequently been inserted, particularly in sociological and historical work, has been a major stumbling block for my arguments. Second, the dominant narratives on consumption within cultural studies have been problematic. These have tended to either subsume the particular ensemble of institutions making up 'commercial society' into the general rubric or idea of 'consumption' or else privileged studies of acts of consumption and the identities of consumers at the expense of a more expanded account of the commercial field.

Getting beyond the limitations of both these sets of arguments has prompted me to consider the conceptual frames through which advertising might be better understood. Drawing upon my earlier work and the suggestive insights of others, I propose that advertising can be profitably conceptualised within the more general framework or idea of 'commercial culture'. The term draws upon the closely related notions of 'consumer culture' and 'consumer society', but can be differentiated from them in the way it seeks to downplay the overly synthetic and epochal bias of those terms and the singular logic of commercialism with which they work. In place of this the idea of 'commercial culture' as I deploy it emphasises the differentiated and multiple forms through which commercial relations and cultures are articulated. It proposes, in other words, that there is no general, universal logic of consumer culture or commercial society (despite the universalising tendencies of commercial relations), but instead only specific commercial cultures. In doing so, it directs us towards the potentially diverse array of institutions, forms of knowledge and expertise making up this social field and the subjective processes constituted through the world of commerce and commodities. The idea of 'commercial culture' also insists on the importance of grasping the generative relations with wider economic, political and cultural formations into which commercial processes are drawn within particular historical settings. Above all, the aim is to establish 'commercial culture' as a discrete object of analysis, one through which advertising might be more effectively explored.

In the first part of the chapter, I reflect on a number of influential accounts drawn from contemporary sociological analysis. I focus on three ambitious analyses in particular: Scott Lash and John Urry's *Economies of Signs and Space* (Lash and Urry, 1994), Scase and Davis's *Managing Creativity* (Scase and Davis, 2000) and Featherstone's *Postmodernism and Consumer Culture* (Featherstone, 1991). I then move on to consider the way advertising and consumption have figured within cultural and historical studies and discuss some of the general features of this work. Finally, I conclude by elaborating further on the idea of 'commercial culture' that informs the arguments that I develop throughout the book.

advertising and the end of industrial society   One of the most widely cited and ambitious accounts of contemporary social and cultural change produced over the last decade is Lash and Urry's *Economies of Signs and Space* (Lash and Urry, 1994). The book offers a bold vision of the role to be played by a re-invigorated sociology shorn of the narrow preoccupations of its classical past and focused upon the mapping of global flows of information, commodities and people. Lash and Urry take as their starting point the dynamic impact of the more intensive processes of com-modification associated with the emergence of 'disorganised capitalism'. This is a capitalism increasingly organised on a global scale in which commodities, capital and human subjects circulate over greater distances and at greater speed, underpinned in large part by new information and communication structures. Alongside these global flows, Lash and Urry also identify a set of countervailing tendencies that have contributed to the distinctiveness of contemporary social formations. These derive from the increased possibility for human agency and reflexivity thrown up by the new social order ushered in by 'disorganised capitalism'. It is this mixture of both high speed global flows and new forms of reflexivity that form the lynchpin of their account and which lie at the heart of their ambition to develop a 'sociology of flows' and 'reflexivity'. Both these concerns are brought together in the central idea that drives their account. This is the idea of 'reflexive modernisation'. Lash and Urry derive the term from the work of Ulrich Beck and share with him a concern to periodise a new phase or stage of modernity – what Beck calls 'reflexive modernity' or what Giddens defines as 'high modernity' (in Beck, Giddens and Lash, 1994: 91) or sometimes 'late modernity'. In fact, it is Lash and Urry's recourse to and elaboration of the concept of reflexive modern-isation that does much to distinguish their account from other contemporary arguments about economic and cultural globalisation with which it other-wise shares much common ground (Robins, 1996).

For Lash and Urry, reflexive modernisation refers to those social processes that are dissolving the contours of industrial society. Reflexive modernisation in this sense represents the progressive deepening of modern-ity's corrosive powers and, in Beck's terms, the 'radicalisation of modernity, the creation of a new modernity' (Beck, 1994: 75 cited in Beck, Giddens and Lash, 1994). A notable feature of this process is the way social subjects – individuals – are freed from the collective structures of industrial society; freed, that is, from the structures of class, family and work-based forms of collective organisation (Lash and Urry, 1994: 37). It is this 'freeing' of social subjects from 'social structure' that forces individuals to take more respon-sibility for the conduct of their lives and to reflect upon the contingency of their social existence. In other words, it is the 'freeing' of individuals that provides some of the necessary conditions for reflexivity.[1]

Lash and Urry have most to say about how this process of reflexive modernisation works in relation to economic life. Their attention to what they call the progressive 'freeing of agency from structure' within this domain is especially germane for my arguments. This is because they give the cultural industries, and advertising in particular, a paradigmatic role in the emergence of new forms of reflexivity at work. At the heart of these changes within economic life lies the consolidation of what they call 'reflexive accumulation'. Reflexive accumulation refers to the increasing dominance within Western economies of more knowledge and information intensive forms of economic activity both within the manufacturing sector and within the burgeoning service sector.[2] They use the term to distinguish their claims from similar arguments that have described the same kind of transformations within economic life under the rubric of flexible specialisation or post-fordism. For Lash and Urry these other conceptualisations are limited because they fail to grasp both the increasing importance of services to Western economies and, more importantly, the defining feature of reflexive accumulation: the increasing penetration of economic life by culture. As they emphatically put it, reflexive accumulation refers to the way 'the economy is increasingly culturally inflected and that culture is more and more economically inflected' (Lash and Urry, 1994: 64). Underpinning this claim is an assertion that economic activity – including manufacturing processes – are more design and research and development intensive, and more concerned with the production and deployment of knowledge, images and aesthetic symbols. One consequence of these developments is that workers within key economic sectors are required to be more innovative and creative, able to initiate ideas rather than be guided by rigid rules and divisions of labour; required, in a word, to be more reflexive. Whilst Lash and Urry do acknowledge that this process is not universal and that there are 'reflexivity winners and losers', they see increased reflexivity at work as characteristic of the leading edge of economic activity. In further exploring the distinctiveness of these forms of reflexivity at work, Lash and Urry devote a good deal of space to the cultural industries. These sectors are important to their argument because they represent the most advanced cases of individualisation and reflexivity at work and provide the model upon which other sectors are developing. Thus, they argue that the cultural industries have long been innovation and design intensive and the sectors in which the labour process has been most rapidly reconstituted around the ideas of flexibility and individualisation. This is evident in the way these industries have led the way, they contend, in developing organisational structures that have broken from the forms of vertical integration and bureaucratic organisation that characterised earlier forms of industrial organisation. Further, they argue that the cultural industries are increasingly organised around the ownership and control of intellectual property rights and less around control over the production of cultural forms. Their economic success derives from the packaging and presentation of a portfolio of assets: artists, images and sounds. In this sense, Lash and Urry contend, the cultural industries are becoming less like 'industrial commodity producing firms . . . [and] more like post-industrial firms such as business services' (Lash and Urry, 1994: 137). More like, in fact, as they suggest, the advertising industry. It is this expertise in packaging, promotion and branding that gives the advertising industry its new exalted position within the political economy of 'disorganised capitalism'. For Lash and Urry, the advertising industry not only contributes to the increasing 'culturalising' of goods and services characteristic of reflexive accumulation (and through this the wider aestheticisation of everyday life), but is paradigmatic of trends occurring within the cultural industries and the wider economy as a whole in which control over knowledge and information are more central to economic success. There is also an inference in Lash and Urry's account that advertising agencies represent models of business organisation and ways of working that are themselves emblematic of wider organisational restructuring, though their comments on agency structures are, as I suggest below, eccentric.

In privileging the role of advertising and the cultural industries more generally in their account of a transition from the epoch of industrial society to 'reflexive modernity', Lash and Urry's argument chimes with a range of other contemporary sociological accounts in which the consumer and cultural industries have loomed large. Like these other accounts – particularly of Baumann, Wernick, Harvey, and Scott – the strength of their book lies both in its ambitious sweep and in the more mundane descriptive fit between its account of changes in economic life and widely reported trends in ways of working, workplace organisation and the growing importance of the media and cultural industries to Western economies (see Pratt, 1997; Smith, 1997; Leadbeater, 1999). However, there are significant problems with both the general account of reflexive modernisation that Lash and Urry advance and the particular argument that they develop about the cultural industries. Let us take the idea of reflexive modernisation first. Lash and Urry deploy the term in part to distinguish their work from the closely related debates about modernity and postmodernity. As Lash acknowledged, it was out of a sense of frustration with this latter debate that they were prompted to find a different language and conceptual framework for making sense of contemporary cultural and social change (Lash in Beck, Giddens and Lash, 1994). Their recourse to the idea of reflexive modernisation, however, represents only a very partial break with the tropes of the modernity/postmodernity debate in that the term (reflexive modernisation) follows the same epochal model of change. The style of argument and conceptualisation is similar in both cases. The account is structured around a 'before' and 'after' dualism in which the characteristics of competing eras or epochs are captured by recourse to a limited range of defining features. As Thomas Osborne has argued in relation to other kinds of epochal change theories, such accounts 'tend to overdramatise the characteristics of social change and reduce such change to one or two fundamental elements' (Osborne, 1998: 19). He suggests that ideas like 'postmodernisation' or the 'information society' or – I would add – 'reflexive modernisation' – are 'gestural categories' not amenable to sustained empirical evidencing. Certainly, Lash and Urry's argument in *Economies of Signs and Space* is poorly evidenced and tends toward the use of illustrations rather than sustained evidence. Their argument is repeatedly couched in terms of generalisations and a reductive model of social and cultural change.

These problems are particularly acute in relation to the central idea of reflexivity itself. As we have seen, the term functions in their argument as an integral component of a new epoch of human social organisation. However, in casting reflexivity in these terms, Lash and Urry are guilty of over-generalising some rather specific (if undoubtedly widespread) processes of cultural change. Thus, if we take the area of economic life, it is clear that the increasing importance of 'reflexivity' at work (for some managers and groups of workers at least) is a product of particular processes of organisational reform that have sought to shape workers as autonomous, self-regulating individuals (du Gay, 1996; 2000: 64). These are moves distinct from those employed to open up personal relations and family life, for example, to a greater degree of choice and ethical reflection. In no way can these distinct developments across discrete social domains be reduced in an *a priori* way to some general notion of reflexivity. As Paul du Gay's work on organisational reform has demonstrated, these developments are the product of specific technologies and practices. The extent to which they are generalisable within the limited arena of economic life is also open to question. The depth and extent of the impact of these moves to foster 'reflexivity' at work needs to be tested and may vary from sector to sector and between organisations within the same sector. This is certainly the case, as we will see, in relation to advertising.

These problems with the idea of 'reflexive modernisation' are further compounded by some of the specific, concrete things Lash and Urry have to say about trends in the media and cultural industries. We have seen how they want to place great store on developments in these industries as prefigurative of wider processes of economic restructuring, particularly as regards ways of working and the 'outputs' of this work (information, knowledge, cultural representations). While these developments correspond to their arguments about reflexive modernisation within economic life, they also make use of the notions of fordism and post-fordism to explain changes in these sectors. Their deployment of these terms is a little confusing given that elsewhere they problematise them in favour of the idea of reflexive modernisation. None the less, they are emphatic in deploying the terms indicatively to refer to changes in the structuring of organisations and production processes within the cultural industries and suggest, for example, that the 'culture industries were post-Fordist *avant la lettre*' (Lash and Urry, 1994: 122–3; see also 113 and 134). The deployment of the terms Fordism and post-Fordism to these sectors couldn't be more unhelpful. Neither the model of Fordist mass production nor that of post-Fordism are directly applicable to the media and cultural industries. The film industry is the sector that has been most frequently fitted into these boxes – Lash and Urry, in fact, draw heavily upon Christopherson and Storper's well known account of Hollywood (Christopherson and Storper, 1989). Even Hollywood film production in the era of the studio system is not best understood through the model of industrial organisation derived from the manufacture of consumer goods. While the studio system may have displayed many of the features of vertical integration characteristic of fordist enterprises, film as a cultural form was not (and indeed, is not) amenable to the kind of product standardisation associated with mass production. Further, film production was not caught up in the drive to produce ever more complex machines that defined the classic Fordist sectors. The Hollywood studios may have worked to produce a relatively stable set of genre films and broadly conceived of its audience within the rubric of the mass market and in both senses been drawn into a wider culture of 'mass production', but film production was not, *per se*, Fordist. This is an important distinction to hold onto.

Similarly, contemporary developments in film production do not neatly fit the claims that it has become post-Fordist. As Helen Blair has shown, the persistence of semi-permanent film production work groups within the UK forces a recasting of general claims about the impact of 'vertical disintegration' within the sector (where vertical disintegration is seen as classic evidence of post-Fordist organisation). The peculiarities of the domestic film industry – which historically had a more fragmented production base than Hollywood and was made up of a large independent sector alongside studios like Rank – also problematises the idea that the UK film industry can be fitted into the model of a transition from 'Fordism' to post-Fordism. Furthermore, some of the most distinctive features of recent changes within this sector do not neatly follow this pattern of economic change. These include the increasing dominance of large companies over the distribution of film (despite the rise of independent production) and their transformation into global conglomerates that act as 'image empires' across a range of media (Blair and Rainmie, 2000: 191).

The general problems with these models of economic restructuring are additionally compounded by some specific shortcomings with Lash and Urry's account of advertising. In a dizzying formulation they claim that 'advertising in effect evolves from a free-professional type business service to, in Fordism, an industry and, in post-Fordism, to a fully-fledged 'culture industry' (Lash and Urry, 1994: 138). The British industry, they contend, became from the late 1970s 'simultaneously Fordist and neo-Fordist' (ibid: 139). Such formulations do great damage to the organisational structures and institutional forms that have historically characterised the advertising industry in Britain. As I suggest later, the advertising industry in Britain is a distinctively bifurcated sector split between a smallish number of large, often multinational, businesses and a larger number of small enterprises. This is a pattern of sectoral diversity that goes back to the inter-war years at least. The business forms that have dominated throughout this history among the great swathe of agencies (and which continue to be important) are the partnership and limited company. These represent forms of commercial organisation that have a long history, both being legally consolidated by the Companies Act of 1862. Many contemporary advertising agencies in this sense would not have looked out of place in nineteenth century London. Alongside these small scale enterprises, the big agencies have typically developed by building bureaucratised organisations, with well defined ways of working (often embodied in organisational handbooks). While in this sense large agencies were, and remain, bureaucratic in structure, they are not (and were not) 'Fordist' or neo-Fordist, unless the terms are expanded to meaningless limits. Moreover, the large global agency networks that have emerged from within the British industry in the last twenty years have recurrently organised themselves as holding companies, itself an old business form dating back to the establishment of the first multinational companies. In many ways, then, the advertising industry in Britain does not fit into the models of industrial change that Lash and Urry deploy. Their account offers an unhelpful characterisation of the sector that cuts across a more nuanced sense of the institutional and organisational structures of the industry.

Some of the shortcomings of *Economies of Signs and Space* are addressed in a book that could not be more different from it in terms of style of argument and approach. Rooted in the tradition of empirical sociology, Scase and Davis's *Managing Creativity* develops a more grounded account of trends within what they call the 'creative industries'. It too, however, has ambitious claims to make about the place of these sectors in wider processes of economic change; claims that, in this regard, echo strongly Lash and Urry's general arguments despite the differences in approach between the two books. Similarly to Lash and Urry, Scase and Davis are interested in long term trends that are transforming Western economies and identify the increasing dominance of knowledge, information and science-based areas of employment within the West as part of a broader global realignment in which manufacturing goods production shifts to the 'Tiger' economies of South-East Asia (Scase and Davis, 2000: iii). They contend that what they call the 'creative industries' (the media and cultural industries) are at the 'leading edge of the movement towards the information age [as] their outputs are performances, expressive work, ideas and symbols rather than consumer goods or services' (ibid: 23). In particular, they claim that it is the requirement of workers within these sectors to exercise intellectual and creative skills that makes them paradigmatic of broader changes in economic life. While they acknowledge that plenty of occupations continue to rely upon their workers engaging in repetitive and routine tasks (such as important growth areas in the UK like call-centre operators), they argue that the demand for workers to work creatively ('to think the unthinkable, to be original') become more important in this shift to an information society (ibid: vii). It is this broader recomposition of work that gives the 'creative industries' their new significance to the economy.

While these contentions strongly echo Lash and Urry's arguments, Scase and Davis's claims are more particularistic in focus and more carefully grounded in empirical evidence. One of the strengths of the book, in fact, consists of the supporting evidence that they bring to bear on their arguments. Part of this concerns a more informed account of the make-up of the 'creative industries', including some assessment of the numbers of individuals employed in these areas of work (ibid: 32–4). At a more conceptual level, Scase and Davis are also concerned to challenge the appropriateness of those models of economic restructuring associated with Fordism/post-Fordism to the 'creative industries' that I have just discussed. Importantly, they suggest that historically there have been limits to the impact of processes like vertical integration within the creative industries arising from the uncertainties of cultural production itself. As they note, the core cultural producers in these sectors have often been – and continue to be – only weakly integrated into the larger organisations that tend to dominate these fields of cultural production. These core workers are often linked by agents and short-term associations, or else operate in partnerships or small businesses. As a consequence self-employment and small-scale enterprises represent important economic structures within this area of cultural activity (ibid: 37).

Scase and Davis are also concerned to draw out the differences between the companies that constitute the creative sector. They delineate four general ideal type kinds of organisation: the commercial bureaucracy, which are large scale, hierarchical organisations within the private sector with well defined job descriptions and formalised mechanisms of control; the cultural bureaucracy, large scale hierarchical organisations in the public sector (they cite the BBC as an example); traditional or charismatic organisations, by which they mean small businesses run by owner-managers, with tacit understandings about the division of labour and weakly formalised structures and ways of working; and network organisations, which are either self-employed individuals or very small companies with little or no formalised control and coordination mechanisms (they cite the example of independent television companies) (ibid: 98–100).

Scase and Davis argue that these models cut across the creative industries and can apply to different companies within the same sector. They make good use of these distinctions in their comments on the advertising industry and offer, for example, a relatively nuanced sense of the differences between large agencies as commercial bureaucracies and those small agencies as traditional organisations. They are also particularly good at drawing out the way work is organised in small companies. As they suggest, 'the conduct of work tasks are based on informal procedures, personal negotiations and team working. In these circumstances, the organisation operates as a constellation of projects and processes with loosely defined and continually fluctuating parameters' (ibid: 51). While this formulation tends to downplay the division of labour that continues to exist within even small agencies between core practitioners, it none the less points to something important in the structuring of these small advertising enterprises.

Scase and Davis's account, then, in its concreteness and attention to specificity has much to offer as a corrective to the more grandiose claims of Lash and Urry. However, their argument is not without its own problems. There are two central dimensions to this. The first concerns a problem we have already encountered with *Economies of Signs and Space* and derives from the epochal model Scase and Davis invoke in attaching their insights about the creative industries to a grander argument about the coming of an 'information society'. The idea of 'information society' that they mobilise suffers from those shortcomings noted earlier in relation to the idea of 'reflexive modernisation'. Rather than attend to the 'specificity of the present', as Thomas Osborne recommends, Scase and Davis slide into a dualistic model of cultural change.

The second problem with their argument concerns the analytical limitations that arise from constructing ideal type models from empirical evidence and then attempting to place organisations within them. While they acknowledge that individual organisations will always be hard to precisely place within these models and remain dynamic and changing entities, the decision to construct ideal types works to fix the organisational attributes they detail and remove them from the historical process. As a consequence, locating the current structures of the advertising industry within a longer historical narrative is difficult: the analyst is forced to place an organisation within one of the four types, rather than draw out the historical formation of particular kinds of business organisation. The types they establish also tend to abstract the creative industries from the wider economic and cultural formations with which they are articulated. The abandonment of this historical setting stems from an over-emphasis on an internal, institutional account of this sector.

Another notably underdeveloped feature of Scase and Davis's book is any conceptualisation of the cultural role played by the practitioners working within the creative industries that they describe. This is surprising since their text is littered with the voices of practitioners working in these fields. However, this question is central to Mike Featherstone's account of the media and cultural industries. In an influential set of essays collected together as *Postmodernism and Consumer Culture*, Featherstone explores the emergence of 'postmodern culture' and the role played within this new cultural epoch by consumer culture. To this end, Featherstone has a good deal to say about those practitioners working in the media and cultural industries who have acquired, he argues, a new significance and salience within cultural life. He deploys the term 'new cultural intermediaries' to describe these practitioners and gives them a central role in the establishment of postmodern culture.

Featherstone appropriates the term 'new cultural intermediaries' from the writings of Pierre Bourdieu and he closely follows Bourdieu's description of this group. Bourdieu has most to say about these workers in his discussion of middlebrow culture in his mammoth book *Distinction* (1984), where he identifies 'the producers of cultural programmes on television or radio or the critics of 'quality' newspapers and magazines and all the writer journalists and journalist-writers' as the 'most typical' of this group (Bourdieu, 1984: 324). Elsewhere he includes practitioners in design, packaging, sales promotion, public relations, marketing and advertising within this category, and also cites the example of those people involved in the provision of medical and social assistance (such as marriage guidance counsellors, sex therapists and dieticians). For Featherstone, like Bourdieu, these occupations expanded in the last quarter of the twentieth century and have become increasingly important within the occupational structure. The expansion and greater salience of these jobs stems from the bourgeoning of the consumer sectors of the economy and the associated consolidation of large broadcasting and media organisations. Featherstone is particularly concerned to reflect on the role played by new cultural intermediaries as the shapers of tastes and the inculcators of new consumerist dispositions among the wider population. The cultural authority they are able to exercise in these areas derives from their position within the increasingly important cultural institutions.

Featherstone further develops Bourdieu's arguments by suggesting that the new prominence of these practitioners stems from the alliances they have entered into with politicians, government administrators and the worlds of finance and business. These alliances mark a significant turnaround in the relations between these groupings, since cultural intermediaries were previously more marginal to the centres of economic and political power. It is their enhanced status, however, which for Featherstone, underpins the authority of new cultural intermediaries as taste shapers and accounts for their central role in the forging of a 'postmodern culture'. Through the work of cultural production and circulation, Featherstone contends that the new cultural intermediaries play a key role in the aestheticisation of everyday life and the accompanying breaking down of cultural hierarchies consonant with postmodern culture. As he suggests, 'effectively they [new cultural intermediaries] help to collapse some of the old distinctions and symbolic hierarchies that revolve around the popular culture/high culture axis' (1991: 95).

Featherstone's claims about the role played by new cultural intermediaries usefully add something to those accounts we have already considered about the increasing centrality of knowledge and information intensive forms of work to economic life (practices like design, promotion, research and development). In doing so, his account not only foregrounds those practitioners who tended to be subsumed in the more general institutional accounts of economic change (such as Lash and Urry's), but also draws attention to an important set of dynamics within these institutions that stem from the particular social make-up of these practitioners. Featherstone's arguments, however, are not without their problems; problems originating partly from the limitations with Bourdieu's original conceptualisations upon which they draw and partly from problems intrinsic to Featherstone's own style of argumentation. We can take the latter first as it can be dealt with quickly. It concerns the contrast between the very large claims that Featherstone makes about the significance of these occupational groups and the very limited evidence upon which these claims are made. In fact, not to put too fine a point on it, Featherstone effectively cites no evidence about an occupational group he sees as central to cultural change. The reader is forced to take a lot on trust. This problem is then compounded by the 'presentism' of the idea of new cultural intermediaries that he deploys (a problem already evident in Bourdieu's formulation). This problem stems from the unhelpful qualifier 'new' that Bourdieu attaches to 'cultural intermediaries'. This immediately throws up the question of periodisation in relation to the emergence of these intermediary occupations. The evidence from Britain suggests the need for caution in talking uncritically about the expansion of cultural intermediaries and assigning to them the epithet 'new'. Certainly, occupations such as broadcasting and advertising, alongside journalism, expanded markedly in the first half of the twentieth century and, in the case of advertising, decline, from a high point in the 1960s, in terms of the numbers employed (Baxendale and Pawling, 1996: 3; see also Chapter 3). In no sense, then, are these occupations particularly new and nor are they necessarily expanding. There is a requirement, if the idea of cultural intermediaries is to have any interpretative value, to separate the question of the numerical status of these jobs from their apparent increasing salience within economic and cultural life. The latter may occur, despite fluctuations in the numerical composition of these sectors. In light of this, it is more appropriate to talk about 'cultural intermediaries', rather than 'new cultural intermediaries'. Featherstone also tends to take for granted the cultural rise of these occupations. One of the arguments that I develop later is that for specific groups of practitioners – those working in advertising – this new centrality could not be taken for granted and was far from guaranteed. While intermediary cultural work as a whole may have become more central to economic and cultural life, this general prominence disguises intense struggles between competing groups of commercial practitioners over the provision of this expertise.

There are other problems with the idea of 'new cultural intermediaries' as Featherstone deploys the term. It remains a very inclusive category, aggregating a fairly diverse range of occupations into a common designation. This throws up some particular problems. The most serious concerns the way the term cuts across distinct occupational formations, cultures and forms of expertise. It also tends to downplay the rather different social composition of discrete intermediary occupations. Thus, for example, broadcast journalists and producers in British television – notably at the BBC – are a very different occupational grouping in terms of social and educational background and occupational ethos from the advertising creatives (as we'll see later) who figure in my account (Burns, 1977). A more differentiated account of these occupations is required; one that can grasp the differences between them as much as 'family resemblances'. Additionally, the idea of new cultural intermediaries as Featherstone uses it is inattentive to the organisational cultures of the enterprises that make up this diverse sector of intermediary work. It is a central claim of this book that exploring these workplace, and broader, industry cultures is integral to an adequate understanding of these occupations. In particular, attention paid to the cultural resources that shape the forms of endeavour engaged in by cultural intermediaries and their own subjective identities can add much to our picture of this area of work. In developing this more culturally-informed account of a specific group of cultural intermediaries (advertising creatives), my account is strongly rooted within the intellectual traditions of cultural and cultural historical studies. However, the way consumption and the consumer economy have figured within work in this area has not been unproblematic for my concerns, despite the suggestive insights of much of this work. It is to the historical and cultural studies of consumption that I now want to turn.

advertising, consumption and historical and cultural studies   The most immediately striking value of much of the social and cultural historical work on consumer culture and the consumer economy is its direct challenge to the narrow contemporary focus of the sociological accounts that I have been discussing. While this field is now extensive and widely dispersed – particularly as it bleeds into cultural studies – there remains one book that has had an enduring impact on the historiography of consumption and which has been seminal in relativising contemporary-focused accounts of the consumer economy. This is McKendrick et al's *The Birth of a Consumer Society* (McKendrick et al, 1982). The book's central claims remain controversial and highly contested and yet it undoubtedly continues to inform more recent historical work on consumption (Glennie, 1995: 167). Their argument is driven by the ambition to revise and interrupt established debates within economic history about the take-off of the industrial revolution in Britain. In particular, the book seeks to challenge the secondary and supporting role given to the expansion of consumption within the conventional historical narratives of industrialisation. For McKendrick et al it is changes in the structures of demand occasioned by a new set of intellectual ideas and commercial practices associated with the consumer economy that form some of the necessary conditions for wider economic change. Detailing these ideas and practices forms the substantive focus of *The Birth of a Consumer Society* and underpins its own account of a decisive 'consumer revolution' in eighteenth century England.

The book centres upon the consequences of social mobility and the desire for emulation within the tightly packed social ranks of eighteenth century England as the central mechanism of the growth of 'modern' consumption. It is emulation, the desire to follow the habits and lifestyles of your social betters, which, above all, accounts for the cascading of new propensities to consume and new levels of consumption through the social body. In exploring these processes of emulation, the authors place great store on the development of a vibrant metropolitan culture in London in stoking up new consumerist dispositions, with exposure to London fashions and shops seen as a key component in the diffusion of consumer behaviour (ibid: 21).

The Birth of a Consumer Society also has much to say about the broader intellectual climate in which levels of consumption expanded, exploring in particular the intellectual origins of the 'revolution in consumption'. McKendrick et al describe the movement from mercantalist 'balance-of-payments' explanations of economic growth in which 'total demand' appeared inelastic to conceptions of the 'elasticity of demand' in which consumers at all levels of society might acquire new wants and desires (ibid: 13–15). This was a shift noted by Adam Smith in *The Wealth of Nations* in which he claimed that the 'doctrine of beneficial luxury' had taken over from the doctrine of the 'utility of poverty'. As McKendrick et al succinctly note, 'it was increasingly admitted that the increased availability of the 'comforts and conveniences of life' could operate as powerful stimulus to industry at all ranks of society' (ibid: 19). Observations of this kind were integral to the larger claims of the book about the significance of the expansion of the world of goods in eighteenth century England identified by the authors. *The Birth of a Consumer Society* stakes much on the argument that expanded levels of consumption was not just about the circulation and consumption of a greater number of goods, but represented the formation of a new social order, one in which collective representations of the good life and social harmony depended upon the smooth operation of commerce and consumption (Brewer and Porter, 1993: 2).

One of the most striking features of McKendrick et al's ambitious account is its attention to the innovations in business practices that formed the engines of the new 'consumer society'. Focusing on the pottery manufacturer Josiah Wedgewood, McKendrick et al claim that it was Wedgewood's use of promotional techniques that was central to his success and made him emblematic of the wider shifts in economic life in which consumer marketing played a key role in the expansion of consumer demand. In their reading, then, Wedgewood emerges as a thoroughly 'modern' entrepreneur, deploying show rooms, exhibitions, trademarks, displays and advertisements as part of a consumer-focused and marketing-led approach to his business. More than that, in naming his factory, together with leading lines of his pottery, Etruria, Wedgewood was as cognisant of the symbolic dimension of commodities as any of those players involved in the regime of reflexive accumulation identified by Lash and Urry. Such observations are important in undercutting the claims of authors like Lash and Urry that somehow the 'culturalising' of goods and services is a new or recent phenomenon. As McKendrick et al show, Wedgewood knew a thing or two about the cultural associations that could be attached through design and promotion to commodities.

Paradoxically, the central role that McKendrick et al attribute to marketing in the expansion of consumption represents one of the more problematic aspects of their argument for my purposes. In foregrounding so strongly these commercial practices, *The Birth of a Consumer Society* produces a reductive account of the establishment of the 'consumer revolution' in eighteenth century England. In this sense, they are as guilty as their sociological congenors of collapsing together a set of distinct developments within the commercial field into a general account of the transition to a consumer society in which advertising and marketing emerge as the central driving force behind more complex economic and cultural changes. The book, thus, conflates a number of distinct developments related to the size of markets, the emergence of new consumption practices, the range of commodities and sectors involved, the levels of investment in the production and distribution of consumer goods and the expansion of related economic and cultural institutions. This is the first of a number of problems with their account for an adequate analysis of advertising and commercial culture. More seriously, *The Birth of a Consumer Society* is limited by the trope of 'revolution' that gives direction to its reading of 'consumer society' and by the epochal logic that flows from this. Again, not only does this place the book close to the contemporary sociological accounts in terms of the conceptions of cultural change with which it works, but it also means that it shares much in common with other histories of consumption.

Paul Glennie has noted that the historiography of consumption has been dominated by various and competing claims about the take-off of consumer revolutions. These have ranged from locating the birth of consumer society in Restoration England, the eighteenth and the late nineteenth century, and between the first and second world wars. Regardless of the period, there has been a recurrent tendency across this work to muster particular versions of a dualistic model of change in which an era in which people were the 'users of things' is superseded by one in which they become the 'consumers of commodities'. As Glennie suggests, what this dualism tends to downplay is the complex use of objects – or cultures of consumption – that predated the more systematic developments in commercial culture (Glennie, 1995: 117).

None the less, the best of more recent work on consumption from within historical studies has filled in the most glaring gap in the account developed in *The Birth of a Consumer Society*. This is an exploration of the specific styles, practices and cultures of consumption that developed alongside the expanded world of goods. This work has offered detailed accounts of the place of commercial cultures in the fashioning of collective and individual identities, on the minutiae of consumer spectatorship, public and national rituals and intimate subjective desires (Steedman, 1986; Schama,

1987; Green, 1990; Alexander, 1994) Erika Rappaport, for example, has offered a compelling account of the links between gender identities and commerce in the West End of London in the late nineteenth century (Rappaport, 2000). She persuasively holds together an attention to the styles and practices of entrepreneurship and technologies of selling deployed by West End retailers with the formation of new kinds of femininity among bourgeois women and their own negotiations of the shifting boundaries between public and private worlds that flowed from the sphere of gendered commerce. She also draws out the relationship between the vision of metropolitan life offered by commercial practitioners and more official versions of the city and its moral fabric. Rappaport is also careful to side-step the temptation to fit such an account into a general model of consumer society or consumption.

Culturally-informed arguments like Rappaport's have much in common with the best cultural studies work on consumption. This, again, is now an extensive field of work and, despite the claims of the editors of a recent collection on advertising and consumption that this had long been a neglected area of cultural studies, it is a field sharing a lineage with the early seminal cultural studies (Nava et al, 1997). Certainly, it is possible to reread many of the studies produced through the 1970s to reveal how questions about consumption and the wider impact of the consumer economy on cultural life were central to their concerns. This is most apparent in a collection like *Resistance Through Rituals* (Hall and Jefferson, 1976), though an attention to the place of shifts in the consumer economy and its relationship to changing forms of moral regulation and political control is evident in other work produced in this period, particularly in *Policing the Crisis* (Hall et al, 1978) and Stuart Hall's study of the permissive reforms of the late 1960s and early 1970s (Hall et al, 1978: 254–8; Hall, 1980; Hebdige, 1979, 1988; Millum, 1975). Throughout this work is a preoccupation with the changing cultural forms through which (principally) class relations and identities were lived. In *Resistance through Rituals*, where these themes were most clearly developed, attention was paid to how the expanded world of commercially produced goods and entertainments had contributed to the remaking of working class culture and, most spectacularly, working class youth identities. And while *Resistance Through Rituals* took issue with many of the dominant stories of postwar affluence, including their proclamations about the end of class as a meaningful social category, it shared with more mainstream cultural and sociological commentators an assertion that consumption formed one of the central building blocks through which the story of postwar Britain needed to be told (see Mort et al, 2000).

This body of cultural studies work has bequeathed a distinctive legacy and continues to shape the way consumption and the consumer economy are addressed within many studies of popular culture and popular consumption. Perhaps the most enduring impact has been the privileging of studies of acts of consumption and the use of commercial culture by particular groups of consumers. In fact, this attention to acts of consumption forms one half of the twin foci that have dominated cultural studies work in this area, the other being a more textually-driven reading of consumption, in which particular commercially produced cultural forms – often visual representations – have been taken as the central object of study. While its direct influence upon the study of consumption has undoubtedly waned, a neo-Gramscian model of cultural power and cultural change also continues to give a distinctive gloss to more recent work (see McGuigan, 1992). Certainly, the rationale for the study of popular pleasures and pastimes organised through commercially produced culture continues to bear the trace of the theoretical labour undertaken through the 1970s and 1980s in which the 'turn to Gramsci' loomed large.

The concern to place cultural forms in a wider map of cultural power and to explore the way specific cultural forms, practices and representations contribute to or disrupt various forms of social hegemony remains the typically unstated, but none the less constitutive ethos, of studies of consumption. This has not been an entirely unproblematic inheritance. As has been well documented, a search for the progressive currents in popular culture and the deployment of a largely rhetorical cultural politics in which cultural forms and practices were read for the contribution they might make to an imagined project of counter-hegemony led to a highly skewed account of the cultural field (Bennett, 1992; 1998; Nixon, 1996, 2000). This was one which notably downplayed the significance of those cultural forms that could not easily be inserted into a dissenting political programme and overplayed the cultural significance of more banal and routine forms of cultural practice within the lives of particular constituents of consumers. In a justifiable move to contest older conceptions of the 'passive consumer', recent studies of commercial culture have been burdened by an equally problematic analytical subject: the resistant or recalcitrant consumer (see McGuigan, 1992; Nava, 1992).

Both the positive strengths of this body of work, and some of its limitations, are evident in Paul Willis' study of young people and consumption, *Common Culture* (Willis, 1990). Willis forms an explicit link between earlier work in cultural studies with more recent studies of consumption. The strength of the book remains its attention to the grounded and nuanced exploration of particular uses and appropriations of commercially-produced culture by groups of consumers. To this end, Willis deploys the notions of symbolic work and symbolic creativity to account for, respectively, the necessary cultural work involving language and other symbolic resources associated with the performance of everyday social routines and the active and innovative process of identity formation integral to social life. Arguing, contra to the thrust of contemporary sociologists that for most people, work – paid employment – now offers limited scope for creativity and innovation, Willis contends that it is in the realm of leisure, and particularly through 'the active, not passive consumption of commercially produced goods, that creative processes of individual and collective self-fashioning occur' (Willis, 1990: 18–19).

The book has been criticised on a number of counts, most notably for the romantic conception of human creativity that it unashamedly employs (Frith, 1996). Further, it has been charged with seeking to merely celebrate commercially produced commercial culture and of falling prey to the more general tendency towards cultural populism that Jim McGuigan, most notably, has identified as a persistant feature of a wide body of cultural criticism (McGuigan, 1992). Other commentators have rightly argued that acts or practices of consumption need to be more carefully differentiated. Thrift and Glennie, for example, attempt to develop an account of shopping and the familiarisation with commodities associated with this practice, which emphasises the inculcation of a consumerist disposition as something which is embodied and inhabited, through routines of 'being and doing' (Thrift and Glennie, 1993: 37).

While there continues to be much that is instructive in this reworked attention to acts of consumption, my own work has been strongly shaped by a concern to open up different aspects of the commercial field. In this regard, it shares something with the moves of other writers to turn to the previously neglected areas of cultural production and circulation in a way that circumvents the recourse to political economy. An early version of this move was signalled by Angela McRobbie in a critique of subcultural analysis. In a suggestive essay, 'Second-hand dresses and the role of the ragmarket' (McRobbie, 1989), she insisted that the focus of subcultural studies upon the transformation of already bought commodities neglected a whole host of commercial activities and forms of entrepreneurship that were integral to the subcultural experience. While she did not take the argument very far in that article, it marked out an attention to the 'cultures of production' that has emerged more strongly in her recent work and also figured in the work of other cultural critics (du Gay, 1996; Nixon, 1996; Mort, 1996; McRobbie, 1998; Negus, 1992, 2002; Jackson et al., 2000). Frank Mort's recent work has been particularly important in developing this approach in relation to the study of 'commercial society'. In his book *Cultures of Consumption* (Mort, 1996), he suggested that the study of the consumer economy might be profitably approached through the idea of the 'commercial domain'. For Mort, the idea of the 'commercial domain' represented a way of conceptualising a distinct and identifiable field of institutions, moral and intellectual entrepreneurship and related conceptions of personhood that were analogous to the field of the 'social' identified by historians like Donzelot and Rose (Donzelot, 1977; Rose, 1991). In *Cultures of Consumption* these pre-occupations emerged not only in the way Mort explored in detail the forms of identity produced through particular systems of provision and the spatial embeddedness of these commercial cultures, but also in his insistence on situating this analysis within a broader project of cultural history. This involved locating discrete studies like his own within a wider set of histories of this domain and its distinctive dynamics.

Mort's comments are suggestive and have considerable strategic value in consolidating the commercial domain or commercial cultures as a discrete object of study. They underline, again, the importance of attending to the particular forms taken by commercial endeavour at specific times and in specific places; the changing kinds of technologies and expertise that are deployed in the enacting of commerce and the need to grasp, above all, the way the world of commerce and goods acts upon social experience and subjectivity. As such they hold out the possibility of revising those general narratives on the expansion of consumption, whether that be in relation to debates about the coming of the mass market in the post-war decades or the transition to an era of 'postmodern culture' or 'reflexive modernity'. Moreover, this approach to the commercial domain reinforces the importance of holding together the mutually constitutive relationship between cultural and economic processes within this field of endeavour – what Mort has described as an understanding of 'culture and economic as reflexively inter-related in ways which are neither pre-determined or mono-causal' (Mort, 2000: 12). Such an approach is distinct from earlier forms of anti-economism within cultural analysis in which the 'relative autonomy' of cultural practices was emphasised while retaining a conceptual ranking of social practices furnished by the notion of determination by the economic in the 'last instance'. It is also distinct from a return to political economy in which economic practices and identities retain a primary and foundational character. My own thinking on this matter has been informed by Ernesto Laclau's work and his emphasis on the contingency of all identities (including the economic) and with it the possibility of reconceptualising the relations between the incompletely formed fields of culture and economy through the notions of imbrication and mutual constitution rather than direct determination by, or interaction between, fully constituted domains (Laclau, 1990: 24).

Such a reconceptualisation is particularly important in relation to the study of advertising. Despite the fact that advertising is widely acknowledged to bring together both 'cultural' and 'economic' practices and calculations in very obvious ways, its study has been dogged by a separation of these components of its practice. The idea of commercial culture as I deploy it builds upon the insistence that these components of advertising practice need to be grasped in their dynamic interdependence. Commercial culture, in this sense, is used to capture the 'cultures of commerce': the cultural meanings and values that cohere within and set the conditions for business and commerce to be enacted. In relation to the study of advertising as a commercial practice, this understanding draws attention to the way the business forms, practices and relations integral to the practice of advertising depend for their performance upon sets of cultural meanings and values. This interfusing is most evident in the way agencies manage the commercial relations between consumers and their clients. While agency practitioners often speak about these markets as if they existed independent of their actions, it is clear that agencies play an active role in helping to constitute and articulate the economic relations between consumers and clients through techniques like planning and market research that they mobilise. In other words, agencies, through the representations of the consumer they deploy, provide some of the necessary (cultural) conditions of existence of these commercial (or economic) relations. This is a process that works in a number of different registers. It includes not only market research knowledge, but also the elaboration of these commercial relations through the promotional forms themselves (such as advertisements). What particularly interests me here, in relation to the concerns of *Advertising Cultures*, is the way the management of these commercial relations depends upon not only formal knowledge (market research data, sales figures, consumer feedback, pre-testing of adverts), but also upon more elusive informal knowledge and dispositions. Information about consumers not known to the client or market researcher, but known to the art director or copywriter, together with their own cultural identifications, can be crucial in helping to clinch these commercial linkages. Furthermore, the informal cultures inhabited by theses practitioners will both set limits upon and provide resources for the performance of the creative execution in which these practitioners are engaged. It is this insistence that informs my contention about why the subjective identities and informal cultures of advertising practitioners matter so much.

There is a further conceptual theme associated with this revisionist kind of analysis of commercial culture that is worth reinforcing. As many cultural critics have argued, the world of commercially produced goods plays an important role in shaping particular consumerist conceptions of identity and social rituals among those populations successfully targeted by commercial practitioners. In fact, there has been a persistent insistence that commercially produced goods and services have the capacity to intervene in and shape particular lived cultures through their capacity to mould subjective identities and shape social habits and routines. Commercial enterprises – be they advertising agencies or retailers – can be thought of in this sense as articulating cultural projects or missions every bit as trans-formative in their ambitions towards specific populations as those pursued by social reformers and policy makers. As Janice Winship's work on Marks and Spencer in the inter-war years suggests, here was a business with ambitions not only to sell its goods, but also to establish certain norms of lower-middle class femininity around the ideals of the 'nice and neat' body and restrained, but modern consumption (Winship, 2000).

Winship's works is not unique. As I noted earlier in this chapter, there are many examples of concrete studies that have foregrounded the role of commercially produced cultural goods and services in helping to shape the cultural identities and expectations of particular populations. Such an analytical focus, in fact, is the *sine qua* of recent cultural studies of con-sumption. What has been less well explored, is the subjective consequences of these commercial strategies upon the practitioners who populate the consumer institutions. It is a central contention of *Advertising Cultures* that the subjective consequences of the world of commerce and its consumerist understandings of identity can also be fruitfully explored through the identities and subjective choices made by practitioners like those central to this book. It is this most neglected aspect of these commercial circuits of provision – the informal cultures and subjective identities of commercial practitioners themselves – that I privilege. In this sense, the ambition of the book is to fill out our understanding of the way subjectivity is constituted through the world of commerce; not, in this instance, of those consumers targeted by the consumer industries, but the subjective consequences of commercial processes upon the identities of practitioners themselves.

commerce and creativity   part **2**

'purveyors of creativity':
advertising agencies, commercial expertise and creative jobs

In his racy, at times, acerbic insider's account of the British advertising industry published at the high point of the sectors economic fortunes in the 1980s, former ad man Martyn Forrester dwelt on the *dramatis personae* of a typical agency in his attempt to communicate this 'extraordinary' business to a wider, lay public. Running briskly through the core professional jobs and the associated support functions, he eventually came to the creatives. These were, he suggested, 'almost the top people in the agency. . . . They're bought and sold like footballers with salaries to match' (Forrester, 1987: 15). Forrester's assessment of the elevated position of creative jobs in the social relations of agency life was not unique. *Campaign*, the leading industry newspaper, in its weekly editorial sometime later, advanced a similar analysis. Reflecting on the quality of senior management within the agency sector, it pontificated, 'the differences between agencies lies in the advertising they create. . . . The creative function is therefore the most important one performed by agencies and the one where the most rigorous standards need to be maintained' (*Campaign*, 16/7/93: 21). Elsewhere the paper reinforced this perception of creative people's central role. In its regular profiles of the industry's shakers and movers, for example, it was creatives, along with Chairmen, Chief Executives and Managing Directors, who dominated the pieces. The unstated but none the less clear assumption of *Campaign*'s journalism was that these practitioners were the protagonists within the agency who could exert a decisive influence upon the commercial fortunes of these businesses. More or less absent from these pieces were the other core professionals who performed the apparently more humdrum business, marketing and servicing functions: the account planners, media buyers and account handlers.[1]

The privileged position given to creative people in agency life evident in these various commentaries owed much to the way developments within the sector in the 1980s had enhanced the standing of creative jobs. While there was a long history of writers and artists being seen as central players in the commercial life of agencies on both sides of the Atlantic (Bogart, 1995;

Lears, 1994), shifts in some of the underlying principles that guided agency practice in the 1980s had done much to strengthen the position of creative people as an agency's key human assets. Looming large in this was the move among a group of agencies to realign the commercial and creative dimensions of advertising practice. Associated with a so-called 'creative revolution' in British advertising, agencies like Saatchi and Saatchi, Yellowhammer and Bartle Bogle Hegarty (BBH) had sought to shift the terms of what counted as effective advertising and to develop a more aestheticised style of promotion. They argued that the commercial fortunes of their clients could be enhanced by a long term process of brand building and a defence of 'brand values'. Railing against short-term measurement of advertising effectiveness and more prosaic traditions of persuasion and selling, they promoted advertising that worked to a greater degree through establishing an elaborated set of emotional meanings and values around products, enticing the consumer through desire (see Mort, 1996; Nixon, 1996).

While these techniques were not entirely new and drew upon precedents from earlier forms of commercial culture, the advocates of 'creative advertising' were distinctive in the way they introduced representational techniques previously marginal to press and, particularly, television advertising. These included the turn to forms of pastiche in the use of retro-imagery, the self-conscious use of black and white film stock, cinematic forms of lighting, very fast editing and jump cuts, and the deployment of new typefaces for the copy that accompanied the visual image. For the agencies most associated with these innovations, the creative department acquired a new centrality as they sought to apply the tenets of 'creative advertising' to their clients' marketing needs. John Hegarty, for example, creative director at the agency Bartle Bogle Hegarty (BBH), reflecting on his newly established department in 1983, suggested that 'the creative department is the powerhouse of an agency, the motor that makes it all work. In the end advertising is all about the leap from brief [the marketing proposition] to creative execution' (*Creative Review*, December 1983: 19–20). For Hegarty, then, creatives were the practitioners able to bring to bear the necessary imagination that could turn the terse terms of the marketing strategy into an advert that connected with audiences and lifted the product through its style, look and feel. The commercial success of agencies like BBH and Saatchi and Saatchi during the 1980s contributed to the wider take-up of these representational techniques in advertising and to a new privileging of creatives in the advertising development process.

The creative people central to this book were drawn into a job that was, in the mid-1990s, still marked by the transformations of the 1980s. Moreover, they worked in an industry whose reputation as a centre of 'creative excellence' continued to be shaped by the enduring impact of the 'creative revolution' upon what counted as effective advertising. But they were also entering a sector that was much less confident of its standing and of its commercial role. The end of the boom in advertising expenditure at the end of the 1980s, greater demands from clients for agencies to be more accountable in the money they were spending and the deep recession that affected the sector in the early years of the 1990s, contributed to a more uncomfortable period of change and flux for agencies and their core employees. The wider political project of Thatcherism that had been important in enhancing the symbolic role of advertising and associated commercial sectors was also unravelling through the early 1990s and this changed the context in which the industry found itself operating. The uncertainty generated by this set of developments impacted on creative jobs in contradictory ways, both helping to reinforce their privileged position while also disrupting some of the taken for granted assumptions about the kinds of work creatives did and the kind of skills and dispositions they needed to possess.

Precisely what the nature of these broader changes was and how they impacted on the organisation and performance of creative jobs forms the focus of this chapter. In the first part I begin by sketching out some of the local conjunctural factors and more deep-seated structural changes that reshaped the commercial and media environment in which agencies found themselves operating during the mid-1990s. These changes posed both challenges to established ways of working within agencies and also offered commercial opportunities.

In the second part, I explore how agencies responded to this moment of crisis and opportunity. In doing so, I focus upon two exemplars of the wider shifts in the sector. These were the agencies Bartle Bogle Hegarty (BBH) and Howell Henry Chaldecott Lury (HHCL). Both companies are instructive because they sought to protect their status (and income) in the face of external pressures on the agency sector by positioning themselves as the trusted business partners of clients and attempted to resist the very different constitution of their identities as the mere suppliers of adverts. This business partner model of the agency was important because it cast agencies as consultants able to operate across the full range of their clients com- mercial needs and to intervene, if necessary, in areas outside of advertising. In stressing this new role, both agencies made much of the unique kinds of expertise and know-how that they could bring to their clients. Central to this was a presentation of agencies as, above all, the purveyors of creativity and a unique source of creative know-how for clients. Delivery of this expanded service also required both agencies to implement major pro- grammes of organisational reform. Detailing these changes forms a key aspect of part two of the chapter.

Getting to grips with these organisational and strategic changes and the wider institutional developments within the London-based advertising industry of which they were a part is important for the broader argument of the book. Not only do they provide an account of the institutional setting in which the practitioners that I interviewed were starting and establishing their careers, but they shed considerable light on the status and standing of creative jobs and the business and organisational strategies within which creative people worked. As we will see, their jobs emerge as central to the internal life of agencies as they deepened a sense of their identities as creative businesses, while at the same time creative jobs remained not entirely foursquare with the main organisational logics that governed other key employees. It is this exceptional status that is key to understanding the place of creative jobs within the social relations of agency life. And what structured this position were assumptions about the 'creativity' they possessed and the limits upon its organisational regulation.

contemporary challenges   In May 1996 *Campaign* offered an upbeat commentary in its weekly leader column on the rather vexed question of advertiser's relationships with their advertising agencies, under the headline 'Accountability benefits both agency and client' (*Campaign*, 3/5/96: 27). The leader had been prompted by moves by the body representing UK advertisers, The Incorporated Society of British Advertisers (ISBA), to make available to its members a common standard for assessing the performance of their advertising agencies. The standard had been devised following research carried out by the ISBA into its members views on the service they received from agencies and, in particular, their views on whether agencies delivered (in that most contemporary phrase) value for money. The researcher, Dr. Ian Cheston, summarising his findings in the press coverage that accompanied the publication of the proposal, noted that 'the high expenditure days of advertising are gone. Clients are looking for people to make their marketing programmes more successful. It's the agencies that are most professional that will survive' (*Campaign*, 26/4/96: 7).

Campaign's response in its leader to Cheston's findings and the ISBA's proposal was to take both firmly on the chin. While it wryly acknowledged that 'it's almost inevitable that when advertisers start to talk about greater accountability, mutinous mutterings emerge from agency boardrooms and creative departments', it went on,

> There is no need [to grumble]. The growing pre-occupation with accountability goes hand in hand with the recognition of the importance of agencies to commercial success . . . If accountability is well managed, each side benefits. Agencies can get to grips with client's needs and any renewed attack on margins can be nipped in the bud (*Campaign*, 3/5/96: 27).

There was more than a good dose of positive thinking, however, in *Campaign*'s response; of reading for the best interpretation among the more uncomfortable meanings of the ISBA's proposal. As the leader writer knew only too well, the demands for greater accountability articulated in the ISBA proposal were the product of a more widespread questioning of agencies by clients. This questioning had gathered pace since the early 1990s and had undoubtedly been prompted by the sharp recession that effected key sectors of the UK and wider international economy during the early part of that decade.

The recession not only put a significant squeeze on the marketing budgets of client companies, but also provoked some serious questioning among them of the commercial value of advertising? Big spending advertisers such as the processed food manufacturer Heinz and the confectionery giant Nestlé, for example, both took the decision in 1994 to promote individual brands through direct marketing – that is, media such as direct or 'junk' mail – rather than through television advertising. Other client companies also began to look much more closely at the effectiveness of above-the-line (principally, press and television) advertising and, in addition, turned a more questioning eye on the overall service they received from advertising agencies (see inter alia, *Campaign*, 10/12/93: 28–9; 13/3/94: 30–1; 25; 14/1/97: 38–9; and 14/11/97: 38–9).

Under such scrutiny a worrying perception emerged among clients and their representatives. This suggested that advertising agencies were generally badly managed organisations that took a frivolous view of both their business strategies and their costs and routinely engaged in some rather sharp commercial practices. Evidence of a whole host of activities appeared to confirm this: that agencies added anything up to a 40 per cent mark-up to the production costs of adverts when charging clients; that discounts gained from media companies were not declared to clients; that agencies made money by delaying payment to media owners and investing it on the overnight money markets; and that agencies were formerly run by meaninglessly large boards of directors, in which it appeared that board membership was routinely confirmed as a way of giving recognition to staff rather than helping to shape effective management practices (*Campaign*, 25/3/94: 12, 23; 10/5/96: 12). Management consultant David Maister, picking up on this latter problem, went so far as to suggest that 'agencies are not so much badly managed as un-managed. They work like Fenian democracies, where everyone wears their sword to the gathering, but nothing gets decided' (*Campaign*, 25/3/94: 12 and inter alia, *Campaign*, 14/11/97: 38–9).

This intensive scrutiny of agencies by clients and the demands for greater agency accountability that it generated were focused upon an industry itself at a particularly low ebb. The agency sector had contracted sharply in the period between 1989–1993. Following its rapid growth in the mid-late 1980s, advertising expenditure fell back from its high point of 1.6 per cent of GDP in 1988 to 1.32 per cent in 1993 (Advertising Association, 1994).[2] The high leveraged nature of most agencies made them especially vulnerable to even relatively small drops in their levels of income and those agencies that had borrowed heavily in the late 1980s to fund programmes of acquisition and expansion were particularly exposed by the decline in advertising expenditure given their need to service payments on large debts. The downturn in advertising expenditure contributed to a sharp fall in advertising employment. By 1993, it had reached a thirty year low. Those employed in IPA member agencies fell from 15,400 in 1989 to 11,600 in 1993 (*Campaign*, 29/1/93: 1; 13/1/95: 1; 19/1/96: 7). A survey conducted by NABS, the advertising benevolence association, in 1993 found evidence that up to 58 per cent of advertising practitioners drawn from across the key professional jobs had been made redundant at least once, while 34 per cent had been made redundant three times (Hull, 1993).

The local difficulties generated by the economic recession – including clients demands for greater accountability – were unfolding at a time when agencies were also having to grapple with other more deep-seated external pressures on their business. One set of challenges came from the increasing importance of global marketing to the big international client companies and their associated ambition to centralise their advertising into a smaller roster of typically larger agencies. The profound segmentation of the agency sector that the demands of these clients had already helped to form by the late 1980s – with the sector split between a smallish number of genuinely global agency networks and other smaller, privately-owned agencies – continued to provide a major structural dynamic that individual agencies had to negotiate (Mattelart, 1991; Daniels, 1995; Nixon, 1996).[3]

Agencies were also facing competition from other groups of symbolic intermediaries in the areas of expertise that they have traditionally monopolised. One set of challenges came from management consultants who, increasingly, were offering their services to clients as providers of rigorous strategic advice about brands. The consultancy firm McKinsey and Co., most notably, garnered a good deal of disapprobation from agencies for its aggressive moves into the communications field in the early 1990s

(*Campaign*, 15/7/94: 29 and 2/12/94: 36–7). Advertising agencies were also experiencing intensive competition from companies known as 'media independents' in the researching, planning and buying of media space as clients became more prepared to separate the media buying services that they required from the other core services bought from agencies. This move by clients had profound consequences. As Mike Yershon noted, whereas in 1973 only the US giant Unilever and a handful of other clients used media independents and did not, as a consequence, integrate their planning, buying and creative work under one roof, by the early 1990s over half of all media buying was carried out at a different location from where the creative work was developed (*Campaign*, 4/6/93: 32–3). Many of the blue-chip clients were integral to this process. In the year to May 1994, for example, £200M worth of media business was centralised into media independents by Boots, British Gas, RHM and Cadburys (*Campaign*, 13/5/94: 30–1).

Both these forms of competition – but most clearly that coming from media independents – were related to a further significant set of external developments bearing upon agency practice. These derived from changes in advertising media. The decade between 1988–1998 saw an acceleration of the process of media proliferation that began in the early 1980s. At the root of this was the policy-driven opening up of media markets – especially television markets – and the emergence of new media technologies and delivery systems. The scale of these developments was phenomenal. For example, in 1980 there was just one commercial television channel in Britain providing 88 minutes of advertising time a day. By 1993, this had risen to 15 channels offering in excess of 1,500 minutes each day. Similarly, in 1980, there were just 16 national newspapers and 1,400 consumer magazines. By 1992, this had risen to 23 newspapers, each typically consisting of a number of sections, and 2,300 consumer magazines. Commercial radio stations also rose from 26 in 1980 to 125 in 1992 (Campaign, 4/6/93: 32–3).[4] Associated with this process of media proliferation was the rising cost of traditional advertising media, particularly television airtime. This rise in the cost of placing adverts was the product of the concentration of media ownership, especially in the television industry. For example, by 1997, Carlton, Granada and United controlled 70 per cent of network TV sales in Britain, while on a global scale News Corporation, Time Warner, Seagram, Disney and Viacom operated from their bases in the USA as an effective oligopoly with enormous power over media pricing (WPP Annual Report, 1997: 36). This concentration of ownership was itself a major spur to the growth of the large media buying groups that had increasingly taken over this function from full-service agencies. The size of these media buyers – which included companies like Zenith and the Media Partnership – enabled them to generate lower media costs for clients in their negotiations with media owners.[5]

Addressing these heterogeneous challenges and, in particular, protecting the status of agencies as the pre-eminent suppliers of advertising and marketing services became a pressing concern for the major players in the London-based advertising industry in the early to mid 1990s. It led, among other things, to a sustained reflection on the commercial role of advertising agencies. Some of the influential players in the London-based industry sought to reorder the kinds of commercial expertise that they offered clients and the way they conducted the business of advertising. In the next section I want to explore these developments in some detail by looking at the way two influential agencies – BBH and HHCL – reorganised their respective businesses.

re-imagining the ad agency

The new debate is about how agencies should market their skills as advisers and theorists. Further down the line, it is also about how they should structure their businesses to do that (*Campaign*, 13/10/95: 29).

The prescriptions summarised by *Campaign*, above, concerning the way agencies should position themselves in the commercial environment of the mid-1990s were contained in an article tellingly headlined 'The ad agency grows up'. As the article acknowledged, agencies needed to embrace the challenging times in which they found themselves and boldly set out a vision of the ad agency as the preeminent source of knowledge and marketing expertise for clients. These prescriptions were evident in the initiatives taken by one of the more significant exponents of this re-invigorated version of the advertising agency, Bartle Bogle Hegarty (BBH). The agency, formed in 1982, was one of the most successful and strongly branded advertising agencies in Britain. As I have already noted, it had quickly gained a reputation as the producer of stylish advertising, particularly for its first and most significant client Levi-Strauss. By the mid-1990s the agency had matured into a significant player within the British advertising industry with a range of subsidiary companies and an office in Singapore.[6] As the agency grew, it sought to address the challenges facing it and the agency sector more generally. Looming large in this was the foregrounding of its role as a trusted business partner to clients. In elaborating this vision, BBH claimed that the way agencies were often seen – and often saw themselves – prevented them from fully developing this more expanded role. As the agency suggested in a business practice document produced for clients:

Agencies work for clients and, traditionally, advertising has seen itself as a service industry. But all the available data shows that the thing clients seek most is creativity. There is a potentially difficult balancing act here. It is not easy to play a responsible role as the specialist source of creative excellence and, at the same time, to be positioned as a service provider (BBH Business Practice, 1996: 3).

Part of the problem for BBH stemmed from the way agencies charged for their services. Two forms of remuneration dominated within the industry: commission-based and fee-based payments. Both had a long pedigree within the industry, with commission-based payment stretching back the furthest. Its roots lay in the establishment of agency practice at the end of the nineteenth century in which agencies had acted as agents of the press. Commission payments were formalised into a legally-regulated system – the fixed commission system – in 1932 and under this system agencies recognised by the Newspaper Proprietors Association (NPA) could receive a 10 per cent commission on the costs of the media space that they bought for advertisers. Although media commission remained an important source of income for many agencies in the mid-1990s, income derived from fees and retainers paid by clients came close to matching it (see, inter alia, *Campaign*, 13/8/93: 22–3; 20/1/95: 25; 23/6/95: 12).[7] BBH, in line with a number of other agencies, sought to develop a form of financial compensation that better reflected the role agencies could play as all-round business partners to clients. To this end, it proposed the idea of the 'agency salary':

Our approach is simple. View the agency as a person. The clients who appoint BBH want the agency to become part of the team and to work in a spirit of real partnership. . . . Salary is not just a semantic re-expression of fees. It represents a different attitude to the issue. If an agency is to become part of the team and operate as a strategic partner, it cannot do so simply via the production and placement of the advertising. It must be able to contribute on a broader front, to take *initiatives outside the specific sphere of advertising development*. . . . We are not seeking to pad out our income. We simply seek a method of remuneration that reflects the scale of our input, the quality of our output and allows us to deliver in breadth to the best of our ability. The fact that one agency may cost more or less than another does not, of itself, make a statement about which offers better value (BBH Business Practice, 1996: 9–10) (emphasis added).

BBH's advocacy of the idea of the agency salary was about more than the technical matter of how agencies were paid. As their statement testifies, in focusing on the methods of agency remuneration it was seeking to dramatise its vision of agencies as trusted business partners to clients who were able to operate across the full-range of their client's business and commercial needs.

At the same time, the focus on financial compensation offered a way of institutionalising this kind of relationship with clients through the financial contracts both parties entered into. The move formed part of its ambition to become what it elsewhere called the 'co-custodian' of its clients brands and able to act as a trusted confidant over wider areas of a clients business, including areas like product development. The agency had some success in pursuing this new kind of relationship and, in the case of its long-term client Levi-Strauss, was represented on the board of the client company.

In pressing for this kind of influence, BBH made much of the distinctive expertise that it could bring to the client's commercial needs; expertise that set it apart from other agencies and, importantly, competitors like management consultants. At the heart of this, as one of the earlier quotes indicated, was its provision of 'creativity' and 'creative excellence'. However, what the agency understood by these terms, was something rather specific. On the one hand, BBH invoked them to connote the broad range of expertise and know-how that it could offer clients. Central to this was its ability to provide 'creative original thinking' (Nigel Bogle, IPA Newsfile, April 1993: 1). This was thinking that could unlock the marketing and wider business problems of a client and pave the way for effective advertising or some other remedial strategy. Creativity and creative excellence, on the other hand, also encompassed the representational techniques evident in the press and television advertising produced for clients. In this latter sense, the agency saw itself as continuing the 'creative revolution' in British advertising.

As we have seen, the agency's reputation had been built on the stylish and highly aestheticised press, cinema and television advertising that it produced in the mid-1980s. Defending this legacy and its particular ordering of the expertise that agencies could deliver was integral to how BBH understood 'creativity' and 'creative excellance' in the mid-1990s. In fact, it was this dual emphasis on creative *execution* and its capacity to generate creative *ideas* and *thinking*, which characterised BBH's deployment of the rubric of creativity. The agency invoked these definitions at every opportunity, drawing attention, for example, in a case study prepared for the Department of Trade and Industry (DTI), to its success at being voted International Agency of the Year for three consecutive years at the International Advertising Festival at Cannes for its creative work. Through moves of this kind, BBH positioned itself as close to the heart of the UK's reputation as a centre of 'creative excellence'.

BBH's concern to position itself as a supplier of 'creativity' to clients and as an organisation able to bring this expertise to bear across the full range of a clients business needs – and not just press and television advertising – was closely shared by Howell Henry Chaldecott Lury (HHCL).

HHCL was formed in 1987 at the height in the boom in advertising expenditure of the mid-late 1980s. By the mid-1990s the agency had achieved significant growth on the back of the steady accumulation of new business and was ranked at number 23 in the listings of agencies in Britain based on billings.[8] By the time it was named agency of the year for the second time in 1995 in the annual *Campaign* awards, it was the fastest growing of the top 50 agencies and had established itself as one of the most high profile agencies in Britain. HHCL placed great emphasis on its iconoclastic approach to advertising and marketing and was self-consciously avant-garde. A central aspect of this concerned its ambition to operate, like BBH, not only in the area of advertising, but across the broader field of marketing and communications. It christened this approach, with characteristic aplomb, '3-D marketing'. 3-D marketing aimed to approach a client's marketing needs by developing a dialogue with target consumers across different media. As the agency put it,

[3-D marketing] expands customer relationships into a series of interlocking experiences. The aim is no longer to align several 'flat' media but to create an experience that actively links the customer, the media and the brand. In other words, the 'brand experience' will exist beyond a set of mental constituents presented on flat media (HHCL, 1994: 27).

The agency cited the example of Niketown, the American company Nike's retailing emporium, as a good example of 3-D marketing, where, as they put it, 'shoes are just one expression of Nike-ness – one ride at the fair' (HHCL, 1994: 21). This conception of '3-D marketing' went hand in hand with the agency's avant-gardism. HHCL described itself as being 'particularly good at working with clients who need to *radically* change the way they communicate with their various audiences' (HHCL, www.hhcl.com). Elsewhere it claimed to be 'an innovative . . . marketing and communications agency, responsible for a number of high impact campaigns which have tested the boundaries of the acceptable in advertising'. The agency's work was certainly distinctive. With widely praised campaigns for Britvic's 'Tango' soft drink, the Automobile Association (AA), Mazda and Golden Wonder, the agency developed a style of communication that was direct and highly cognisant of the conventions of marketing. This led, for example, in the case of its work for 'Tango', to a campaign that cast the company's marketing director warning consumers to be on the look out for 'fake' Tango ads and a television commercial for Mazda that required the viewer to record the ad and then play it back frame by frame in order to see its message (see *Campaign*, 6/11/95: 17).

HHCL's ambition to produce innovative work was also evident in the range of promotional techniques that it deployed. This linked up with its concern to operate across a broad front on behalf of the client. One dimension of this concerned its commitment to what it called 'media creativity'. This referred to the innovative and inventive use of advertising media. Writing in *Campaign* in May 1996, Simon Calvert, head of planning at the group's media buying and planning company Bednash and Michaelides, suggested that 'media creativity' was the key point of difference between what he called old and new forms of marketing. Referring to Miller Pilsner's 'Millertime' television advert that had taken the form of a mini-TV show, and Snapple's soft drink promotion, which consisted of stickers stuck on mango's carrying the copy 'also available in Snapple', he argued that 'these are early examples of where a new kind of creativity in media is at the very heart of advertising development. One where media creativity multiplies the effectiveness of the communication' (*Campaign*, 28/6/96: 23).

HHCL's emphasis on 'media creativity' formed part of its vision of '3-D marketing' and was allied to the agency's positioning of itself as a strategic partner to clients, one that was able to operate across different media and without a bias to the traditional media of press, television and posters. As Rupert Howell, the agency's chief executive put it, '90 per cent of strategies begin with advertising and the advertising solution is forced through. [Our approach] is about thinking about the whole of the client's business – how the telephone gets answered probably has more impact on the business than ads do' (*Campaign*, 4/11/94: 11). This emphasis on the need to think beyond the limits of traditional advertising was integral to HHCL's accenting of the idea of creativity towards that of innovative and original thinking and strategy. Champions of the agency in the trade press often sought to draw a distinction between HHCL's strategy and that pursued by a more established agency like BBH. They argued that HHCL's marketing and communications-driven conception of 'creativity' set it above the advocates of 'creative advertising'. As Stephano Hatfield argued, HHCL was an agency that put 'good ideas before pretty executions' (*Campaign*, 4/11/94: 12). Other commentators were also keen to play up the differences in these competing versions of 'creativity'. Drawing out the argument that agencies needed to get their art directors and copywriters to apply their skills not only to television and press work, but also to areas like point-of-sale and direct marketing materials, Shaun McIlrath, senior copywriter at FCB Impact, cited the example of the versatility of the creatives at his own agency. As he noted, 'a creative team here can be working on a commercial one week and a shelf display the next. It calls for versatility and a highly developed sense of sell. And, as such, its held to be hideously unfashionable among the folk who are in it for the art' (*Campaign*, 19/3/93: 25).

While differences certainly existed in the style of advertising and promotion produced by BBH and HHCL, commentators like Hatfield and McIlrath were guilty of overplaying them. Their comments drew on longstanding tensions between a more marketing-driven version of advertising and one that favoured aestheticised and stylish forms of communication that reached well back into the post-war years. In their study of British advertising in the 1960s, Pearson and Turner, for example, noted that the distinction among practitioners between 'marketing men' and 'creative men' was a widespread one (Pearson and Turner, 1965). Such an opposition has figured as a stock in trade of industry debates on both sides of the Atlantic for much of the past 40 years (Ogilvy, 1983; Fox, 1997; Lears, 1994). However, in the case of BBH and HHCL, the opposition was misplaced. Both agencies embraced a broader view of the marketing and service role that agencies should play as they sought to position themselves as trusted business partners to clients and both were committed, as a consequence, to an approach to solving their clients' business needs that shifted press and television advertising out of its previously assured centrality to the business of advertising.

Differences, however, did appear in the way the two agencies sought to institutionalise this consultancy model within their respective organisational processes. In the late 1990s, both HHCL and BBH embarked on major programmes of organisational change in order to enable them to deliver the kind of service – and 'creativity' – that their respective visions of the ad agency demanded. Central to these programmes of organisational restructuring was the ambition to develop more dynamic and 'creative' ways of working. Rather late in the day compared to many of the client companies they worked with, BBH and HHCL attempted to re-organise themselves along more entrepreneurial lines.

With characteristic bravura, HHCL announced the changes that it was making to its ways of working by re-branding itself as a marketing and communications company. The agency even produced a publication – *Marketing at a Point of Change* – to promote and give intellectual gloss to these changes (HHCL, 1994). The publication proclaimed,

The new company (HHCLandP) will [. . .] involve a radical restructuring of the way work is produced as well as a re-appraisal of what that 'work' is. . . . The company will need a competitive approach on all fronts, in particular it will need innovative strategic and creative skills. It will require a radically new approach to problem solving, one based on a collaborative working methodology that encourages and facilitates cross-discipline working, and one that incorporates the customer into the process. . . . Where emphasis has previously been on integrated execution, it will have to be on integrated *thinking* (HHCL, 1994: 29–31).

Running through the slick language of this passage were pointers to the central organisational changes HHCL introduced in order to deliver this dynamic approach to working with clients. These were multi-functional or multi-disciplinary 'project' teams that were assigned to separate client accounts. Again, the agency was bullish about the rationale for this move:

> Campaigns are owned by all members of the group, and everyone contributes at each stage, thereby facilitating communication between people from different functional backgrounds. This diversity of information sparks ideas that people wouldn't otherwise have as creatives become media strategists and media strategists become account planners. Clients are present at many of the group meetings 'as part of the problem solving not the problem' (HHCL.main.html).

This restructuring marked a significant change from the way agencies had conventionally been organised. The organisational model of the service agency had typically been a departmentalised and functionally-driven structure. The core jobs central to the development of advertising and the servicing of clients were organised into discrete departments: an account handling department, an account planning department, a creative department and a media buying/planning department. Overseen by the traffic department, the process of creating work for clients formally moved from department to department towards the final finished advert. As John Leach, a planning partner at HHCL, noted 'this system was analogous to a relay race'. He counterposed this to HHCL's approach. 'We see the creative process as more like a rugby scrum' (10/11/95: 27). The project teams that the agency introduced aimed to restructure established ways of working in order to generate a more 'creative' and innovative environment.

Bringing these new ways of working to life prompted HHCL to transform the built environment of the agency. After initially considering moving from their Kent House premises behind Oxford Street in London's West End, the agency instead hired a consultant to help them restructure the interior of the building. At the heart of the redesign was the principle of 'romping'[9] or 'hot desking' in which staff were given a mobile phone and a locker and encouraged to occupy a range of spaces depending upon what they were working on, rather than their own permanent desk. To this end, the interior of Kent House was remade as a 'diversity of environments':

> Parts of the office are homes for the client teams, parts of the office are 'streets' where randomly assigned individuals share benches, other space is taken-up with meeting areas of various sizes and designs (including stand-up meeting rooms) or

quiet areas for individual thought. All these spaces are linked via a central, circular walkway where you find people 'walking and talking' . . . In the course of their working week employees could work in a number of different places. This is deliberately designed to induce different emotional states as the environment chances, to constantly change office neighbours, and to expose people to many different ideas. As a result you 'find out things that you didn't think you wanted to know' (HHCL.main.html).

Although there remain big questions about how effective in practice HHCL's organisational reforms were in changing established ways of working, these initiatives demonstrated its conviction to restructure the way the agency's core staff worked in order to improve its effectiveness as an organisation. What was particularly striking about these moves is that they sent out a strong signal about how the agency saw all its key workers – not just art directors and copywriters – as a potential source of 'innovation' and 'creativity'. Project team working, in this sense, sought to liberate the 'creativity' of all the core practitioners involved in the advertising process.

BBH took a similar approach to matters of organisational change and the pursuit of ways of working that could improve the conditions within the agency under which advertising work was generated. The agency hired the industrial psychologists Nicholson McBride in 1993 to help it bring about these changes. At the heart of the restructuring that followed this consultation was the introduction of cross-disciplinary project teams. Martin Smith, the agency's chairman, explained the logic of this move and, in doing so, strongly echoed the arguments made by HHCL:

[Project teams] are very different from how it used to be. Now we have teams who have a set number of pieces of business. There's a symbolic oval table in the middle with more chairs than there are people because we want there to be, if its relevant, somewhere for Motive [BBH's free-standing media department] to sit, Limbo [BBH's direct marketing subsidiary] to sit . . . somewhere for the client to sit, somewhere for the creative department to sit. It's about developing . . . Flexibility is what its all about. What we're trying to do increasingly is to get people to think more broadly, think more interestingly, more creatively. We're supposed to be a very creative business, and yet most of our practices stultify creativity (Smith, 1996).

While on the face of it, BBH's decision to restructure itself along these lines put in on common ground with HHCL, BBH introduced a significant – and highly symbolic – modification to the project team structure, when the teams were established in May 1996. In setting them up, BBH explicitly excluded art directors and copywriters – the advertising creatives – from them. In doing so, the agency maintained the integrity of the creative department and the established system of pairing art directors and copywriters.

This system of creative teams (a copywriter paired with an art director) had been pioneered by the New York agency, Doyle Dane Bernbach (DDB) in the 1960s and quickly became the norm in Britain by the mid-1970s. Prior to this, copywriters had usually sat together in a separate room from the visualisers, the preferred term for those who illustrated or laid-out copy before 'art director' became commonplace. The pairing of art directors and copywriters was unique to creative jobs and was one of the features that gave these jobs their distinctive character. Explaining the logic behind maintaining both the system of creative teams and, particularly, the integrity of the creative department, Martin Smith argued:

> it is important to strike a balance between a kind of openness, where . . . everybody works in a tight group and the fact that there is no doubt about it that creativity works best when there is a controlled tension. There has to be some kind of tension between the business needs that are being articulated by account management and planning and the creative solution which is being offered by the creative department. If it is all too nice and straight line, you end up with Switzerland. You know, something wonderfully efficient and neutral and extremely dull. What you have to maintain is that tension, you have to get a creative tension going. And you still have to have the fevered argument, the temperaments . . . that's important to get good work, because you have to get people feeling emotionally something is right, and someone fighting them and changing it and bettering it. And that's important within a creative organisation. So we've got to maintain the tension where its relevant, and I think it is relevant between the people who are the primary connection with the client and the people who must be the ones who sprinkle pixie dust on the idea and create something which is a leap from where I and others like me would have got logically (Smith, 1996).

Elsewhere he made the same point more succinctly. He suggested, 'advertising ideas are usually the product of 2 creative people, a closed door and a great brief. Everything else we add to that very simple concept is done to help the creative team perform its task' (*Campaign*, 25/6/93: 31). Smith's views were echoed by the agency's head of planning, Nick Kendall. He argued that while project teams were useful in making possible the cross-fertilisation of ideas, there were risks:

> The danger is [creatives] become so much part of the team, so client-focused, that they lose their . . . annoying outside subjectivity! Because we can logic our way to anything, but sometimes the creative process does need to be just like that [able to

make creative leaps] . . . One side of the team are trying to put order into something, and creative teams are non-linear, emotion-based, instinct-based and come from a perspective which says how can I do something different . . . Whereas we [planners] want to do something different, but we want it to be relevant and to the purpose . . . The creative department, though, has a 'ring of guards' around it! (Kendall, 1996).

Both men's defence of the separateness of creative teams and the concern to provide the working conditions under which they could generate the necessary imaginative leaps to bring a clients' brief to life was centrally tied in with BBH's vision of itself as a 'creative agency' and the producer of 'creative advertising'. Thus, while BBH attempted to 'free up' the creativity of all its core workers, it retained a sense that creatives were a special case and the privileged source of creativity. This was different, as we have seen, from HHCL's approach. It attempted to give scope to other practitioners to becomes the source of creativity more broadly conceived and to erode the division of labour within the creative development process – though, it should be noted, that HHCL still effectively paired creative teams within this more open structure. These different approaches carried discrete messages about the relative status and standing of creatives in each agency and were intimately bound up with the broader understanding of the kinds of commercial expertise each agency primarily saw itself as supplying.

conclusion   The organisational reforms pursued by both BBH and HHCL and the positioning of creative jobs within the creative development process that was central to this were not unique to these two agencies. Similar initiatives were evident across the industry and effected even in established, multinational agencies. The WPP Group, for example, introduced project teams into its two venerable agencies, Ogilvy and Mather and J. Walter Thompson. As with the approach taken by BBH, creative teams were exempted from the project teams established by WPP because of the felt sense – expressed by WPP's Chief Executive, Martin Sorrell – 'that creatives need to spark off each other' (WPP, 1996: 55).

Other agencies, conversely, more closely followed the model set down by HHCL. Perhaps the most noteworthy was St. Lukes, another iconoclastic and high-profile 'communications' agency. Like HHCL, St. Lukes deployed project teams and emphasised the creative contributions of all its key staff. The agency even refused to enter its advertising work for the industry's creative awards because these exclusively recognised art directors and copywriters as the producers of campaigns.

The practitioners central to this book worked in agencies where the old departmental system, project teams and revised versions of project teams were all operating. All of them, however, performed a job that remained a privileged one within the structure of agencies, but also one that was subject to a certain flux in relation to its boundaries with other core jobs, as agencies sought to establish their identities as all round marketing consultants. It was also a job, whatever the organisational dynamics of the agency, which entailed coming to terms with new expectations about the kinds of creativity that clients were purchasing from agencies. Certainly, the broad promotional and consultancy role that agencies saw themselves as providing prompted an adaptation of conventional art directing and copywriting skills. As we have seen, these moves encouraged the use of promotional techniques and 'creative solutions' to client's business needs that displaced the 30 or 60 second television advert, in particular, from its preeminent position in the repertoire of promotional forms deployed by agencies. As Robert Campbell, founding partner of the agency Rainey Campbell Roalf, succinctly suggested, 'I hope creative people will get satisfaction from different things [other than press and television work]. You'll have to start giving rewards for ideas, not craft' (*Campaign*, 27/8/93: 36–7). We will see later how creatives themselves responded to these challenges. I will also have cause to return to the internal organisational processes of agencies in Chapters 5 and 6 and reflect further on the characteristics of agencies ways of working. However, in the next chapter, I want to consider further the peculiarities of creative jobs by beginning to explore their distinctive social make-up.

déclassé and *parvenus*? the social and educational make-up of creative jobs

Commenting in his mammoth book *Distinction* on the 'new professions', particularly those associated with cultural production ('radio, television, marketing, advertising, social science research and so on' [Bourdieu, 1984: 151], Pierre Bourdieu famously suggested that these jobs were marked by the openness of their modes of entry and career structures and were especially amenable to 'creative redefinition' by their occupants. As he put it, 'jobs and careers [in the new professions] have not yet acquired the rigidity of the older bureaucratic professions and recruitment is generally done by co-option, that is, on the basis of 'connections' and affinities of habitus, rather than formal qualifications' (Bourdieu, 1984: 151). Bourdieu's comments on these occupations were prompted by a wider discussion of the impact of what he called 'diploma inflation' associated with the opening up of educational access in post-war France and by the tensions that this had created in the correspondence between the social and educational backgrounds of individuals and the social make-up and standing of a range of occupations.

Bourdieu was particularly interested in the consequences of the 'democratising of schooling' and the associated redefinition of jobs for the established trajectories and inherited social positions of both middle-class and working-class individuals. While he argued that the former had to increasingly deal with the problem of downclassing, whereby their educational qualifications failed to guarantee them the assumed social position in the division of labour that an earlier alignment between education and jobs would have delivered, the latter had to manage the limits upon their social aspirations as the new qualifications they had achieved failed to produce the social mobility they felt was their due. These structural tensions bore upon the new professions in especially acute ways. Bourdieu contended that the openness of these jobs made them the preferred destination for those middle-class individuals seeking to protect their social standing against 'downclassing', while the same occupations were appealing to those aspiring working-class individuals seeking to overcome the inertia of established class divisions that structured access to occupations.

Written in the late 1970s and grounded in an analysis of French society and the particularities of its education system in the 1960s and 70s, Bourdieu's comments on the 'new professions' remains one of the few sustained empirical commentaries on these occupations and their relationship to the educational system and established class divisions.[1] Despite the need for caution in translating Bourdieu's claims into a different national setting and historical moment, I want to take his arguments about the 'new professions' as the starting point in this chapter for an analysis of the educational and social make-up of the creative jobs performed by the men and women central to the story this book tells. In Chapter 1, I noted some difficulties with Bourdieu's idea of 'new cultural intermediaries' and, in drawing on his specific arguments about the social make-up of these jobs, I want to propose some further qualifications to his analysis as they pertain to advertising employment. The first concerns Bourdieu's assertion about the openness of these jobs and their difference, in particular, from more bureaucratised occupations. While Bourdieu is right to suggest that the 'new professions' – and specifically, advertising – lack the kind of elaborated career structures and pattern of career advancement (based upon formal and certificated criteria) typical of established professions and bureaucratised occupations and instead rely heavily on informal cultural and social capital in allocating individuals to jobs, he tends to underplay the extent to which advertising in Britain at least has historically pursued a professionalising project and attempted to formalise both its recruitment and processes of career development and promotion. While this project has had some conspicuous limits, particularly in the contemporary moment, it none the less reveals moves to more tightly define and formalise the organisation of these jobs in this sector. Significantly, this project has been applied unevenly to the different categories of core employment in the industry and creative jobs have notably been largely exempted from these professionalising moves. In this sense, they are perhaps closer to Bourdieu's model of the 'new professions' than the more 'professionalised' jobs in advertising.

Being alert to differences of this kind within advertising employment has shaped my concern in developing a more differentiated account of the core jobs in a 'new profession' like advertising than Bourdieu is interested in undertaking. Certainly, the differences between creative jobs and other areas of core advertising employment are not only evident in their exclusion from the moves to professionalise advertising. It surfaces in the educational trajectories of creative people. In this chapter, I also reflect on these differences and consider how they further contribute to the distinctiveness of the social make-up of creative jobs. Taken together, the educational and social backgrounds of creative people and the relationship of these jobs to processes of professionalisation serve to underscore the exceptional status of creative jobs within agencies and the way creative people constituted a distinctive social grouping within the industry.

advertising and the new lower middle class

Bourdieu's most celebrated comments on the new cultural intermediary professions in *Distinction* surface in his discussion of both the 'new bourgeoisie' and the 'new petite bourgeoisie'. It is in the course of reflecting on these class fractions that he has some suggestive things to say about the social make-up of these occupations. In particular, it is as embodiments of a new fraction of the petite bourgeoisie that Bourdieu offers his most sustained reflection upon these occupations. Bourdieu is primarily interested in the distinctive characteristics of what he calls the new lower middle class and the way they are differentiated from the established lower middle classes by virtue of their cultural dispositions. He is particularly concerned with drawing out the way this grouping embodies a new 'art of living' characterised by its opposition to older notions of duty, sobriety, modesty and deferred gratification in their own lifestyles and modes of living. In place of this, he contends, the new lower middle class are instead committed to a 'morality of pleasure as duty' (Bourdieu, 1984: 367). Bourdieu sees in this new morality or ethos a more intensive form of individualism that, he suggests, fits with the demands of a consumer-driven economy. It is this ethos that positions the new lower middle class within what he calls the 'ethical avant garde' of consumer capitalism and its new form of 'enlightened conservatism'. For Bourdieu, this is an ethic or ethos that draws the new lower middle class into a cultural alliance with the new middle class, who share the same anti-puritan values and lifestyles. The new middle class occupy similar key roles in the consumer economy as owners, executives and directors in the cultural intermediary professions (Bourdieu, 1984: 310–11).

If it is the cultural dispositions of the new lower middle class that are Bourdieu's main interest, however, he also reflects on the social backgrounds of those individuals who make up this particular section of middling social groups. In fact, Bourdieu contends that this new fraction of the lower middle class is distinctive in the way its occupants derive from a particularly diverse set of social backgrounds. As he suggests, the 'indeterminacy of the new or renovated occupations means that the heterogeneity of the agents trajectories is particularly marked' (Bourdieu, 1984: 359). This heterogeneity stems from those educational and social changes that I have already alluded to. As Bourdieu himself puts it,

It can immediately be seen that, precisely by virtue of their actual and potential indeterminacy, [the new occupations] offer no guarantees but, in return, ask for no guarantees, [and] impose no specific conditions of entry, especially as regards certificates, but hold out the promise of the highest profits for non-certificated cultural capital, which guarantee no particular career prospects . . . but exclude none, not even the most ambitious. [As such they] are adjusted well in advance to the dispositions typical of individuals in decline endowed with a strong cultural capital imperfectly converted into educational capital, or rising individuals who have not obtained all the educational capital which, in the absence of social capital, is needed to escape the most limited of middle positions (Bourdieu, 1984: 358).

For Bourdieu, then, these occupations stand out in being composed of a mixture of *déclassé* middle-class individuals and socially aspirational individuals from lower middle class and, particularly, working-class backgrounds. It is this social mix that gives these occupations much of their distinctive character.

Bourdieu's compelling observations on the make-up of these jobs beg an immediate question. To what extent do they correspond with the social composition of advertising employment in Britain? Evidence about the social backgrounds and trajectories of advertising people, including those working in the London-based industry, is difficult to come by and this occupational grouping as a whole has been conspicuously ignored by empirical sociologists of both stratification and the sociology of work.[2] A small sample of 102 practitioners that I surveyed, however, offers us some suggestive pointers. This revealed that 43 per cent of those in the core professional jobs were drawn from middle-class backgrounds, with an identical percentage coming from lower-middle-class families. 14 per cent were from working class families.[3] While these figures can only be indicative, they do suggest that the make-up of these jobs is more solidly lower middle class in terms of background than Bourdieu's account would indicate, while also confirming his overall claim about the heterogeneity of the origins of individuals in this field of work. The mixture of social origins that my data reveals certainly contrasts sharply with the more uniformly middle-class backgrounds of those professionals working in an adjacent field, like the City of London, surveyed by McDowell at around the same time (McDowell, 1997: 132). She found that City professionals were solidly bourgeois in origin (ibid). In a larger, more ambitious study of the middle classes in the 1990s, Savage et al also noted that the professional middle class was strongly self-recruiting (Savage et al, 1992: 134).[4] However, it may be that the heterogeneous make-up of advertising jobs is typical of lower middling occupations, at least if we are to judge by Tony Fielding's evidence about the lower-middle-classes (Fielding, 1995).[5]

Among the advertising practitioners that I surveyed were important differences between types of practitioners in terms of social backgrounds.

Specifically, the make-up of creative jobs was more clearly skewed towards individuals from subaltern backgrounds. Thus, among the creatives surveyed, 37 per cent came from middle-class backgrounds, of which 52 per cent were from professional middle-class families; 45 per cent came from lower-middle-class backgrounds, of which 52 per cent came from families with small business or petty commercial interests; 18 per cent were from working-class backgrounds. This distribution contrasted with the more solidly middle-class make-up of media buying and planning jobs. Among these practitioners, 56 per cent were from middle-class backgrounds, of which 64 per cent were from professional middle-class families; 40 per cent were from lower-middle-class backgrounds, of which 50 per cent had some business or commercial connections; 3 per cent were from working-class backgrounds. The group of men and women whom I interviewed were representative of the more lower-middle-class origins of creatives. For example, 46 per cent of them came from lower-middle-class families, while 36 per cent of them came from middle-class backgrounds.

More difficult to read off from these figures, given that they represent a snapshot of this sector at one point in time, is whether this social mixture was generated by the same structural conditions identified by Bourdieu in his analysis of the new professions in France. What is clear is that the relationship between the formal education system (specifically in England and Wales) and the labour market in Britain has been subject to significant and ongoing transformations. These have been driven by the increasing importance of credentials to employment and the expansion, in particular, of higher education. The latter changes have been especially important. Prior to 1962, higher education in England and Wales was dominated by the elite Oxbridge Colleges and the Victorian civic universities and attended by just over 7 per cent of the population, mostly young men (Scase and Brown, 1994: 35). Following the Robbins reforms of 1963, together with the founding of the Open University in 1969 and the expansion of provision by the Polytechnics, participation increased to 20.3 per cent by 1990 (ibid).

The increasing number of undergraduates, however, did little to shift the proportion of students from manual and non-manual working class backgrounds attending higher education institutions, though more working class students in absolute terms did enter HE. The most significant changes through this period of reform came from the numbers of women participating in HE. This rose from less than 25 per cent before the Second World War to 43 per cent by the end of the 1980s (ibid). The subsequent creation of a unified higher education sector in 1992 and the further policy drives from central government to extend participation rates have led to 32 per cent of young people entering HE by 2000/1 (Universities UK, 2002).

This expansion of HE has had a number of important consequences. First, it has deepened the division between graduates and non-graduates and, in particular, made it more difficult for the latter to enter into or progress within professional and semi-professional occupations (Scase and Brown, 1994: 27). Second, the expansion of graduate numbers have undermined the status of established graduate careers and led to a process of 'cascading' whereby higher levels of certificated education and training are required to perform jobs that previously placed greater emphasis on on-the-job and hands on experience (Roper, 1994; Scase and Brown, 1994; Lockwood, 1995). Third, the greater emphasis on credentials has intensified divisions between graduates, with professional employers making further distinctions between graduates on the basis of their degree awarding institution. As McDowell notes in relation to professional City work, for example, a credential-based system has reinforced the dominance of individuals from an elite group of Universities among City firms (McDowell, 1997: 129). While the particularities of these developments are different from those detailed by Bourdieu in relation to the 'democratisation of schooling' in France, they have none the less reproduced some not dissimilar conditions with regard to the relationship between education, certification and employment.

The status of advertising as a career has certainly been caught up in these broader changes. From the late 1950s, the advertising industry, through the recruitment and training committee of the IPA, was keen to establish advertising as a graduate career, forming links with the University Appointments Board in 1959. The scheme involved second and third year undergraduates visiting agencies during the summer vacation (see further Nixon, 2000: 65). At the same time it continued to recognise the necessity of attracting non-graduate applicants into the industry. Thus, as the IPA's in-house publication for its members suggested in 1957, not only was it important to attract more graduates, but also 'public school boys and the cream of the secondary schools into advertising. There is a place, to, for the products of the modern schools and plans are afoot for producing an integrated pattern of recruitment' (*Institute Information*, vol 4., no. 12, 1957: 1).

The leading agencies of the period were less inclusive than the IPA and many revealed an ambition to enhance their standing by selecting their top people from public schools and particularly from among graduates. In fact, by the mid-1960s, Pearson and Turner suggest that the big agencies had a preference for graduates with generalist degrees, including a bias towards Oxbridge, among their core employees (Pearson and Turner, 1965: 119–131). There was also a strong smattering of individuals with private school backgrounds. Agencies like J. Walter Thompson were well known for the educational calibre of their staff and Pearson and Turner rather savagely suggested that, 'in the lush advertising years after the war, [JWT] had . . . earned a reputation for hiring Etonians with carnations rather than brains. Sandy Mitchell-Innes (himself an Etonian and one of JWT's two deputy chairmen) retorted that the only Thompson [JWT] man he could remember wearing a carnation was a Harrovian, but the reputation stuck' (Pearson and Turner, 1965: 41).[6] Other agencies, such as Robert Sharp and Partners, deliberately set out to hire Cambridge men. As Pearson and Turner noted, they even put a series of adverts in the Times asking for young men with Firsts (ibid: 122). And other key protagonists in Pearson and Turners account – such as John Hobson and John Metcalf of the agency, Hobson Bates and Partners – were both Cambridge men, with degrees in classics and English respectively (ibid: 133).

Contemporary evidence indicates the continuing preference for individuals of this educational provenance among agency recruiters, particularly as this bore upon those destined for the upper echelons of the industry. Around half of all senior agency personnel (chairman, chief executive and managing directors) that I surveyed were graduates with a wide variety of degrees from elite universities – Oxford, Cambridge, London School of Economics, Warwick and University College London. 50 per cent of these senior figures, moreover, had been to Oxford or Cambridge. Individuals from private school backgrounds continued to be well represented.[7] Among those employed at lower levels within agencies, the percentage who were graduates was high. Among the core jobs, in fact, the overwhelming majority were graduates, with the jobs of account handler, account planner, media buyer and planner explicitly identified by the IPA as graduate jobs (see IPA, 1995). A survey of media buyers and planners, for example, revealed that they all had generalist degrees from a range of 'old (pre-1992) universities'.[8] Perhaps most striking were the figures, again, for creative jobs. They emerge as less overwhelmingly graduate dominated in their make-up. Among the creatives I surveyed, 63 per cent had honours degrees, while 19 per cent counted an HND as their highest educational qualification. The subjects studied by creatives were also markedly different from their professional colleagues. While 44 per cent had taken a generalist degree, the remaining 56 per cent had studied either art or graphic design degrees. In fact, they were five times more likely to have studied a degree or HND in art or graphic design than any other subject. Those who had studied generalist degrees typically had additionally taken a further postgraduate diploma in art direction and copywriting, or else been through the D&AD's creative workshop, which offered technical training in the same skills.

These different educational routes were bound up with assumptions within the industry about the kinds of technical or craft skills required to perform these jobs. In a moment, I want to explore further these institutional processes, particularly those driven by the sectors leading corporate bodies, and consider what further light they shed on creative jobs. It is clear that the educational experiences of creative people, together with their generally more subaltern backgrounds, combined to socially distinguish them from their colleagues working in the other core jobs. Equipped with more technical and quasi-vocational training and more likely to come from lower middle class or working class backgrounds, they formed a distinct social grouping within the industry. As Paul Holt, the executive creative director at Klein and Hart, romantically put it, 'I tell people in my department that we're the C1s, we're the skilled workers, the skilled artisans'.

This educational and social mix was reflected in the group of practitioners that I interviewed. The following examples give a flavour of this. Teresa Walsh, for example, a 36-year-old art director, came from a lower middle class background. Her father had run his own small business, while her mother was a care-worker. She went to the local secondary school, leaving after completing her 'A' levels. After initially training as a nurse, she eventually went to a northern polytechnic to study animation and left with a degree in graphic design. Phil Chantler, a 31 year old art director, came from a skilled working class family, where his father was an electrician working on the North Sea oil rigs and his mother was a hairdresser. He too went to the local comprehensive and took 'A' levels. He then spent 4 years at the local art college, doing first a graphic design course and then an HND in advertising. Chris Bradshaw, a 35 year old art director, came from a lower-middle class family. His father worked in the motor-trade as a sales-man and his mother was a housewife. He took 'A' levels before completing a degree in graphic design at St. Martin's School of Art. Dylan Wrathall, a 32 year old art director, was from a comfortable middle class background, growing up in Hampstead with his father a psychiatrist and his mother a journalist. He attended Westminster public school and read a degree in History and Philosophy of Science at Cambridge. He then did an MA in graphic design at St. Martin's School of Art. Mark Stephenson, a 38 year old copywriter, also came from a secure middle class background. His father was in the armed forces and Stephenson became a boarder at Dulwich College. He then went to Cambridge University, completing a degree in English. He took the D&AD workshop before getting his first creative job. Murray Wright, a 35 year old copywriter, was from a working class Norwich family. His father was a school caretaker and his mother had done a variety of ancillary jobs, including cleaning and kitchen work. He won a scholarship to the local grammar school, before reading Modern and Medieval Languages at Jesus College, Cambridge.

As I have already suggested, institutional processes within advertising played a central role in reproducing this distinctive social make-up of creative jobs and the class divisions within advertising employment of which they were a part. These institutional processes were brought sharply into focus by the modernising of agencies ways of working and the wider dislocatory effects upon agency life that I detailed in Chapter 2. I want to reflect further on these developments now. Opening up these processes is important because they reveal attempts to formalise recruitment and selection within advertising that Bourdieu's conception of the new professions tends to underplay.

raising the standard

Most agencies realise that advertising is under pressure to become a more professional profession . . . Agencies within the IPA are in the vanguard of this move towards a new professionalism. They'll continue to set the standards, and their clients will be the first to reap the rewards (IPA Information Pack, 1998: 10).

Throughout the 1990s, in the wake of the recession that effected the advertising industry in Britain and bound up with the commercial changes that bore on the sector, a concern emerged among the industry's corporate bodies about the levels and standard of training and career development within the industry. This was particularly evident in the initiatives of the two preeminent corporate organisations, the IPA and the Design and Art Directors Association (D&AD). The IPA, in particular, was preoccupied with the professional standing of the industry. Agencies had a poor record on training and professional development and many leading figures in the IPA and beyond were especially concerned about the disparity between the amount of training advertising people received and that typically received by marketing managers of client companies. In addressing this problem, the IPA set itself the goal of elevating the standing of advertising by positioning it as a sector with high standards of training and professional ethics. For example, in 1998 it relaunched its programme of continuing professional development, the IPA 7 Stages programme. Stage 1 was aimed at trainees while Stage 7 catered for senior managers (AA, 4/2a). Deploying the language of professionalism, the IPA saw the programme as contributing to its central objective 'of developing and helping to maintain the highest possible standards of professional practice within the advertising business' (IPA, 1998: 9). It also sought to bolster its bi-annual awards, the IPA Advertising Effectiveness Awards, in order to (as it put it) 'promote advertising accountability and the continuous improvement in professional standards' (IPA, 1998: 12). At the same time the Institute consolidated its guidance to its members on best practice in relation to the process of pitching for client accounts and laid down models of business contract for agencies to follow. Through these moves, the IPA sought to codify a set of professional ethics (ibid).

Maintaining the industry's ability to attract high quality graduates and sustain its profile as an attractive graduate career on a par with competing professions formed a further key element of the IPA's mission. Through the period from 1993-8, evidence suggested that advertising remained a popular career choice for many graduates. Larger agencies, for example, regularly received 2–3,000 applicants for the handful of graduate training programmes that they ran (*Campaign*, 20/6/94: 5; *Independent*, 24/8/94: 19; *Independent on Sunday*, 20/6/96: 19; *Campaign*, 2/10/98: 4). A nagging concern surfaced amid the popularity of advertising as a career choice to university leavers. This centred on the felt sense that advertising was losing out to other occupations – variously, accountancy, the City, the civil service, law and management consultancy (*Campaign*, 29/6/90: 33; 6/1/95: 5; 11/7/97: 18–19; *Independent*, 24/8/95). Thus, while the industry remained inundated with graduate applicants, the top graduates were in many instances bypassing the sector and being scooped up by occupations with better starting salaries and more well-established professional career structures.

The IPA was certainly concerned that the age-profile of the industry gave the impression that advertising offered only the possibility of a short career (IPA, 1995). The Institute's own figures did appear to support this supposition. They revealed that 50 per cent of those employed in IPA agencies were less than 30 years of age, with 80 per cent under 40 (IPA, 2000: 11). The publication 'Graduate careers in advertising agencies' produced by the Institute attempted to allay such fears by insisting, 'an oft-punted fallacy has it that advertising people reach burnout at thirty. Not true. The industry offers lifetime careers. Healthy progress, professionally and financially, comes with the territory' (IPA, 1995: 6). The fact that the IPA needed to labour this point, however, suggested that there was a deep-seated problem with the structure of the career when compared to more established professional occupations.

The IPA increasingly saw its role as helping to redress this perception and improve the quality of graduate applicants. It attempted to put in place mechanisms that would filter out weak applications and raise the standard of those who applied to agencies. This included developing stronger links with universities, in particular those elite institutions that had traditionally supplied the sector with its top people.[9] The IPA also established a graduate 'clearing house' in 1995 to formalise a notoriously informal set of labour markets. As the IPA conceded, 'getting a job in advertising has traditionally been more of an art than a science: personal contacts, luck and a dash of eccentricity were once the pre-requisites' (*Independent*, 24/8/95).

If these moves to formalise recruitment practices and training were recurrently glossed in the language of professionalism, it is clear that there were some conspicuous limits to the IPA's embrace of a professionalising project. The Institute certainly tended to see its training initiatives – like the IPA 7 Stages programme – as complimentary to the training provided by agencies themselves. As such, the IPA conceived of its role as filling in the gaps left by the limited training and career development provided on the job by agencies. In this regard, it subordinated its embrace of professionalism to a model of 'practical education' and, in so doing, placed itself at some remove from the conventional role played by a professional qualifying association.[10] In fact, while the IPA attempted to bolster the standing of the industry through recourse to the language and some of the trappings of professionalism, it mixed this with a more business-orientated model of advertising and the increasingly dominant understanding of advertising as a 'creative industry'. Thus Chris Powell, the IPA's high profile President in 1993, set specific limits on the pursuit of professional status. While he emphasised the importance of raising the standards of conduct within the industry and saw the IPA playing a key role with regard to training and staff development (as well as propagandising for the industry), he suggested, 'I don't think we can do this [raise the standing of the industry] by creating an exclusive pre-entry club, an impractical route in a trade where anyone can, thank goodness, set up and challenge the orthodoxies' (*Campaign*, 23/4/93: 30). Elsewhere he repeated the same point, insisting, 'advertising is a trade. By definition it is not a profession in its literal sense, and if it were people wouldn't be able to start an agency and have a crack at everybody else' (*Campaign*, 2/9/94: 22).

Powell's commitment to an entrepreneurial model of advertising – one that emphasised its dynamic, small business ethos – was indicative of a deep-rooted commitment from many agency people to the world of commerce and entrepreneurship that cut across the moves towards professionalism. Other IPA insiders combined this faith in commercialism with an emphasis on advertising as a creative business. For example, Nick Phillips, the IPA's Director, questioned the value of the industry attempting to follow the model of the established professions and instead emphasised the autonomy of advertising agencies as creative businesses in which 'creativity' was allied to, not antithetical to, the commercial needs of clients. He contended that:

We shouldn't spend too much time looking at accountants, barristers and architects. A much closer and more helpful role model is Michelangelo. He was committed to the clients needs (though not necessarily his first stated brief), original in conception and passionate about standards of production, prepared to work in all media and orientated to the effect of the finished work (*Campaign*, 2/9/94: 23).

In combining an embrace of an attenuated professionalism with other understandings of advertising's occupational identity, both Powell's and Phillips' views were undoubtedly informed by the legacy of earlier moves within the IPA to professionalise advertising in the post-war years. The question of professionalism, in fact, was one that ran very deep in the institutional rationale of the IPA. The Institute had been established in 1927 as the corporate body of advertising agencies in order to promote professionalism. Through the 1950s and 1960s, it had engaged in an extensive and sustained push to consolidate professional standards of conduct within the industry (Nixon, 2000).

Among its chief ambitions at the time was the pursuit of a form of occupational closure in the provision of advertising services based upon certificated education and training (that is, professional qualifications). These moves were motivated by the Institute's vision of the advertising practitioner standing on a par with doctors, lawyers and even accountants as trusted professionals. Despite the optimistic tone of the IPA's pronouncements during these years and its belief in the inevitability of the onward march of professionalism within advertising, this expansive drive to consolidate it as a profession ultimately ran into the sands by the late 1960s. The reasons for this were various, but partly stemmed from the commercial success of agencies in the buoyant years of the post-war consumer economy. Agencies were able to consolidate their position as the preeminent suppliers of advertising services in this period without recourse to the assurances of professional qualifications that the IPA had felt were necessary. In addition many advertising people had clearly felt uncomfortable with the idea of being seen as professionals. Certainly the pull of the identity of the businessman was key and achieving the status of a professional seemed not to have been a high priority for the majority (Nixon, 2000). A sense of themselves as 'artists' and 'creative people' also cut against the pursuit of professionalism in the same period (ibid). What, in fact, emerges from this earlier moment in the history of post-war advertising is the composite character of the occupational identity of the industry. This has been one of the more enduring legacies of the sectors' formation in Britain through the twentieth century.

The IPA's contemporary moves to raise the industry's professional standards were not only striking for the way they were shaped by the legacy of the sectors' formation. They also revealed the uneven way they applied these limited professionalising initiatives across the industry's core jobs. Conspicuously outside its programmes were art directors and copywriters. Thus, in developing a course to extend the professional standing of the industry, the IPA placed creative people outside this exercise. The decision to do this sprung from the unstated assumption that there was something exceptional about creative jobs, and creativity itself, that resisted moves to systematise advertising training. I'll come back to this point in a moment. The IPA's approach to creative jobs further arose in part out of the different educational pathways, which the majority of creatives followed en route to a career in advertising. As we have seen, the most important feature of this was that creatives tended either to have a specialist degree or else not have followed undergraduate studies at all. In both cases, they did not neatly fit into the IPA's graduate training model. As the IPA's publication 'Graduate careers in advertising agencies' openly acknowledged, its advice was not centrally aimed at creatives: 'It is the other core jobs that opportunities for graduates principally exists. Creatives may be graduates, but they are equally likely to come from other educational backgrounds' (IPA, 1995: 18).

Being outside the training and career development programmes run by the IPA generated its own problems for those industry insiders concerned with the training and skills levels of creatives. If the industry was generally critical of much of the vocational advertising training provided by HE and FE institutions, then its views on the specialist training provided for art directors and copywriters was even less sympathetic. The D&AD, the IPA's sister organisation that represented creative practitioners, was especially vocal in its comments, suggesting that much of the education offered by colleges was poor: 'To call it lamentable would be polite. Too often we've had students from colleges . . . who were well short of any idea about what it takes to create an advert because they've been taught by people who have never practiced advertising or practiced it badly' (*Campaign*, 16/7/93: 22). For some commentators these problems stemmed from the fact that 'creativity' could not be taught beyond the acquisition of basic craft skills. Certainly, formal qualifications in art directing and copywriting were seen of little value given that creatives were judged by their last piece of work. As Barbara Nokes, creative director of CME KHBB argued, 'the trouble with the creative area is that it is more of an art than a science. People exist on their track record rather than by virtue of a certificate issued ten years ago' (*Campaign*, 4/9/93: 24). Other leading industry figures like Dave Trott, former creative director at GGT, contended that it was the working environment of agencies, which forged creative skills. As he suggested, 'it is the agency environment which provides the spark. CDP in the 1970s was a world away from anything a college could teach (*Campaign*, 16/7/93: 22).

Such views were not shared by the D&AD and the organisation was adamant that the industry's 'creative future' required appropriate levels of investment through education and training. Reflecting at its annual student awards in 1998, David Kester, the D&AD's education offer, argued,

> The assumption that creativity is an innate talent which develops naturally on the job is ripe for challenge, and D&AD will do so with a research project into the training needs of creatives to be launched in the autumn (D&AD Student Awards, 1998: 1).

Addressing the education and training needs of creatives, in fact, became one of the central elements in the D&AD's conception of its role as it restructured itself in the early 1990s.[11] In 1995, it published the first in a new series of 'mastercraft' books that aimed to raise the skills levels in creative departments. The first of these was 'The copy book'. This offered its readers exemplary instances of advertising copy, with commentaries on them by their creators. 'The art direction book', published in 1997, followed the same format for art directors. The DandAD billed the series as part of a 'long-term counter-attack against the training crisis in the industry' (*Campaign*, 27/1/95: 35; 6/10/95: 27).

The association also promoted its 'Creative workshops' with renewed vigour at around the same time. The workshop had been established in 1978 and ran four times a year. They gave the successful applicants the opportunity to work on briefs and have their work assessed by established creatives. Competition to get a place on the workshop was intense, with only 22 applicants being accepted on the six-week course. The workshop was widely recognised as a good source of training and an established way into the industry (see D&AD Advertising Workshop, 1997). The course did not guarantee success, however, and the experiences of the young creatives taking the 'Creative worskshop' were sharply different from those of their peers in other core jobs. This difference was clearest in relation to the transition from training to full-time employment. Unlike the graduate training courses run by agencies for account handlers or planners, courses like the D&AD Creative workshop typically led, in the first instance, not to a salaried job but to a creative placement. Placements were one of the most distinctive features of the career trajectory of creatives relative to other specialisms. Creative placements were job trials in which creatives worked in agencies, typically on 'live' client accounts, for little or no payment.

The use of placements by agencies expanded rapidly from 1990 and developed into effectively a system by the mid-1990s. The precise form that placements took varied from agency to agency. A survey by *Campaign* in 1996 revealed big differences between the duration of placements and the kind of remuneration individuals received. BBH paid placements £150 per week and limited the placement to a three month fixed term. O&M, on the other hand, paid £50 per week for a two-week placement, while HHCL put its placements on a freelance contract (*Campaign*, 18/6/96: 12). Anecdotal evidence suggested that the experience of many teams was far harder. Some placements were retained for up to nine months and paid as little as £35 per week. Agencies often colluded in fraud by tacitly encouraging individuals to sign on for social security during placements. In the majority of instances there was no guarantee that, even if they had performed well during the placement, the creatives would be offered a full-time job.

The issue of creative placements generated considerable debate in the trade press, with the letters page of *Campaign* and *Creative Review* period-ically including (often) anonymous letters from young hopefuls berating the industry for a practice that was experienced as exploitation. Much of the problem with placements arose out of the unhappy coincidence of the contraction of the industry in the early 1990s and the increased supply in the numbers of would-be creatives graduating from HE and FE colleges. The rapid institutionalising of the placement system was also underpinned by a belief that they were, in the words of Tony Cullingham, the course director at West Herts College, 'a necessary evil' (*Campaign*, 18/10/96: 12). As the leading creative Trevor Beattie argued, 'it is still the best way for agencies to take a look at a team in a work experience situation, and for the team to get a taste of what the industry is all about' (ibid; see also, *Campaign*, 25/5/90: 42; 13/9/91: 41; 16/4/93: 30; IPA, *Portfolio People*, 2000).

Recruitment for creative jobs was undertaken via the submission of a creative portfolio, a collection of completed work and speculative adverts produced by the team. Creative directors typically reviewed this submitted material and then interviewed a shortlist of candidates on the basis of their portfolio of work if and when jobs became available. Anecdotal evidence from creative directors suggested that teams were often difficult to separate on the basis of their portfolios. For some industry commentators this prob-lem had become particularly acute because of the proliferation of advertising courses that offered training in art direction and copywriting skills. This had led, it was felt, to an increasing homogeneity in the portfolios submitted by teams. Placements were an attractive option for creative directors in this context, since they provided further ways of discriminating between teams and enabled creative directors to assess how teams performed on 'live' accounts (see *Campaign*, 16/7/93: 22–2; 5/2/99: 12; 19/3/99: 7).

It was evident that many aspiring art directors and copywriters saw placements as an unavoidable experience to be undertaken en route to the hoped-for financial rewards of a career as a successful creative. Certainly the salaries of top creatives offered a tantalising glimpse of high material rewards. A creative director in a London agency could expect to earn in excess of £159, 000, with added bonuses like share options, private medical insurance, club subscriptions and a clothing allowance (Campaign Report, 19/1/90: 7; 22/11/96: 5) If a creative moved into freelance directing and established a 'star' reputation, they could earn in excess of £750, 000 a year. Account handlers, media buyers and account planners at a similar stage in their careers were likely to earn between £55–75,000 (ibid). The labour market in creative jobs was noteworthy, however, for the wide variations in salaries. Whereas there was a more established salary ladder for the other core jobs, creative salaries ranged from the low levels of young teams on placements taking home under £5,000 a year to a team with five years experience earning around £40,000, to the mega-salaries of star individuals (ibid). More so than other core jobs, then, the labour market for creatives was highly differentiated and placements contributed to this situation. The job market for these jobs was also characterised by the mobility of creatives between agencies and career advancement typically rested upon moving between agencies rather than promotion within one agency. This characteristic of creative jobs placed great weight on visible markers of a teams standing and, in particular, wining peer recognition through the system of creative awards was central to career success for art directors and copywriters. These awards were the currency upon which creatives could trade and progress in the industry.

This feature of the labour market in creative jobs encouraged a career-orientated approach to work, rather than loyalty to one particular agency. It also made networking at both formal and informal industry events a more important prerequisite for creatives than for other core practitioners. Being known on the industry circuit of award ceremonies, launches and the wider social networks of the industry was central to career success. Two of the women creatives I interviewed, Samantha Jones and Miranda Harris, were explicit about the importance of these forms of networking. As Samantha Jones put it, 'we're quite sociable people, especially Miranda, and that's how we'll get our next job. I mean, our portfolio is as good as the next person's, but that is how we will get on, by drinking with the right people, and talking to the right people [. . .] even if we feel really knackered, we will go, because nine times out of ten you will meet someone who is useful there. You just have to play the game'. Social capital, in this sense, was integral to the pursuit of the successful art directing or copywriting career.

conclusion   The structure of the labour market for creative jobs formed one central element in differentiating creative people from their colleagues employed in other core agency jobs. Offering greater scope for rapid career advancement and higher material rewards, it was also marked, as we have seen, by the absence of structures that facilitated smooth career development and progression. This characteristic of the market for these jobs was symptomatic of the way employment in them fell outside moves to formalise recruitment and training by the industry's corporate bodies, the D&AD's ambitions notwithstanding. Shaping this exclusion were, as we have seen, deep-rooted arguments about the technical skills and, specifically, 'creativity' possessed by good creatives. The latter capacity was, in particular, seen, by its very definition, to be resistant to attempts to contain and organise it within professional or bureaucratic structures. Despite the initiatives taken by agencies to 'free up' the creativity of all their core workers that I discussed in Chapter 2, it is clear that recruitment into the industry and patterns of career advancement continued to differentiate between the special attributes of creative people and their 'professional' colleagues.

Absenting creatives in this way from the limited process of formalising recruitment and training in advertising employment, placed creative people close to Bourdieu's conception of the 'new professions' with which I began this chapter. In their social make-up, they also confirmed his account of the diverse social mix of these new occupations. As we saw, the educational and social backgrounds of art directors and copywriters revealed a combination of *déclassé* middle class and aspiring lower middle class and working class individuals, though the balance overall was towards individuals from more subaltern origins. This skewing of their social make-up, combined with the fact that the job was less overwhelmingly graduate dominated, again set these practitioners apart from their colleagues. Creatives thus emerge as a distinctive social grouping within the social relations of agencies. This distinctiveness was profoundly reinforced by a further dimension of the social make-up of these jobs that I haven't yet considered, but that is fundamental to the arguments of the book. This concerns the way the jobs of art director and copywriter were overwhelmingly male dominated. I turn to the gender make-up of the job in Chapter 5. However, before doing so, I want to reflect further on the way ideas of creativity were bound up with the occupational ethos of these jobs. Moving from the level of institutional practices and the pronouncements of the corporate organisations, I want to consider how the rubric of creativity surfaced in the subjective identities of creative people themselves. In doing so, I also want to bring greater clarity to how we might understand what creativity is in relation to advertising practices.

the cult of creativity: advertising creatives and the pursuit of newness

> I want this industry to catch up with areas like music, fashion, design and film. In dance music alone you have techno, handbag, garage, trance, trip-hop, swing, gangsta, rap and on and on. There is so much originality. In advertising you are called original if you thieve something first (Dave Buonaguidi, St. Lukes, *Guardian*, 26/2/96: 14)

> There is a new school of creative, I suppose, because there's a lot of young teams giving two fingers to the industry. [. . .] People are communicating in so many different ways that the old mainstream ideas and means of communicating are becoming irrelevant. [. . .] You can reach people through clubs, through records, through the Net – and that's just the beginning. The old school of ads, all the gentlemanly press work and refined messages, don't work and the old boys of advertising don't like that idea. . . . It's time for a change (Mark Taylor, Cogent, ibid).

Dave Buonaguidi and Mark Taylor's comments appeared in a profile of a group of young advertising creatives published in the *Guardian* in February 1996. The group, who worked across a range of agencies, had gained notoriety through their association with a set of controversial adverts produced in the mid-1990s. The adverts included work for the television channel TNT, for Holsten pils lager, for the leisure operator Club 18–30, the jewellers Great Frog and the motorcycle manufacturer Harley Davidson. The campaigns were certainly striking. In the most talked about – Saatchi & Saatchi's poster and press campaign for Club 18–30 – the adverts deployed explicit sexual puns to sell the holidays as opportunities for young male heterosexual adventure, with one poster leading with the immortal copy 'Beaver Espania'. In another campaign – Viv Walsh and Jo Tanner's advert for the Great Frog jewellery – the promotion ended with the telling line 'If you don't like our jewellery, fuck-off!'.[1]

Industry grandees reacted with consternation to the campaigns. For example, Adrian Holmes, chairman of the agency Lowe Howard-Spink and the 'doyen of London's creative establishment' (*Campaign*, 24/3/95: 11) used his speech at the prestigious Monte Carlo television event in 1995 to challenge what he called the 'new unpleasantness, the new brutishness, the new yobbishness' that he saw as characterising the communicative ethos of these adverts (*Campaign*, 17/3/95: 8). Other practitioners at the upper echelons of the industry similarly balked at the campaigns and rallied to Holmes' side. For Chris Powell, President of the IPA, and Frank Willis, director of advertising and sponsorship at the ITC, the highly targeted nature of the adverts threatened not only to offend the wider public, but also to damage the standing of the advertising industry at a time when it was trying to promote itself as a responsible and business-like sector (*Campaign*, 24/3/95: 6, 11 and 24; 31/3/95: 26; 7/4/95: 26; 21/4/95: 22).

While the exchanges between these rather differently placed practitioners registered some enduring questions confronting advertising practice, including its sometimes fraught negotiation of the dominant codes of public discourse relating to taste, decency, propriety and politeness, the debate was telling in other ways. Buonaguidi's and Taylor's comments in particular point us towards models of creativity and accounts of the creative process that circulated widely within the London-based advertising industry. Running through both men's comments was an assumption that producing new and original work was the central goal of advertising creatives and, moreover, that this work had to be produced in the face of those constraints set by 'mainstream' advertising and the dominant communicative ethos of the sector. Thus, both Buonaguidi and Taylor marked out their ambition to produce challenging and innovative work that pushed at the boundaries of advertising convention. At the same time, they allied themselves with broader innovative currents within the culture, including, in Buoanaguidi's case, what he saw as more dynamic and creative areas of cultural production. In asserting this vision of the kind of work they strove to produce, Buoanguidi and Taylor were drawing on a well-worn critical analysis of cultural production that counterposed 'authentic creativity' with the restricted, formulaic or instrumental forms of commercial practice. Significantly, however, both men reworked this opposition as a division *within* advertising practice. Thus, Buonanguidi, for example, offered an analysis of the sector in which he worked that closely echoed familiar critical commentaries upon advertising. Like Raymond Williams's haughty dismissal of the ascription of the term 'creative' to the kinds of cultural production that took place within advertising, Buonaguidi spoke of advertising as guilty of producing only second-rate, imitative cultural products and as devoid of the dynamic creativity of a cultural form like dance music (Williams, 1976: 84). The implication of his comments, though, was that he was precisely interested in pursuing 'authentic creativity' within the commercial framework in which he found himself. Mark Taylor similarly sought to ally his own ambition to use advertising and marketing techniques that were distinct from dominant advertising forms – notably long-copy press advertising – with the production of genuinely innovative and creative work.

Buonaguidi and Taylor's comments are an appropriate place to start because they were not alone in drawing on this opposition between 'authentic' and 'second-rate' creativity. Similar oppositions loomed large in the accounts of the practitioners that I interviewed. In this chapter, I want to explore their accounts of the creative process. As we will see, there was no consensus among them on how the work they performed should be understood within the rubric of creativity and it is the divisions between the competing models of creativity that they held, as much as common themes that united them, that I want to explore. While their accounts of the creative process were clearly distinct from the actual performance of their jobs, that is, from the phenomenology of cultural production itself, the models of creativity that the practitioners deployed surfaced with subjective force in their accounts and are revealing about the occupational identities they inhabited. In fact, what we can see in the recourse they make to competing models of creativity is a handling of a central occupational dilemma: was it possible to produce authentic creativity in advertising or were they merely commercial hacks? As we will see below, in taking up different positions on this question, individual practitioners attempted to centre their identities as creative people within this world of commercial work with rather different effects.

Attending to the links between the rubric of creativity deployed by the men and women I interviewed and the occupational standing of their work, however, does not fully explain the rhetoric of creativity that flowed freely from these practitioners and the place of this trope in their accounts. In pushing further at their ideas of creativity and the creative process, I want to engage with Keith Negus's suggestive arguments about creativity developed in relation to his work on popular music. Negus's work is shaped by a number of concerns. One overriding insistence is his ambition to move beyond the opposition between 'commerce' and 'creativity' that has dogged critical discussions of commercial cultural production. To this end, he has argued that music corporations – the embodiments of commercial and business calculation – play a key role in according recognition to certain kinds of musical creativity and in shaping the context in which claims about the 'creativity' of particular kinds of musical production can be made – and contested – in the first place. Underpinning this contention is a broader argument about creativity. Drawing on well-established precepts within cultural analysis, Negus suggests that creativity is not best thought of as being about sudden bursts of originality or invention, but rather consists of working with established genre codes, conventions and expectations. It involves the introduction of some element of novelty or difference within a recognisably familiar constellation of meaning. As he succinctly puts it, what is usually at stake in identifying some cultural practice as creative is the combination of both newness and familiarity to which audiences and other practitioners themselves respond. It is this slight different-ness, rather than absolute novelty, which is usually at stake in debates over creativity. However, Negus also acknowledges that these critical discussions about the value of a particular cultural form or practice can also be driven by a struggle over the genre worlds themselves and the genre hierarchies within these worlds (Negus, 1995; 1998; Negus and Pickering, 2000).[2]

These observations, despite being derived from the study of popular music, are pertinent to my arguments about advertising and creativity. They allow us to conceptualise the forms of cultural production in which art directors and copywriters are engaged as involving tightly defined, if not static, representational genres. Press and television advertising, most clearly, are characterised by a well established and relatively limited set of genres. Individual creative teams conventionally work with these genres, introducing or attempting to introduce elements of novelty or difference within the frameworks of well-established rules and expectations. Thus, despite the grandiose claims often made about the work they did or would liked to have done, we might profitably interpret the rhetoric of creativity mobilised by creatives as an extrapolation of quite small differences or degrees of different-ness. In this sense, their cult of creativity was partly bound up with a 'narcissism of minor difference' in which creative teams sought to differentiate themselves from other practitioners in the advertising that they produced.

The valorisation of creativity was tied up less, in this sense, with making a client's product stand out – the manifest commercial reason for finding new ways of communicating with consumers – so much as with drawing attention to the creative teams in an intensely competitive occupation. Moreover, as Taylor and Buonaguidi's comments suggest, the pursuit of newness often came to be bound up with struggles over genres and genre hierarchies and further coded in generational terms, with the young creatives whom I interviewed allying themselves with 'newness' in order to steal a march on more established colleagues. In this latter sense, we might read into this pursuit of newness and creativity a form of social fantasy in which the striving for difference was bound up with 'making it' in the industry.

commerce and creativity

Its [advertising] one of those businesses that's a little bit like . . . at worst, it's a little bit like making a car. If you tick all the right boxes, then you will create a car. Whether it's

> a very good one is irrelevant half the time. And so what I'm always trying to do is find
> a style. I mean, I want to make Ferraris, or I want to make something that's a little bit
> more extraordinary than just a car.

Paul Cantelo was a 33 year old art director working for Serendipity, a smallish but rapidly expanding agency in central London. He occupied a central role in the shaping of the agency's creative work and was evangelical about the direction in which the agency ought to develop. At the heart of this was a general antipathy towards the rest of the industry in which he worked and an elaborated concern to produce genuinely creative and original advertising. While the taking up of an anti-advertising position was not uncommon within the industry, his comments on these issues defined him as the most enthusiastic exponent of the cult of creativity among the practitioners I spoke to. Integral to this was an almost doctrinal conviction that only low levels of 'creativity' currently existed within the London-based advertising industry. As his comments, above, indicate, he saw the industry as organised around standardised production procedures in which the making of adverts was as devoid of individual creativity as the mass production of motor cars.

Echoing familiar critiques of mass society Cantelo identified this malaise within advertising as part of a wider process of cultural standardisation in which the innovative currents in contemporary culture were being subsumed by mediocrity and conformity. This was a world in which the search for the 'winning formula' meant that 'all cars look like Austin Montegos, all homes look like Barratt homes, and everyone dresses in denim'. Advertising was, for Cantelo, a guilty partner in this process of 'levelling down'. As such it was an industry that prompted his contempt. Adding to his earlier comments, he vented his spleen about advertising mixing together a moral Puritanism with an emphasis on the pursuit of authentic creativity:

> I loathe the business, I can't stand the business. I think its full of shit. I don't like the fact that a lot of business has just been grown out of money, because I think that's the biggest, that's the dirtiest thing. And you know, it should be a creative business, and people kid themselves it's a creative business. And I can't think of an ad that I've ever seen on TV that I've really liked. . . . I used to find that really worrying. But then you think, 'well that's good because it sets me apart'. I think you just have, in the end, to challenge everything.

This aggressive, moralistic attack on the industry in which he made his living served to underpin his own sense of himself as a dissident or outsider seeking to bring creativity to a moribund world. He further marked his distance from the 'mainstream' of advertising by identifying with rule breakers and difficult creative types. Thus, he contended,

I like really angry people who've got a problem, people who are never satisfied with doing things the expected way. I don't like professional creatives. You get painters whose whole life is painting. But in advertising you can do it on a part-time basis. You know, make a living out of it and then go home and eat sushi all the rest of your life.

What was important for Cantelo was that advertising people fully immersed themselves in the creative process in a way analogous to the fine arts and were not merely luxuriating in a comfortable life ('eating sushi all the rest of your life'). During the course of the interview he emphasised on a number of occasions how he attempted to live out this model of creative immersion. He described how he spent much of his spare time painting and making decorative objects from salvaged materials. In reflecting on his painting, he emphasised the way he strove to find and 'sort out' his own style. This emphasis on developing a unique style was, as we have already seen, important to him and not restricted to his hobby painting. Railing against the forms of explicit cultural appropriation and pastiche evident within advertising over the last twenty years, he further argued,

Yes, go and see as many galleries and all those kind of things as you want to do, but when you start working on your own stuff [ads], then make sure it comes from you rather than Damien Hirst or someone else, because otherwise you've let someone else do the hard work. Originality is the only thing that matters . . . creativity is all about originality.

In expressing this opinion, Cantelo touched on a central and rather vexed question for creative people working in advertising, particularly given the trend that Cantelo alluded to: of explicit cultural referencing and post-modern irony that had become a feature of some advertising throughout the 1980s and since[3]. This concerned the legitimacy of appropriations from other cultural forms into advertising. Periodically the industry was faced with claims by fine artists that agencies had illegitimately reworked their ideas. For example, in June 1998, the Turner Prize winning artist Gillian Wearing accused the agency BMP DDB of using her idea for its commercials for Volkswagen. In 1994, Bridget Riley successfully challenged O&M over an advert for Sun Pat peanut butter that she claimed was based upon one of her paintings (*Campaign*, 19/6/98: 12). One influential response from within the industry was to recognise that advertising was indeed a cultural practice that necessarily worked through cultural appropriation rather than outright innovation. As Trevor Beattie, executive creative director at GGT, argued, 'advertising is a world of magpies and we steal sparkling things. . . . We go to a club and steal a trend and go on to appropriate whole chunks of youth culture. . . . Advertising never sets trends, it only follows them' (ibid).

This view was some distance away from Cantelo's lofty vision of creative originality as something that was not culturally founded but sprung from deep within the individual. Cantelo saw his task as stripping away cultural influences to allow his authentic 'voice' to come through. However, other practitioners whom I interviewed, despite often sharing his ambition to produce inventive advertising, conceptualised the sources of creativity in terms closer to Beattie. This saw creativity as emerging not so much in sudden bursts of absolute originality, as coming out of the manipulation and reworking of cultural influences. Generating 'creative solutions' in this sense was a craft that could be learnt. Murray Wright, a freelance copywriter, echoed Beattie's analysis in spelling out clearly this model of creativity:

> You've got to have a magpie eye for shiny things. Creativity in relation to campaigns is not about picking ideas out of the air and coming up with something original. Not least because the deadlines are so tight . . . what you need to have is the sort of mind that stores all sorts of bits of information – that can be a song you've heard, programmes or films you've seen, pieces of art or whatever. And suddenly you have a brief to work on and somewhere in the back of your mind you think, 'Ah, that's relevant, I can use that. The job is really problem solving.

Andy Hanby, a creative director at Paul & Rogers, made a similar point:

> I am a consumer. I take influences from everywhere. Being a passionate consumer really does help. Just seeing and absorbing things. . . . And then just storing all the images and replaying them when you've got an appropriate brief. . . . It's about keeping yourself up to speed with what's going on in real life. If I don't know who's in Coronation Street, then I'm pretty much out of touch. If you're constantly in touch with what happens in the real world, then you can hopefully try and give it back to people in the form of some kind of advertising. And talk to them in their language.

While the notion that being *au fait* with Coronation Street is the same as being in touch with real life is a rather extraordinary claim to make, Hanby's comments emphasise the need for creatives to be fully immersed in the widest possible set of cultural currents. It is out of this immersion that creatives could draw inspiration and channel these influences into inventive advertising. Phil Chantler, an art director at Rowlands & Partners, made a similar point. His comments were additionally interesting, however, because they revealed how both an emphasis on the cultural sourcing of creativity could be combined with an understanding of creativity as something that emanated from within the individual. Thus, having suggested that it was important to be a 'cultural omnivore' (echoing Hanby and Wright's comments), he claimed,

> Being fascinated by everything is really important. Like tuning into something that's already there. Being receivers for that. Being interested in everything, culture, aeroplanes, books, films, everything. And then eventually, if you let yourself, *it can come out of you* in the work (emphasis added).

What is significant in Phil Chantler's comments, then, is the way he sees creativity as something that is essentially internal to the creative, as something that 'comes through' him, while simultaneously understanding the process of creation as dependent upon the cultural resources available to him. Such a heterodox understanding, which was also hinted at in Hanby's comments, pointed to an understandable difficulty among the practitioners I interviewed of marrying critical understandings of creativity with their actual experience of generating ideas and executing adverts. As with the musicians that Negus discusses, there was almost inevitably an unbridgeable gap between the way these men formally talked about the creative process and the lived, phenomenological experience of 'being in' the act, in the moment of cultural production. Hence, the recourse made by Chantler to both culturally sourced and more mystical understandings of the creative process.

The competing models of creativity that could be applied to advertising and the porous boundaries between them, however, were not only the product of this phenomenological distance between the act of creating and the subsequent process of describing these practices through language. The tensions thrown up by the contrast between mystical and culturally-sourced conceptions of creativity in their testimonies was itself the product of tensions built right into the kind of training these practitioners had received en route to becoming advertising creatives. Looming large here was the influence of art and design education. As discussed in Chapter 3, the majority of art directors and copywriters had entered advertising via degree, HND or diploma level studies in either fine art or graphic design. The remainder, who had entered via generalist humanities degrees, had typically encountered elements of this kind of art and design training through taking either postgraduate diplomas in art direction and copywriting or the D&AD workshops.

Training was important because it exposed the practitioners to two influential, co-joined models of creativity embedded within the teaching of art and graphic design. These sprung from the separation within the art schools of the 'fine arts' and the 'applied arts' and represented a distinctive version of the established opposition between 'authentic' and 'derivative' creativity that had a wider critical currency. Institutionalised through the Coldstream reforms of the 1960s, this division within art and design education drew a clear line between how the creative process was to be understood on either side of the pure/applied division. While in the former, ideas of romantic individualism were encouraged and creativity was understood as emerging in sudden bursts of originality from gifted individuals, in the latter creativity was understood in more circumscribed terms as a form of commercial craftsmanship involving the mobilisation of cultural resources to solve externally set problems (Frith & Horne, 1987: 27–48). These models, as is clear from the testimonies we have encountered, exerted considerable authority over how the practitioners I interviewed thought about the creative process. For example, Phil Chantler, unsurprisingly, clearly drew upon the graphic design training he had received at Newcastle Polytechnic, to describe his practice largely in terms of a model of applied creativity. Paul Cantelo likewise mobilised ideas of creativity derived from the arts foundation course he had taken at Epsom College. Interestingly, however, the fit was not always straightforward. Andy Hanby had studied fine art at University of Belfast and yet understood the commercial practice he was engaged in within the model of applied creativity. In doing so, he was clearly registering the difference between the kind of cultural practice that he had been trained in and that which he undertook as paid employment.

There was something more at stake in the choice these practitioners made in the way they conceptualised the creative process than simply the reproduction of the languages of creativity that they had learnt within further and higher education. How they represented their work tells us something about their broader occupational identifications. Centrally, it sheds light on how they handled the cultural standing of the form of commercial practice in which they were engaged. In the 1960s, the IPA had neatly captured this as the dilemma of the 'artist in advertising'. Addressing an audience of would-be illustrators and designers, it posed the following question: was the 'artist in advertising' a mere executant of a client brief, a 'hack', or were they a fully engaged thinker and source of genuine creativity? Cautioning its readers against imagining themselves as on a par with genuine creative artists ('It would be wrong for an art school to judge any of its students work from a commercial point of view. You must understand that it would be equally wrong for a commercial body to judge an artists work solely from an art point of view [. . .] Grasp this truth and you will save yourself a great deal of disillusionment later' [IPA, 1965: 4]), the document none the less sought to delineate some space for the 'commercial artist' to exercise discretion and influence over the work he or she produced for clients, a space that offered advertising people some limited autonomy (IPA, 1965).

Despite both the different commercial and cultural climate and the changes in the organisation of creative jobs themselves since the mid-1960s, the practitioners I interviewed experienced the same dilemma as that drawn out by the IPA. Specifically, they had to negotiate the ongoing subordination of 'commercial art' to apparently more autonomous fields of cultural production. This was despite some moves to reconcile commerce and creativity within critical analysis. These had opened up the possibility of recognising the value of cultural practices shaped by clear commercial imperatives. Thus, the design critic Stephen Bayley, inverting the usual cultural hierarchy, claimed that 'the people with the real visual talent don't bother to call themselves artists; these people are too busy making potent modern art, like television commercials' (Bayley, 1989, quoted in Whiteley, 1994: 122).

The D&AD also assertively drew on this understanding in the late 1990s in its publications. As the preface to the 1997 D&AD Annual put it, 'our creatives enjoy an unrivalled international reputation – in particular for their willingness to take chances and to break new ground. But this is not simply innovation for innovation's sake. Creatives and clients alike recognise the link between creativity and commercial success' (D&AD, 1997: 1). Practitioners like Cantelo, most notably, as we have seen, remained troubled by the older denigration of 'commercial art' and sought to valorise the commercial work they performed by aligning it with the fine arts in order to counter the negative associations of commercial practice. Others, like Hanby, embraced their role as commercial technicians. It is worth reflecting upon this latter response. In shying away from the move to elevate their working practices by aligning them with the fine arts, Hanby et al none the less foregrounded their role as independent cultural translators and intermediaries. It was their capacity to connect with cultural trends and to be extremely sensitive to the felt movements of culture that gave creatives authority over the cultural practices in which they were engaged. Other practitioners I interviewed signalled this move even more strongly. They cast themselves as 'conceptualisers' and creative thinkers who were a cut above more dependant commercial artists, like graphic designers. As Samantha Jones, a copywriter at Direct Arts claimed, she and her partner were 'conceptualisers with specific [craft] skills. . . . We fundamentally have the same discipline which is conceptualising, and then we have our separate craft – if there's long copy in an ad I will go and craft it and Miranda will craft the way it looks'. Paul Davenport, a creative at Klein & Hart, on the other hand, suggested that 'graphic designers did menial stuff and what we do is think up ideas'. He further underlined this distinction by derogatorily referring to much of the day-to-day work done by graphic designers (such as tracing type and blocking in areas of colour) as 'wristing'. This invoked the intensive manual process of working on type and layout, but also played upon a masturbatory image to downgrade the practice.

What is significant about the responses of those practitioners who embraced their role as commercial technicians and cultural translators, as well as those who sought to identify with the fine arts, was the way their moves sought to bolster the standing of the commercial practice in which they were engaged. And while the different responses among these practitioners revealed distinct occupational personas, they shared a common concern to elevate the status of the work they performed. The common ground between the art directors and copywriters I interviewed was further evidenced in the way they aligned themselves with the moves away from the absolute centrality of the television spot advert within advertising strategy. In this sense, cutting across the competing models of creativity that they held were arguments about advertising genres and genre hierarchies. Practitioners who held contrasting views on how the creative process worked were often in agreement about the need to challenge what Buonaguidi earlier referred to as the 'mainstream' of advertising and its distinctive generic forms. It is to these arguments over genre that I want to now turn.

the pursuit of newness

> You look at Levi's, why are they still doing 'pop promos' [television and cinema ads] and then running them on the most expensive type of medium? Why don't they just discover young bands, and then run it on MTV or the cinema? But I would go even further than that. Why not give a musician a brief for Midland Bank and say, 'Here's 750 grand, what will you do with that?' And they'd go, 'Well, I wouldn't do an ad. I'd do a bit of music'. And you think, 'Oh, that's interesting, already'. Or a playwright would write a play . . . rather than doing a TV ad (Paul Cantelo).

As part of his diatribe against the industry in which he worked, Paul Cantelo became very animated about the need to not only enhance the existing (low) levels of creativity within advertising, but also to do this through deploying promotional techniques that broke with the established conventions of above-the-line advertising. As his comments above indicate, he was prepared to take on what was regarded in many quarters as one of the most 'creative' and effective television campaigns of the past fifteen years – BBH's long-running work for Levi-Strauss – in order to make his point. In attacking the Levi's adverts, Cantelo was seeking to break free of the established genres of (especially) television advertising and the genre hierarchy that positioned the 30 or 60-second television spot advert as the preeminent form of advertising communication. For Cantelo, challenging the approach embodied in the Levi's adverts released creative people from the familiar and derivative styles of representation that dominated the industry's output and enabled creatives to produce genuinely innovative and inventive work. In Cantelo's terms, then, breaking from 'mainstream' advertising opened up new opportunities for creativity.

Cantelo's views were shared by Steve Message, another established creative who had spent most of his career on the less glamorous side of agency life working for a direct marketing company. Message shared with Cantelo a strong commitment to advertising and marketing techniques that were not reliant upon the classic above-the-line media. A large part of this antipathy sprung from his experiences working in direct marketing and this undoubtedly gave an edge to his views on creativity. Reflecting on his career he emphasised the importance of innovating in the forms through which products and services were marketed. He remarked that:

> I want to be able to achieve what you had with the Heineken campaign in the 1970s without having to go into television or the press . . . to create something like that through other media. [Something] that people will look back on and say that everything changed a little bit at that point. In that sense, I've got a broader view of creativity that is that it's the ability to create surprising ideas in any medium. At the moment, for most creatives, I think it's a rarefied environment that exists. A lot of people only want to do TV ads. It's lovely to do, but it's not the be-all-and-end-all. Why limit yourself to one medium and a very controlled one at that. My view is that creatives of old existed in a lovely situation, but one that isn't destined to last. [Their] reference points were East European cinema and what's happening at the Tate and that's all well and good, but its very limiting.

Message's comments here reveal more than a hint of regret at the passing of an older advertising order, while at the same time they position him on the side of necessary change. If the tide of history in this sense appeared to be with him, it was also clear in his comments that Message strove to ride these currents and to leave his mark by producing a paradigm-shifting piece of work. In this latter sense, his comments are striking for the ambitious nature of his claims. I will come back to this later.

Some of the concerns that preoccupied both Message and Cantelo were also evident in the testimonies of Steve Goode and Mike Walker. They were a pair of young creatives working for Direct Arts and they too emphasised their desire to develop a new communicative ethos as part of their ambition to produce new and inventive work. The pair had met while at college and been working full-time for two years. When I pressed them on whether there was anyone whose work they admired within the industry, Steve Goode replied,

> Chas and Jim just have no respect for anyone in the industry and for what they've done. And they have their own ideas about how things should be done and they've gone and done it. We try and do things differently all the time. We'll always try and do a different route. But we get knocked back so often. Sometimes its clients and sometimes its internal [the creative director or planner]. People are not ready for change. The more traditional teams at college just wanted to do nice headlines and a visual. We were taught – especially when Chas and Jim came to give us a lecture – to think differently. Why not put an ad on the steps of a tube station, rather than in the press and TV?

This passage is striking in a number of ways, but particularly for the opposition around which it pivots. Goode counterposes what he calls 'traditional' teams against original and inventive advertising. He is damning of those students whom he perceived wanted to produce work that fell within the recognisable formulae of above-the-line advertising and, at the same time, seeks to place on a pedestal the work of 'Chas and Jim' whom he felt embodied new and inventive thinking. Chas and Jim – Chas Bayfield and Jim Bolton – were, in fact, a relatively young team who had, at an early stage in their career, already won a number of awards and considerable industry recognition as the exponents of quirky and distinctive work. Elsewhere in the interview, Goode again praised his heroes for the way they sought to 'tear up the industry norms'. In identifying with Chas and Jim, then, Goode revealed something about how he and his partner understood the cultural practice in which they were engaged and the ambition they had to produce new work that contested the established genre hierarchy of advertising.

Not all the practitioners I interviewed were as concerned as Goode and Walker, Cantelo and Message, with challenging established advertising genres. One of Goode and Walker's freelance colleagues at Direct Arts, Murray Wright, aligned himself with the tradition of what he called 'well crafted, erudite, thoughtful long-copy'. He cited the work of Tony Brignull at CDP in the 1970s and David Abbott of AMV as exemplars of the kind of work he admired. Both men were highly respected copywriters and Brignull, for example, had won considerable recognition for his work on CDP's celebrated press and poster campaign for the metropolitan police in the 1970s. For Wright both men's literary skills had raised the status of advertising and distanced it from the brasher forms of promotion and hard sell.[4]

Wright's identification with this tradition of long-copy press advertising was influenced by his own academicism. This was, after all, a man with a degree in Modern and Medieval languages from Jesus College, Cambridge. His identification with Abbott and Brignull was telling in other ways, though, since it revealed an inter-generational continuity in which he saw himself working within a style of advertising established by his illustrious precursors. This emphasis on a connection across generations further set Wright apart from many of the other practitioners I interviewed. Their views on advertising styles were, like those with which we begin this chapter, strongly bound up with a generational model of succession and change. Steve Message's comments earlier, for example, linked his preference for 'new' styles of marketing with his distance from the 'creatives of old'. A similar theme was implicit in Goode and Walker's identification with the youthful iconoclasm of Chas and Jim. This generational dynamic of challenging an established grouping of practitioner was, however, most brutally expressed by Andy Hanby. He explicitly joined together his embrace of new promotional styles with a marking of generational distinctions. He suggested,

Advertising has skipped a generation. Young people in the business tend to think much more 360 degrees [take an all round view] than older people. The older people tend to think, TV commercial, press ad, radio ad, which is very blinkered. . . . It's difficult to teach old dogs new tricks, dare I say it.

This recourse to generational stereotyping is one familiar from other accounts of the world of business (Roper, 1994). Casting those in established positions as 'dead wood' and mobilising a model of inter-generational relations in which the ambition is to aggressively unseat and replace those above you has a wider cultural currency. The advertising industry was riven with these understandings of career hierarchy and succession and the opposition between the established and the ambitious was, as we have already seen from the 'yobbishness' debate, often subscribed to (see especially, *Campaign*, 24/3/95: 23; *Independent on Sunday*, 3/9/95: 10; *Guardian*, 26/2/96: 14–15). The very youthful age profile of the industry also meant that there was a heightened sensitivity to and consciousness of age, together with a valorising of youth. In this context, 'youth' was often positioned as the source of newness and invention. Anthony Simonds-Gooding, Chairman of the D&AD, for instance, spoke almost deferentially of the need for his organisation to 'ensure that we continue to keep very close to the young' (D&AD Annual, 1996: 6), by which he meant young creatives. For many of the practitioners I interviewed, it was clear that a self-consciousness about their generational status as aspiring practitioners was linked with attempts to position themselves as embodiments of the 'new'. Their accounts, thus, often drew an equivalence, as we have seen, between generation, the development of new promotional techniques, and creativity. Moreover, it was clear from the vigour of their assertions and the grandiosity of their claims that a good deal of psychic investment was at stake in their pronouncements. In this sense, the rhetoric or cult of creativity among these practitioners served to support a social fantasy in which they imagined themselves 'making it' within the industry and gaining the 'star' recognition they sought. Whereas, then, one might have expected these practitioners to be content with producing work that clients liked and with doing the job to the best of their ability, they recurrently invoked a narrative of career success analogous to that of pop stars in which transcending established ways of doing things and making it big became the goal.

These desires did not always take such an overblown form. They could also be expressed in more prosaic terms in their accounts and in these instances the link between the pursuit of newness and career advancement were often more explicit. One important way in which this desire for success was more directly expressed was in their stated ambition to win industry awards. We get a clear sense of this in the comments of Miranda Harris, an art director at Direct Arts. Harris was more explicit than most practitioners in elaborating upon the importance of trying to turn every piece of work that she and her partner were given into an opportunity for career advancement. Thus, she suggested,

> everything that lands on your desk, you have to look at it and think, 'Is this gonna win me an award? How can we make this work for us?' I mean 9 times out of 10 it won't because, you know, the brief's really shit, but every time a brief lands on your desk, you think, 'This could be it! I want this to be it!' Or, more importantly, you have to make your own opportunities . . . like we made this speculative ad. You've got to be looking for that, for that sort of thing all the time. You know, what sort of projects can we work on that will help our career?

Steve Goode and Mike Walker were also frank about the motivations that drove their approach to their work. Steve Goode confessed that 'in the end a creative is working for himself, to impress his peers'. This emphasis often made teams impatient about clients' views of the advertising they were buying. As Chris Bradshaw and Steve Dempsey, senior creatives at Knight & Stewart, complained,

for us, when you start on a project you aim to take on the world, to produce the best fucking thing. And its weird, but there's a hell of a lot of businesses [clients] which, seriously, don't want to be edgy, they don't want to be progressive, they don't want the next generation of people to switch onto them, they just want to copy the trends because its safe.

While their comments again emphasised the importance of breaking new ground and innovating in the work creatives produced, they also speak of an anxiety about being held back in that ambition by what they saw as conservative clients. This agitation stemmed from a perception, not entirely without substance, that 'safe' advertising – advertising that repeated well worn techniques of selling and promotion – was unlikely to win awards for a team. Being 'edgy' and 'progressive', on the other hand, more clearly fitted into the D&AD's vision of 'creative excellence' and (most especially) into the criteria by which the association and its jurors awarded its annual prizes. As the D&AD's President for 1999, Larry Barker, emphatically put it,

It's no small feat to get an idea from first thought to finished ad without being compromised. That's what we reward at D&AD. Yes, [we are] strict. No, [we don't] let much in [the annual]. And, yes, there's lots of stuff that's popular and/or effective that will never get in. The Direct line telephone worked. So, is it good advertising? No, its crap and I don't care how effective it was ('Proud to be Cool', *Campaign*, 14/6/99: 25).

In practice what lay behind comments like Barker's was a preference amongst D&AD jurors for adverts and promotions that drew upon the newer currents in graphic design, photography, subcultural style and music. The D&AD was also strongly committed to forms of minimalism in design and an aestheticised and tasteful conception of advertising (see D&AD Art Directors Book, 1998).

There was good reason for the teams to place such emphasis on tailoring themselves to these criteria and to the winning of awards. As we saw in the previous chapter, the labour market in creative jobs was much less formalised than that for other core jobs and the process of both getting a job and making progress in the career was not based upon clear recruitment and promotion criteria. What mattered – and what gave creatives the possibility of rapid career success – was the winning of creative awards. These formed a large part of the currency upon which reputations were made and careers advanced. The possibility of incremental advancement within one agency over a long period of service was an unlikely one for most creatives and the mobility of creative teams between agencies made winning awards an essential goal for an ambitious team.

What is striking about the testimonies of the practitioners is how fully they had embraced the rules that structured the market in creative jobs and how they cultivated a habitus, formally at least, appropriate to prospering in this intensely competitive world. In addition to those practitioners from whom we have already heard, there were other examples. Thus, Jack Scott, a copywriter at Peterson, emphasised the need to be highly mobile and expressed a preparedness to change and adapt. Drawing the analogy with the chameleon quality of certain pop stars, he suggested that 'there is always the danger of repeating past successes. You've got to constantly move, re-invent yourself'. Like other practitioners, Scott was *career*, rather than company, orientated.

The sense of urgency about getting on and gaining recognition evident in these comments was intensified by the short-lived nature of advertising careers. In part out of recognition of this, creative people often suggested that they did not see themselves staying in advertising all their working lives. They aimed to establish themselves in advertising and then saw themselves moving into video and film production on the basis of contacts they had made. Steve Message, on the other hand, worried that he might need to start up his own agency because of the 'cult of youth' within the industry. As he noted, 'I think that's got to be a serious consideration for anybody who's getting on in terms of status and age in the business. I'm 34 and I'm considered to some extent a veteran. In five years time there'll be a guy getting paid half as much as me going "I'll work weekends".'

The structure of the labour market in creative jobs and the individual-ised conception of careers associated with it were important in encouraging the practitioners I interviewed to valorise creativity and to play up the importance of generating new and original work. As such their pursuit of newness represented a strategy of distinction in which they sought to establish the 'different-ness' of their work. In doing so, they were engaged in a process that comes close to Freud's description of what he called the 'narcissism of minor difference'. Freud used the phrase to refer to forms of cultural nationalism in which quite small differences between ethnic groups who were otherwise culturally close came to carry intense symbolic sig-nificance (Igantieff, 1994). For the creatives I interviewed, the cult of creativity worked in a similar way to heighten what were in reality generally only small differences between the advertising they produced, or strove to produce, and that generated by other teams. However, in important ways, the rubric of creativity represented a way of dramatising the desires and insecurities generated by needing to mark out these differences in order to succeed in an intensely competitive world of work.

conclusion I have ended by reflecting on the motivations and desires that fuelled the insistent recourse to the tropes of creativity, newness and invention in the accounts of their working lives given by the practitioners. Much of their valorisation of creativity appeared, as we have seen, paradoxical given that the forms of cultural production in which they were involved were tightly regulated by the genre worlds that made up this sphere of commercial practice. As I have argued, following Keith Negus, what was generally at stake in their claims to creativity were quite small degrees of difference.

Despite the formal constraints on the work they produced, the practitioners were also concerned to contest some of the more negative understandings of this kind of commercial practice that they performed. Looming large here was their handling of the pejorative views of 'commercial art'. And while there were clear differences between how the practitioners understood the creative process in which they were involved, they all sought to bolster their status as creative thinkers and autonomous practitioners in their own right. This move was further evident in the way many of the creatives embraced styles of advertising and promotion that were not dependent on classic above-the-line media. Their embrace of new media and marketing techniques represented something of a displacement of established distinctions, derived from divisions within art education, between 'authentic' and 'formulaic' creativity. In recoding this division, the practitioners cast television advertising as formulaic and identified themselves with other styles of promotion that they saw as genuinely new and creative. The embrace of these promotional forms also carried, as we saw, further symbolic significance. In positioning themselves on the side of these developments within advertising strategy, they aimed to set themselves apart from more established practitioners. Their valorisation of creativity, in this sense, was shot through with generational dynamics in which they sought to embody 'newness' against an established cohort of creatives. What also came through strongly in their pursuit of newness were the career-orientated models of their working lives that they embraced, and their distance from notions of company loyalty and incremental advance within one organisation. The cult of creativity was, in this regard, bound up with their embrace of entrepreneurial and individualistic ways of working.

There is something else in their testimonies that has great significance for the arguments of this book. This concerns the way their ideas about creativity and the creative process could come to carry a set of gendered meanings. Certainly, the bravado and confrontational nature of some of their claims to creativity that have surfaced in this chapter point to a link with youthful forms of masculinity. It was no accident, in this sense, that the industry debate with which I began this chapter should concern a set of adverts aimed at young men that deployed the idioms of laddishness. Opening up the links between gender and creativity and the gender dispositions of creative people forms the focus of the remaining chapters of the book.

gender, creativity and creative jobs

part 3

a homosocial world? masculinity, creativity and creative jobs

Pick a career. Any career. Make it progressive, forward thinking, fluid. Fill it with people with an anti-establishment attitude. Make them radical, creative, equality-minded. What would you call it? Advertising, maybe? An industry, surely, with all the above qualities and one where, of course, men and women get on in equal measure (Belinda Archer, *Guardian*, 13/9/99: 4).

The London-based advertising industry was, as many industry-insiders were fond of repeating through the 1990s, one in which women were highly visible and constituted half of all those employed. It was also an industry, it was claimed, that was open and meritocratic, which sought out the brightest and the best people and where ability and drive were rewarded regardless of age, gender or social background (Baxter, 1990). Wasn't it, as Belinda Archer's rhetorical questions suggested, a progressive industry in which 'men and women got on in equal measure'? An industry, moreover, in the words of Marilyn Baxter, author of a report on the position of women in advertising, which was 'short on prejudice and tradition and long on risk taking' (Baxter, 1990: 10). Despite the currency of these themes in the industry's self-imaginings, the answer was, as Belinda Archer and Marilyn Baxter both forcefully acknowledged, 'well, no, not really'.

Peeling back the public image of the industry revealed some uncomfortable truths. We have already seen that the industry was a youthful one, with 80 per cent of those employed being under 40 years of age and 50 per cent below 30 (see Chapter 3). While this helped to support the industry's image as a contemporary and vibrant sector, it also suggested that advertising was not a sympathetic place to work for those over forty years of age or seeking a long and sustainable career. Evidence of the industry's racial and ethnic mix also challenged its progressive profile. While the IPA's annual census did not officially record the number of individuals from black and minority ethnic backgrounds who worked in advertising, it estimated that they represented less than 1 per cent of the workforce (*Guardian*, 4/12/00: 8).[1] It was the figures for the gender composition of the industry, however, which, for industry insiders, did most to trouble and disturb the progressive image of advertising. These pointed to a strong pattern of both vertical and horizontal gender segregation in advertising employment. At the highest levels of the industry men remained the visible social actors. Only 22 per cent of board directors were women, while among the most senior agency staff (managing directors, chairman and chief executives) only 9 per cent were women (Klein, 2000: 9). This placed advertising close to famously con-servative sectors like the law and medicine in which women occupied 17 per cent and 14 per cent of senior positions, respectively (ibid: 26).

Unsurprisingly, at the other end of the occupational spectrum, women were over-represented among secretarial, clerical and junior administrative staff, with nearly 100 per cent of secretaries being women and 60 per cent of finance and administrative work also being performed by women. Within the core areas of advertising employment – the jobs of account handler, account planner, media buyer/planner and creative – the picture was more complicated. 54 per cent of account handlers were female, up from 33 per cent at the start of the 1990s. Among media buyers/planners, the figures showed a more or less stable picture through the 1990s with 44 per cent of practitioners being women. And in account planning there was a similarly stable picture, with figures pointing to the job being split equally in terms of its gender composition (Baxter, 1990; Klein, 2000). These figures led some credence to the image of advertising as a women-friendly occupation. How-ever, there was one area of advertising employment that remained striking in terms of its gender mix and which did most to disrupt the progressive image of the industry: employment in creative jobs. Only 18 per cent of those performing this job were women and through the decade the percentage actually declined. Thus, whether it was a large creative department like Saatchi & Saatchi's with 100 employees or a small one like CDP's with just 12, the gender mix remained more or less consistently skewed (*Campaign*, 9/2/96: 31). This gender bias had consequences in turn for the numbers of women acting as creative directors (effectively the heads of creative depart-ments), and only 2 women occupied this position in the top twenty agencies (Klein, 2000: 30). Given, as we've seen earlier, the privileged position of creative jobs in agencies and their symbolic centrality to the business of advertising, these were significant figures.

The gender bias in creative jobs, and the apparently intractable nature of this problem, generated much soul-searching within the industry. In fact, between the publication of the first IPA report on the position of women in advertising in 1990 and its follow-up report in 2000, the industry returned again and again to this issue and it moved centre-stage in the concerns, in particular, of the IPA and D&AD.[2] While public pronouncements within the industry on this matter were informed by the longer established debate within the business world on gender equality (especially at senior levels),[3] the continuing urgency of the industry's reflection on gender employment in creative jobs owed much to those processes of modernisation that I discussed in Chapter 2. Certainly there was the felt sense, often only tacitly expressed by industry folk, that the bias in the composition of creative jobs cut across agencies'attempts to present themselves as modern and business-like to clients. This was especially pertinent given the numbers of women holding the position of marketing manger in client companies. This had risen to approximately 50 per cent by the end of the 1990s (Klein, 2000: 41). This meant that the client – or at least their immediate face – was as likely to be a woman as it was a man. Agencies were clearly concerned that the bias in creative departments risked being seen as anachronistic and conservative by clients.[4]

The debate about creative jobs and gender within the industry was instructive in other ways. It revealed the currency of a circumscribed, but none the less sustained gender critique within the industry and the presence of a formation of practitioners and associated trade journalists concerned to improve the position of women in creative jobs. This grouping was notable for the terms in which they pitched their critique. From Marilyn Baxter's report onwards, journalist and practitioners sought to downplay the political or moral motivations behind the calls for greater gender equality at work.[5] Sensitive to being cast as feminists and the association of social engineering that went with that, practitioners tended to foreground the commercial or human resources problems of continuing gender bias. Marilyn Baxter, for example, in the *Women in Advertising* report that acted as an important spur for this debate, had argued that the industry needed to make better use of the under-exploited talent of its female employees. Others, such as journalist Susannah Richmond and IPA author Debbie Klein, emphasised the commercial advantages of bringing more women into creative jobs by citing figures suggesting that 70 per cent of television advertising was targeted at women and that they accounted for 80 per cent of total consumer expenditure (Klein, 2000; *Campaign*, 11/9/92: 27). Noting the level of complaints received by the Advertising Standards Authority (ASA), the industry regulator, concerning portrayals of women in advertising, both women contended that breaking down the 'bastions of male prejudice' that were creative departments would allow agencies to produce advertising that avoided the twin pitfalls of either alienating or patronising this key market (*Campaign*, 11/9/92: 27; *Independent*, 15/6/99: 11; *Guardian*, 13/9/99: 4; Klein, 2000).

As the tone of some of these comments suggests, despite their carefully weighted arguments industry critics were robust in making public the scale of the problem they felt the industry faced and in seeking solutions to it. In doing so, they repeatedly circled around the link between the informal cultures that developed within creative departments and the limited headway women had made in creative jobs. Debbie Klein was typical of the critics as a whole when she contended that (what she called) the 'laddish behaviour' that predominated in creative departments represented a fundamental barrier to women's entry into and progress within creative jobs. She cited evidence that suggested that it was perfectly acceptable in many agencies to make lewd remarks to female creatives and that football talk and going drinking as a group was commonplace among male creatives (Klein, 2000: 32). Other evidence revealed the strongly, and at times, wildly excessive masculine cultures within creative departments and a series of individual horror stories from women creatives that conveyed the deep-rooted misogyny of many creative directors. In a *Campaign* article on what it called the 'stone-age attitudes' to gender equality within creative departments, two female creatives recalled that their current creative director called them 'the birds' and that he was apparently embarrassed to offer robust comments on their work in case they burst into tears. Such treatment, however, seemed benign when compared to the initiation rite they were subjected to at another agency. When they arrived for work on their first day, the two women found their entire office covered in sanitary towels as a greeting (*Campaign*, 9/2/96: 30). The agency, DMB&B, held the 'Always' sanitary towel account and their male colleagues clearly thought that such an exercise was an appropriate form of welcome. Juvenile initiation rites of this order were not unique to these two young women. In the same article, journalist Emma Hall described how an anonymous male creative director liked to drop his trousers and press his genitals against a glass wall as an initiation ceremony for creatives. Andrea Smith told an even more striking tale in a letter to *Campaign* that followed up this article. While she was particularly direct and her experiences especially troubling, Smith was not untypical when she offered a revealing commentary on what life could be like for a young woman in a creative department. She claimed,

I left advertising 18 months ago after eight years because I no longer wanted to have to deal with childish chauvinism in the creative department. I was routinely humiliated in front of colleagues and had to endure endless criticism and insults . . . I know from fellow female creatives that my experiences aren't unique, and that the successful women in your article are more likely to be the exception than the rule. Is it surprising, then, that some women choose not to subject themselves to abuse? . . . Until creative directors even consider educating themselves and change their Neanderthal attitudes, there is little hope for women creatives (Andrea Smith, letter to *Campaign*, 1/3/96: 24)

It is these workplace cultures associated with creative jobs and the links, more broadly, between gender and creative jobs that this chapter sets out to explore. In particular, picking up on the views of trade commentators like Klein, I am concerned to reflect on the ways the culture of creative departments helped to not only shape the way this work was experienced, but also to colour the image of creative jobs within the industry as strongly, if not unambiguously, masculine forms of endeavour. My focus in doing so is on the creative departments in which my group of practitioners worked. While agencies often made much of the distinctive cultures of their departments, I foreground in what follows the strong continuities that existed across these departments in terms of how creative jobs were thought about and creative people managed. Drawing on the testimonies of the practitioners central to this book, as well as those of the creative directors who ran the departments in which they worked, I explore the ways in which these departments were infused with a set of diffuse, but none the less strikingly gendered representations of the creative person. These representations drew on wider cultural repertoires in which the links between creativity and masculinity were forged. In particular, they owed much to the distinctively masculine set of attributes associated with the figure of the artist, which had deep roots within the cultural milieu of advertising and beyond. To begin with, I explore these conceptions of the creative person active within creative departments and the cultural scripts upon which they drew. Then, I move on to consider the forms of management deployed within these departments and reflect on the way they helped to reproduce the links between creative jobs and particular styles of gendered conduct. Not only did male creative directors often condone excessive behaviour perpetrated by male creatives when it arose, but relations between creative directors and (typically) younger male creatives formed a central dynamic of life in these departments. These relationships were often characterised by both identification and rivalry between older and younger men, and it is the structuring of these homosocial relations that gave the departments, in many instances, their particular character as robustly masculine domains.

creative people   In 1997, D&AD published a booklet to accompany its annual series of Advertising Workshops (D&AD, 1997). Sponsored by the specialist creative headhunters Canna Kendall, the booklet detailed the up and coming programme for the year ahead. Alongside practical matters relating to the workshops, the booklet contained short pieces written by established creatives offering advice on how to succeed at getting into the industry. Among these was a piece by the art director Tiger Savage. Her advice took the form of a cartoon representing the essential attributes of the successful creative [see figure 5.1]. Identifying various dispositions through reference to parts of the body, Savage's cartoon detailed the importance, for example, of 'eyes – to see things differently', 'gut instinct', pointing to the abdomen, and 'thick skin'. Most striking of all, however, was the depiction of male genitals on her generic creative and the pithy description 'balls (and that goes for the girls too)' at the end of the line pointing to the genitals. The inclusion of these physical characteristics and the subjective dispositions that Savage derived from them suggested an ironic – one might say tongue-in-cheek – reference to the bias in the social make-up of creative jobs within the industry. We might read her cartoon as a wry commentary on the state of gender equality in relation to creative jobs. In another sense, Savage's representation of the generic creative as male appeared to confirm the link between the attributes of the creative person and maleness. Even aspiring female creatives, she seemed to be saying, had to imagine themselves acquiring culturally, if not biologically, the attributes of assertive masculinity.

The link that Savage drew between masculinity and the make-up of the creative person was not unique to her. Her comments drew upon well-established cultural precepts with a currency both within the advertising industry and beyond. Looming large in these cultural repertoires was the long historical shadow cast by the decisive linking, from the eighteenth century onwards, of creativity with the fine arts and, in particular, the positioning of the artist as the privileged possessor of the faculty of creativity. It is around the figure of the artist as a distinct category of person that gendered meanings have most strongly accrued. Parker and Pollock have argued that by the mid-nineteenth century a set of exclusively masculine attributes had accumulated around the artist as a creative individual, throwing up in turn distinctively masculine persona, most notably the bohemian and the pioneer (Parker and Pollock, 1981; Orton and Pollock, 1996). They also show how the gendering of the artist was not without its ambiguities. The attributes of the creative artist – dependent, insecure, expressive, over-emotional and prone to infantile egotism – placed him at odds with more upstanding versions of masculinity. This ensemble of attributes gained much of its power by also being set simultaneously against representations of femininity that suggested that women could at best express taste, rather than true artistic genius. From assumptions that their association with biological reproduction precluded them from the possibility of profound cultural creativity to assertions that the social responsibility of mothering cut against the form of 'passionate discontent' necessary to drive creativity, femininity was understood as incompatible with the full acquisition of the attributes of the creative person. Women could only express creative impulses within such circumscribed domains as the decorative arts.

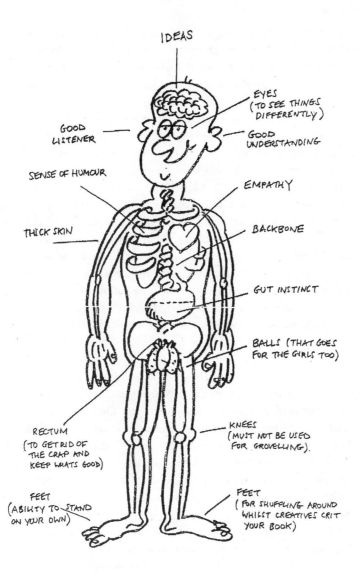

IDEAS

EYES
(TO SEE THINGS
DIFFERENTLY)

GOOD
LISTENER

GOOD
UNDERSTANDING

SENSE OF HUMOUR

EMPATHY

THICK SKIN

BACKBONE

GUT INSTINCT

BALLS (THAT GOES
FOR THE GIRLS TOO)

RECTUM
(TO GET RID OF
THE CRAP AND
KEEP WHATS GOOD)

KNEES
(MUST NOT BE USED
FOR GROVELLING).

FEET
(ABILITY TO STAND
ON YOUR OWN)

FEET
(FOR SHUFFLING AROUND
WHILST CREATIVES CRIT
YOUR BOOK)

Figure 5.1

A cartoon representing the essential attributes of

the successful creative

(D&AD Worshops 1997)

Pollock and Parker suggest that some of these conceptions of artistic genius were contested through the twentieth century – most notably by conceptual and abstract art – but that the romantic conception of the artist, with its baggage of gendered attributes, has persisted within advertising. It was certainly evident in the public personae of leading advertising creatives at the time when the practitioners I interviewed were starting and establishing their careers. Perhaps the two most noteworthy were Tony Kaye and Paul Arden. Kaye was one of the most sought after commercial directors and was best known for his work for Dunlop, Intercity and Volvo. He had formerly been art director at CDP. Arden was also a freelance director having resigned from his job as creative director at Saatchi & Saatchi in 1993 in order to pursue directing work. Both men cultivated the attributes of the difficult artist and troubled social outsider. In Kaye's case, this included smashing cameras and being generally difficult to work with. Eccentric, wilful and petulant, he described himself at various times as an 'emotional cripple' and 'a fucking alien'.[6] Arden, on the other hand, had a reputation as the account handler's worst nightmare – derived in part from his preparedness to destroy work on the brink of deadlines if he felt it wasn't good enough – and was known for what Graham Fink deftly described as his 'whim of iron' (Fink, 1996).

The flamboyant public profiles of these two men did not go uncontested and competing scripts of the advertising creative served to complexify the links between masculinity and creativity. One alternative version – exemplified in the public personae of consummate ad men like John Hegarty and David Abbott – was that of the creative as aesthete and man of taste. Urbane, sophisticated and thoughtful, Hegarty and Abbott both cut quiet but none the less authoritative figures within the 'creative community' and were without the vanities and maverick individualism of men like Kaye and Arden.[7]

While this script offered an antidote to that of the creative as artist, it tended, however, to reproduce the same link between masculinity and creative jobs. The force of this linkage was underlined by the fact that trade commentators often had difficulty in representing female creatives in anything like an elaborated way. In *Campaign*'s profiles, most notably, these women often appeared anonymous and underdeveloped figures. Alternatively, they occupied wildly eccentric public personae or else appropriated the dominant cultural tropes of masculinity. Tiger Savage herself was a case in point. The assumed name and the flamboyant dress sense for which she was known hinted at more than a dash of eccentricity in her self-presentation.[8] We'll see later how the female creatives I interviewed handled this dominant conception of the creative person in advertising.

The association between masculinity and creativity signalled by Tiger Savage in her D&AD piece recurred within the fabric of the departments in which the group of men central to this book worked. This was despite the formal ambition of these agencies to open up creative jobs and their often strident claims that they were concerned to recruit the best people regardless of gender. Certainly the creative directors who ran the departments in which the practitioners worked – and who were primarily responsible for recruiting them – strongly held to the view that creative recruitment was especially open and based upon conspicuous talent. As one of the creative directors I interviewed angrily and defensively argued, in response to a question that there did not seem to be very many women in the department that he ran, 'I'd hire a dog with a spanner up its arse if the work was good enough'. Another creative director, again underlining the way they had been sensitised to the question of gender bias by the contemporary trade debate, claimed – in response to a question about the qualities he sought in a potential employee – that what he looked for in the candidate was 'that they were a woman'.

This assertive tone was often coupled with claims that they (creative directors) saw very few women among those applying for jobs in creative departments and, hence, were not to blame for the bias. There was some truth in this claim. Certainly the available evidence suggested that women were under-represented on the more specialist training routes into creative jobs and among the body of practitioners signed up with headhunters and within the placement system. Figures from 1996 for the intake on the well-known postgraduate course in art direction and copywriting run by West Herts College, for example, revealed a gender split of 8 women to 27 men (*Campaign*, 9/2/96: 31). This bias was confirmed by the headhunters Canna Kendall who revealed that only 24 of the 108 practitioners they had on their books in 1992 were women (22 per cent), while Andrew Cracknell, a senior creative director, claimed that only one eighth of those who applied for creative placements were women (Dougary, 1994: 25). However, among those students taking degrees in subject areas that were important feeders for employment in creative jobs, the figures suggested no obvious pattern of gender bias. UCAS figures for the period 1995-9, showed that those undergraduates accepted onto courses within the subject field of design studies were split 45 per cent male and 55 per cent female.[9] This headline figure did obscure potential differences in the gender composition of particular degree programmes. The UCAS subject field of design studies certainly included subject areas with rather different traditions of recruitment. Fashion and textiles, for example, had long been a female-dominated enclave (McRobbie, 1998), while industrial and product design were overwhelmingly male-dominated with only 2 per cent of students being female. Graphic design was an area that was, anecdotally at least, split 50/50 in terms of gender, although graphic design degrees that taught illustration tended to have more women students.

While we need to treat these figures with caution, they do suggest that women graduates were not choosing to move into the recruitment process for creative jobs, despite being qualified in the appropriate degrees. While there is no available evidence to fully explain this situation, we might speculate that the reputation of creative departments as 'bastions of male prejudice' (to invoke Susannah Richmond's description) and the more general dominance of men in creative jobs combined to discourage women from applying for this kind of work.

Despite their formal commitment to recruit more women, the creative directors I interviewed were also complicit in reinforcing the link between masculinity and creative jobs. Their commentaries revealed that the subjective attributes they looked for in creatives were far from neutral. In fact, throughout the interviews I conducted, some strikingly consistent understandings of what made a good creative emerged. These were not all, by any means, exclusively bound up with gender, but it was clear that a set of gender assumptions ran through some of the attributes they were looking for in a prospective art director or copywriter. Perhaps the most significant related to an oft-repeated concern that good creatives should have the capacity to be open and able to see things differently, to be unencumbered by convention and dogma. David French, executive creative director at French Harris Smith, for example, suggested:

> what you're looking for is an openness and an ability to engage other people . . . because you're trying to convince people of perhaps a different point of view and only by being able to disarm them can you inform them. . . . And that skill, that ability comes from an openness and a kind of *naïveté* in the creative person in that they're prepared to try all sorts of things and then articulate it in such a way that it captures the imagination of the person you're talking to.

Later in the interview he elaborated a little further:

> I think good creative people have a sense of fun and *mischief* about them . . . and irreverence . . . and what irreverence breeds is a kind of preparedness to try something which hasn't been tried before (my emphases).

French's attention to the ability of a good creative to approach a brief from a fresh angle and to have the necessary naïveté to try something different was re-iterated by Ian Harding, creative director at XYZ. He contended that a creative required, 'egotism, the artistic reflect, the ability to take something and put a spin on it, without losing the plot. It is the person who can take the brief, spin it around and do something completely odd and yet it is also instantaneously entirely logical, but just done in such an odd way which is, I think, probably art'.

The 'egotism' of creatives was key, for Harding, in underpinning this capacity of creatives to approach problems with fresh insights and not to be swayed from that by others involved in the creative development process. Reflecting on the importance of this 'egotism' he saw it as linked to what he called 'unreasonableness'. He tellingly cited Paul Arden as an exemplar. Arden was the one brilliant creative in London, Harding claimed, and his 'trick is his ability to remain effectively 12 years old': to be childishly unreasonable and uncompromising.

Paul Holt, executive creative director at Klein & Hart, also emphasised the childishness and juvenility of good creatives. Alongside detailing the importance of curiosity, he contended,

The very best creative people, you want them to have their minds in a state of arrested development. When you can see and think like a child, then you tend to produce stunning advertising. If you think of the most famous beer campaigns of the last 10 years, they're little fairy stories with George the bear [for Hofmeister lager]. This is Paddington bear, this is the stuff of a five year old, of bedtime stories and yet it turned John Webster, the creator of these characters, into a multi-millionaire.

A senior colleague of one of the creative directors I interviewed underlined the currency of this idea. He suggested that the creative director in question, an urbane and sophisticated man credited with a good business brain, also had the ability to remain in some small way 'a child at heart'. This recurrent attention to the capacity of good creatives to approach advertising problems through the 'eyes of a child', to be unreasonable, irreverent and awkward, appeared, on first inspection, to have little to do with masculinity. Pushing further at the testimonies of the creative directors revealed how these capacities were linked, in many instances, to deep-rooted ideas about gender that they held. Paul Holt, for example, made it clear in his comments that the attributes that he had described as essential to creativity were primarily to be found in men. Reflecting on his ambition to bring more women into Klein & Hart's creative department, he claimed that he had to strike a balance between 'hiring pretty feisty sassy women' and the need to keep young male creatives in a 'child-like state'. The implication of his comments was that 'feisty' women threatened to force the young male creatives to grow up and thus erode the essential juvenility that was crucial to performing the roles of art director and copywriter. In Holt's comments, then, women appeared as a supplement to the core creative role that was necessarily performed by young men who possessed the appropriate irreverence, naïveté and unreasonableness to create effective advertising. This link between inventiveness, irreverence and masculinity was more explicitly stated and elaborated upon by David French. Understandably cautious about voicing his views, French none the less offered a sustained argument about the links between masculinity and the attributes of a good creative:

> I think within the nature of men is the ability to think inventively more so than in women. Women are about preserving things and keeping the home and . . . you know that all sounds terribly chauvinistic and I don't mean it to but, you know, actually women are from Venus and men are from Mars – it isn't to say that one is better than the other . . . maybe its that [imaginative] leaps are made by, by this irreverence, by breaking things down. Women's attitude is about homemaking, creating security. Men are about breaking boundaries down, that's where great creativity comes from. Maybe it's all to do with the absolute individualism that is required and that is less a trait of women than of men. It seems to me that the male species is able to focus on one thing and not care about anything else and that's what you want. You want that total absorption in trying to resolve the problem. Yes, being open to other things around you, but not trying to always assuage them.

French's analysis offered a powerful sense of the essential links between masculinity and the dispositions required by the effective creative. His contentions drew much of their authority from wider cultural scripts about gender and about creativity. On the one hand, his arguments were informed by popular ideas about sex and gender derived from socio-biology.[10] On the other, they owed much to those longer established cultural repertoires that I have already noted. Such conceptions certainly informed the way the creative directors I interviewed most clearly thought about the ideal creative. These gendered meanings were explicitly present in French's and Holt's comments and were implicitly invoked in Ian Harding's emphasis on the unreasonableness and quirky insights of creatives.

It was not only in the approach to recruitment pursued by creative directors that these representations of the creative person surfaced in departments. They were also active in the cultures that developed within creative departments. Certainly there appeared to be some descriptive fit between the attributes of the ideal creative and the culture of masculine immaturity and juvenility given free rein within creative departments. We have already seen that the trade debate on gender bias in creative jobs had pointed up the privileging of laddish forms of masculinity. The experience of the practitioners I interviewed reaffirmed this. Teresa Walsh, for example, an art director at CTRL, complained about the juvenile behaviour of the men she worked with. She suggested, 'this department's very laddy. When they're on their own they're really nice, but when they're together they don't even speak to me. . . . It's like they're 16 [the men were in their 30s] and they have things like a Barbie doll tied up by her arms and legs on the office door. And I used to make cakes . . . I made a cake for everyone when it was one of their birthdays – and one of them shouted, 'what's in this, nipple milk!'

Two other young women creatives at Direct Arts, Samantha Jones and Miranda Harris, while they were more phlegmatic about this kind of culture, revealed that they were known in their department by the derogatory titles of the 'tampon twins' or, alternatively, 'Beaver' and 'Pussy'. Paul Holt also complained about the manifestation of this laddishness. As he suggested, 'when I arrived here the atmosphere was unbelievably boysy and macho, and the manifestations of that culture were not terribly pleasant. . . . For example, the Christmas tree was hung with tampax and condoms'.

Evidence of this kind pointed to a certain dovetailing of the attributes of the creative person sought by creative directors and these particular forms of masculine culture. Not that these cultures of masculinity were reducible to the conceptions of the creative as juvenile and irascible that we have looked at. Clearly, the forms of masculinity privileged within these departments were shaped by other factors. In particular, the young male creatives were able to draw on wider cultural resources in living out their gender identity at work and these cultural scripts – particularly that associated with the cult of laddishness within popular culture – were not reducible to ideas about the creative person. None the less, there was a degree of assonance or fit between these forms of subjectivity. Understanding this linkage, however, means reflecting further on the internal life of creative departments. Why was it that 'laddishness' was able to flourish? Why did these forms of masculinity become dominant? Why were the cultures of departments gendered as masculine in this specific way? Answering these questions means looking at the role of creative directors in the management of departments and opening up their contribution to the cultures that developed.

managing creative people

You have to flatter their egos. Its an enormous process of charming them, persuading them, treating them a bit like naughty schoolchildren (Tim Bell, in Fletcher, 1990: 67).

Because outstanding creative ability is so rare, the creative manager who finds and employs talented people must learn to live with their whims and tantrums (Winston Fletcher, in Fletcher, 1990: 32).

Creativity isn't a science. It's an art. It's blood sweat and tears. It's about throwing expensive televisions through plate glass windows. Its about doing nothing for two weeks and then drinking unfeasible amounts of vodka before coming up with a brilliant idea two minutes ahead of the client meeting, and expressing it in a crayon drawing on the back of a bank statement. You can't distill that. You can't 'manage' that. You just have to find brilliant people and let it happen (*Campaign* 'Creative Conference' advert, 2/3/01: 19).

How creative departments ought to be managed and how creative directors should get the best out of creative people were central preoccupations for the advertising industry. They had even generated a small literature of their own.[11] Approaches to these problems were typically bound up with those conceptions of the creative person that I discussed in the previous section. As the quotes from Tim Bell, Winston Fletcher and the *Campaign* advert suggest, there was a collective wisdom within the industry that a good creative director had to somehow create the conditions within which the temperamental, irrational, childishness of creatives could flourish. We have already got a sense from Chapter 2 what this tended to mean in organisational terms. Many agencies created a protected space within the structure of the business where creative teams were partly shielded from the commercial and bureaucratic logics that drove the organisation. Free – in the words of Martin Smith – to make the necessary imaginative leaps to bring clients' briefs to life, creatives often existed within a sequestered space within the internal structure of the agency. This didn't mean that they were totally outside organisational logics and creative directors played an important role in linking creative departments to the wider demands of agency business. More than that, the generally loose organisational structure of agencies and their weakly bureaucratised processes gave creative directors particular influence and authority over the departments they ran. Like many other so-called 'creative businesses', the main constraints upon the running of agencies tended to be set by the external demands of clients. Moreover, the management of work, as Scase and Goffeee have suggested, was shaped by project deadlines rather than by highly bureaucratised work routines (Scase and Goffee, 1995: 36). The role of creative directors, then, involved not so much bureaucratic control over the creative labour process, so much as inspiring and stimulating creatives and overseeing the quality of their work. As such it rested upon a form of charismatic rather than bureaucratic authority. For the creative directors I interviewed, a central part of this role was to protect and reinforce the separateness of the creative department from the rest of the agency. Geoff Rowlands, creative director at Rowlands and Partners, expressed this view particularly forcefully. He suggested,

It is part of my nature to put the creative department against the rest of the agency. And protect them. I'm always shouting at account people or planners. I never have a go at creative people. I am their champion. At another agency, I put up a sign next to the creative department which stated 'Us- this way', Them – that way'. My soul is in the creative department. Spiritually I'm part of that.

Steve Buckland, creative director at Jones Walters, also emphasised the physical and symbolic separation of the creative department he ran. The department was based in a suite of offices around an open central area and demarcated from other parts of the agency, notably the adjacent account planners, by a large heavy door. Buckland joked as we walked through it before I interviewed him that it should have a sign on it addressed to other agency folk stating 'Abandon all hope ye who enter here'. His reference to the sign reinforced the idea of a boundary around the creative department and he underscored this by describing it as a 'community'. Pointing to the open area enclosed by the offices and replete with apple Macintosh computers, he suggested, 'this is the village green'.

Buckland's oddly quaint, bucolic conception of the creative department was rendered in more contemporary terms by David French. For French, the creative department was less a 'village community', more a club:

I think the creative department is like a club, its like a place you come to have a good time. It's a place you come to relax, to talk about the things you would like to talk about. So by a club I mean a place where you go not to necessarily work but to be inspired . . . I am a great believer that if you're enjoying something you're doing it better. It is about how to get to the real you . . . how you get to that self. If I can create an atmosphere which allows that to happen, then I'm well down the road of making this a good place to be.

French's conception of the department as a club suggested that it was a space, on the one hand, defined by common, shared interests and bonds, but was also, on the other, an exclusive space with definite barriers to entry. Like both Rowlands' and Buckland's views of the creative department, French sought to emphasise both the strength of the internal relations of the department and its separation from the rest of the agency. French's approach to the department he ran was significant in other ways. It revealed a more general feature of the way departments were run that was not evident in the comments of Rowlands or Buckland but was in practice widely subscribed to. This was the emphasis on fun and relaxation as essential elements in the organisation of creative departments. French is clear in his comments on the rationale for this. It was bound up with getting the best work out of creative people. However, it is worth reflecting on how this conception of creative departments as 'fun spaces' was realised. At French Harris Smith, where French worked, it took the form, among other things, of providing pool tables, soft chairs and an encouragement of forms of 'play'. Steve Dempsey, one of the men I interviewed who had worked at French Harris Smith, recalled that the department was often brought to life by people strumming guitars. Such a scenario was far from unique. Katy Smith, creative director at Henry Brown, described the creative department as being 'filled with a pool table, some chairs, a Nintendo and a television'. It was a familiar picture of what a creative department looked like. Marcus Lawson, who had worked at Hepworth Rowe, even recalled that the young creatives were allowed to play football down the office corridors of the creative department. What is notable about these 'relaxed' cultures is the way they connected to established forms of masculine culture. In other words, creative directors, in many instances, encouraged creatives to express themselves in the workplace through activities derived from young male culture outside of work. The over-exuberant manifestations of this – such as that evidenced by Teresa Walsh and Paul Holt, for example – were gener-ally condoned since what creative directors were looking for was an environment in which these practitioners could create great work. Other rituals of office life directly orchestrated by creative directors in order to strengthen the social bonds of the department also tended to draw, tangentially at least, on the stock of young male culture. Weekly or monthly department meetings, for example, were lubricated by beer and pizza.

There were other features of the way departments were run that were even more important in helping to shape the culture of masculinity that developed across creative departments. These were the management prac-tices that formed the corollary to the emphasis on relaxation that I have just described. In setting out to motivate their charges, the creative directors I interviewed also recurrently emphasised the role of intense competition as integral to how they built the necessary pressure on teams to get them to produce good work. This emphasis on competition was allied to robust styles of management. Andy Hanby, creative director at Paul and Rogers, was more explicit than most in elaborating on how he motivated teams. He remarked that:

> creative people are generally incredibly lazy up until the last three days before the work is needed. And then they work like idiots. And I try and create this last three-day culture – which is basically, everyone is given a chance to work on a brief. I will go round each team, look through the work. Teams get eliminated as the process goes on. So, if one team cracks the brief, I leave two teams out in the cold. [They] will fight

it out amongst themselves to try and be better than the one team who've cracked it. I will take them off it, which is a kind of psychological trick to say 'you're work isn't good enough'. That will generally make the teams stay behind later and see if they can get something better. And it works on some occasions.

This ruthless system of competition over briefs was given added piquancy by the fact that Hanby and his partner were also involved in the competition. Explaining the reason for this, Hanby argued,

The creative department consists of 5 teams (including myself). That's one of my philosophies. . . . If the creative director isn't seen to be producing work that everyone else wants to have done, then there's no sense of competition. The department becomes terribly lethargic. I want them to get my job. I want them to beat me!

Mark Stephenson, though he ran a slightly larger department consisting of eight teams, placed similar emphasis to Hanby on competition over briefs and used the fear of losing out on a brief in order to motivate teams. The aim, as he succinctly put it, was to 'get them staying an extra two hours at work' in the hope of coming up with the goods. Geoff Rowlands again developed a similar approach. He felt strongly that creative people needed competition and recalled one of the forms he had used in the past to foster this:

We (GR and another creative director) oversaw between 12 and 20 teams. And we set them against each other. We hothoused them. It was called the 'playpen'. Part of me thought it was cruel and a very negative system. But they didn't. Every Christmas they used to take me and Mark out. You know, it was a bit like Uriah Heep. It was hard in that it expunged people who . . . were not as good. But I found it really enjoyable, working with them in that hothouse atmosphere. So I feel creatives need competition. They tend to need competition. They manifestly need competition. The people that are the [foot] soldiers, the writers and the art directors, will tend to compete and will be very aware of what the others are doing . . . I've even had fights. Creatives literally fighting over briefs. It's like school.

This emphasis on competition and robust styles of management was also evident in the comments from Steve Buckland.

I'm not convinced that the right way to run a creative department is to have a nicesy-nicesy department, where everyone gets on and its all lovey-dovey and flower-power. Some competitive edge and a little bit of angst going round – 'this bloody person got that brief'- is absolutely vital and I think that if this place has a fault its that we do get slightly cosy over time and we need to stir ourselves up and be a bit more competitive, be a bit more aggressive. I worry that I haven't made it all a bit too orderly and even. There's not a great deal of horseplay that goes on. The wildest thing that we've got is the table football table. At CDP we used to have 2 snooker tables in the creative department and people would play in the afternoons.

Taken together these testimonies tell us much about how the management of creative teams worked to create the conditions in which assertiveness and the ruthless pursuit of self-interest became the attributes most required by teams to succeed. What creative directors were aiming for was the generation of the necessary levels of creative angst and tension between teams to forge good advertising. While this emphasis appeared to pull in a different direction from the emphasis on informality that we encountered earlier, it is clear that both the more directive interventions of managers and the encouragement of 'fun' and 'play' were complimentary strategies. 'Freeing up' creatives to help them generate ideas and then applying the appropriate pressure to crystallise out these ideas were integral elements in the management of creative teams. Both worked to cultivate an atmosphere that not only encouraged creatives to develop thick skins (as Savage had suggested) and hard hearts, but also made tension-releasing rituals an important part of the informal life of the departments. As the creative directors themselves recognised, with so much at stake for teams in the competition over briefs, handling not only the pressure of coming up with good ideas, but also the associated feelings of hostility and envy towards others, required various means of letting off steam. While there was nothing inevitable about the linkage, it is possible to see why laddish exuberance and juvenility might have been resources that enabled the young men to handle these conditions with some degree of comfort and success and why creative directors were prepared to condone this behaviour.

The accounts given by Hanby et al are striking in other ways. They reveal the closeness of the relations between creative directors and the teams they managed and the intensity of feelings this generated. This was typically expressed through both identification with the teams and a sense of rivalry with them. Both elements were clearly closely related. Rivalry sprung from the sense that both parties (the creative director and the team) were in competition for the same prize (the brief and beyond that recognition) and shared similar motivations and ambitions. Both Hanby and Rowlands, for example, reveal this dual intensity of the management relationship very clearly. In Hanby's case it is expressed through the challenge of teams to beat him, whereas for Rowlands it is evident in the enjoyment of working closely with teams in the 'hothouse' atmosphere of the creative department. These intense relations with (usually) younger men did not only encourage generally positive feelings of closeness. Steve Buckland's comments – and particularly his drift into auto-analysis – are particularly interesting in this regard. What surfaces towards the end of the passage I quoted earlier, is a great anxiety about his standing as man and manager. Perhaps, he wonders, he was becoming a bit soft and complacent. The department he ran, taking its cue from him, had become 'too orderly'. Mark Stephenson also expressed this anxiety about becoming soft and complacement. In his account it was combined with the identification with certain young male teams. Reflecting on why he liked hiring young placement teams he revealed:

> I get a big buzz out if it because they're scary these guys [the placements]. And that's very stimulating for me. You know, it keeps my eye on the ball. If I get too, you know [stuck in my ways]. . . . I have to keep thinking freshly about things otherwise these guys are gonna get ahead of me. I like to be a bit scared. I also get genuine pleasure out of taking people on and seeing them do well.

The closeness of the relations between male creative directors and younger male creatives evidenced here raises questions about how these men (the creative directors) managed women creatives? Getting at these relationships was extremely difficult in the interviews. The creative directors were generally reluctant to be drawn on this issue or else were insensitive to how women might cope within the departments they ran. Andy Hanby, for example, in characterising his department, suggested, 'ours tends to be terribly lager loutish and football-based. If you're a woman in that environment, you'd have to, I'd imagine, fit in'. However, occasionally a creative director would let down his guard and reveal something about these relations. Steve Message was a case in point:

> I have to walk down here [the corridor where the creatives were based] every so often and scream at teams about something that's happened. I have to know I can tell them off. In the past – we have a few all girl teams here – I've had tears in the toilet. And men (sic) don't know how to deal with that. I think people (sic) have a problem disciplining women. In the way that men turn round to each other and tell each other to 'fuck off'.

The passage is telling in the way Message switches from the personal to the collective (from 'I' to 'men' and 'people') in order to distance himself in the telling of the account from the difficulties he clearly had in managing women. More than that, however, it reveals the way management relations were, in Message's case, highly gendered. This was further underlined by the way Liz Sheldon, one of the female creative directors I interviewed, described her approach to management. While she shared some of the ruthlessness of her male peers, she set out to demonstrate to me her deployment of distinctively feminine management skills:

> I think that male creative directors are generally rather heavy handed. And I think women are different. My view of how to get great work out of creative people is to treat them as toddlers. . . . If a toddler's learning to walk, if it's surrounded by loving adults who, every time it falls down, pick it up, kiss it better and say 'you can do it', they learn to walk. If on the other hand, every time they fall over the adults said, 'you're a fucking idiot', they'd never learn to walk. . . . So my view is, you support people, you pick them up, you say 'you can do it'. After a bit, if they can't do it, then they have to go.

Sheldon's comments, like those of the male creative directors, reveal how deeply a set of gendered assumptions informed the approach to the management of creative people. For the men who formed the overwhelming majority of creative directors, their relationships with typically younger men were structured by both identification and rivalry with them. Both dynamics revealed the intensity of relations between men within these social relations. It suggested – as Steve Message's comments made explicit – that creative directors might have difficulties managing women, particularly if they failed to fit into the robust masculine cultures that they fostered. Taken together, what these accounts reveal is how management techniques within creative departments set some of the conditions for assertive forms of masculinity to become institutionalised. The actions of creative directors were integral to the creation of spaces of work in which 'shrinking violets' – whether male or female – had little chance of flourishing.

conclusion   I have ended by reflecting on the role played by management practices in shaping the cultures associated with creative jobs and have suggested that the accounts given by creative directors reveal one of the ways in which the link between masculinity and creative jobs was reproduced within the industry. This linkage was also forged by those deeper understandings of creativity and the creative person that were active within departments. Taken together, they suggest that the jobs of art director and copywriter were understood – implicitly and often explicitly – as masculine forms of endeavour; in short, as men's jobs. This explains why, even though they claimed to want to recruit more women creatives and sometimes publicly criticised the juvenility of the young men they worked with, creative directors were locked into a way of thinking about creative jobs that was shot through with gendered understandings of the creative person in advertising. These understandings were underscored by the forms of identification that linked creative directors with the male creatives they managed, and intensified by the sense of separateness and difference from the rest of the agency that characterised the creative departments that I have discussed. Creatives were seen as a special case and creative departments were seen to fall outside many of the normal organisational rules that guided the internal life of agencies. By extension this 'exceptionalism' and the peculiarities of the job constituted further blocks to opening up creative jobs to gender equality.

It is clear why these characteristics of creative departments and their general recidivism regarding gender equality so exercised other practitioners, especially those armed with an elaborated gender critique. In fact, it is possible to see in the way these departments were viewed by other agency folk, a division within the gender culture that existed within agencies. Planners loomed large among the critics of gender inequality in creative jobs and these practitioners tended to be those with the most socially progressive attitudes in advertising – certainly if an industry survey is to be believed (*Campaign* Report, 22/11/96: 3–6). The debate about gender and creative jobs that I began this chapter with hints at this disjuncture and the existence of differently constituted gender cultures within and across agencies associated with different formations of practitioners.

The robust gender cultures of creative departments raise a number of other questions. How did the young creatives themselves negotiate these cultures? To what extent did they bring to the job dispositions and cultural resources that helped to shape these cultures as robustly masculine? How did the performance of such strongly gendered jobs shape their subjective identities as men? And how did women creatives find a place and an identity for themselves within this culture? It is these questions that I will turn to in the next two chapters.

between men: masculinity and the dynamics of creative partnerships

> They always describe it [the partnership between art director and copywriter] as a marriage because there's no better description. I worked for 8 years with Karl, and I was working with Steve for 7 years. And in those years him and his wife had 3 kids, but I still say that he spent more time with me than he did with his wife. Easily. Because you work night and day in advertising. You just never stop. And it is a marriage. 'Cause you've got to trust each other, with each other's ideas. But I always say that an idea comes out of a misunderstanding really. And you can't misunderstand yourself and that's why it is better to work as a team [. . .] The idea is the child of the marriage. (Mark Taylor)

We saw in the previous chapter how creative jobs were overwhelmingly male-dominated in their social make-up and the way creative departments were characterised by the robustly masculine cultures that typically developed within them. Opening up further the social relations of these departments and pushing at the way individual creatives negotiated the cultures of work that developed around them forms the focus of this chapter. At the heart of it are the unique working relationships between art directors and copywriters.

These partnerships garnered much attention within the industry because of the privileged role given to creative people in the processes of advertising development. What made these partnerships tick acquired considerable importance in the business of running a successful advertising agency. As Mark Taylor's comments indicate, industry insiders were often drawn to foreground the special dynamics of these relationships and the intimacies they involved. Taylor's comments are noteworthy for their emphatic description of his relationships with two long-term male creative partners. Specifically, it is his use of the metaphor of marriage to explain these working relationships that is particularly striking. Taylor was not alone in deploying this surprising metaphor to describe creative pairings of this kind. As his comments suggest, the metaphor enjoyed a wide currency within the industry, figuring most prominently in the profiles of art directors and copywriters produced by the advertising trade press. The widespread use of the metaphor was closely associated with the predominance of all-male creative partnerships within the industry through the 1990s.

While precise figures are hard to come by, it seems that up to 80 per cent of creative teams were all male. The next most popular pairing were all-female teams, with a smaller percentage of teams being mixed. For the majority of male creatives, collaborating closely with another man in a creative partnership formed a central part of their working lives. This was certainly the case for most of the men I interviewed and, significantly, the metaphor of marriage, together with associated themes drawn from hetero-sexual romance, figured repeatedly in their accounts. While these were not the only metaphors they used, their accounts suggested that the tropes of marriage and heterosexual romance had considerable power to illuminate their experience of working in all-male teams. Their choice of metaphors was all the more striking given that the women creatives I interviewed typically – and conspicuously – failed to use them, opting instead for rather different ways of describing their creative partnerships. Unpacking the symbolism of the metaphors of marriage and heterosexual romance in the accounts of the men I interviewed forms a central ambition of this chapter. In particular, I want to explore what the use of these metaphors tells us about the dynamics of creative partnerships and, most importantly, about the gender identities of the men who deployed them.

In opening up these concerns, I want to engage with a body of recent writing that has been very good at shedding light on close, often institution-alised, relationships between men in all-male or male-dominated settings. Looming large in this body of work has been Eve Kosofsky Sedgwick's suggestive arguments about male homosocial desire in her book *Between Men* (Sedgwick, 1985). For Sedgewick – and the subsequent work that has taken its cue from her – the key was to introduce 'desire . . . the potentially erotic' (Sedgewick, 1985: 1) back into accounts of the social bonds between men (Roper, 1994, 1996; Hearn and Parkin, 1987). This move was parti-cularly important, Sedgewick argued, because a potential continuum exists between the social and sexual aspects of men's relationships with each other. However, this continuum remains largely hidden or obscured by contem-porary assumptions about compulsory heterosexuality and by homophobia. As a consequence it is difficult for heterosexually identified men to name these homosocial desires, with close friendships between men subject to anxieties about homosexuality and the wider cultural divide between homosexuality and heterosexuality.

Breaking open these all-male intimacies, however, has considerable analytic value. As Mike Roper has argued, it is precisely the erotic sub-texts – the potential continuum between the homosocial and the homosexual – that often gives relations between men in formally heterosexual settings their particular character and intensity (Roper, 1996). For example, in his work on senior managers, Roper describes the way inter-generational relations between men and the process of succession in management often work through 'circuits of homosocial desire', with men being drawn to management, in part, because of the opportunities it offered for the expression of these intimacies (ibid).

In opening up the accounts of their partnerships given by the men I interviewed, I want to argue that they reveal the same structuring presence of forms of homosocial desire. In particular, the use of the metaphors of marriage and heterosexual romance points to the way questions of intimacy and desire were caught up, in both their experience of these close-working relationships and in their sense of broader public perceptions of them. In exploring the forms of intimacy and desire articulated through these metaphors, I am less interested in the way they help us to account for the reproduction of gender inequalities in this area of advertising employment – an important dimension of recent appropriations of the concept of homosociability – than with the light that the deployment of these metaphors sheds on the masculinities of the male creatives I interviewed. Exploring these tropes, I want to further distinguish between the different levels of representation at which the metaphors circulated and to separate out the range of ways in which they were inflected across the accounts I consider. One aspect of this concerns the important dissonances that existed between the way the metaphors signified within the journalistic codes of the trade press and the way they surfaced in the testimonies of the practitioners I interviewed. The second aspect follows on from this. Across the accounts I consider, there were important differences in the meanings being carried by these tropes. In many instances the metaphors worked to precisely contain within normative heterosexual bounds the forms of homosocial desire active (or perceived to be active) in these relationships. Thus, in comparing the partnerships to an intimate relationship like marriage, journalists and practitioners were able to both give public expression to these homosocial desires, while diffusing the homoerotic associations of this intimacy by routing it through a heterosexual form. Often – particularly in the accounts of the men I interviewed – a contractual model of marriage was implicitly emphasised. This foregrounded the co-dependency, commitment and the sense of a shared project associated with marriage over and above questions of sexual desire. In deploying the metaphors in this way, the journalists and the practitioners were reinscribing the break in the homosocial continuum and fixing their identities (in the case of the practitioners) as robustly heterosexual.

This was not the only inflection given to these tropes. In some instances the metaphors worked in more sexually ambivalent ways to actively articulate quite strong erotic desires. Thus, while these men still expressed their feelings through a heterosexual form, their accounts began to blur the line between homosociability and homosexuality. In doing so, they composed a sense of identity more open to the possibility of sexual ambiguity.

These latter accounts force us to qualify the conceptualisation of homosocial desire derived from Sedgwick's work. While it is axiomatic in her conceptualisation that the continuum is radically disrupted for heterosexual men, the accounts I discuss reveal that this disruption was far from universal. On the contrary, they point to the formation of heterosexual masculinities that are not defined so exclusively or defensively against homosexual masculinities. In a different way, the representations produced within the trade press also raise questions about Sedgwick's assertion. Rather than conceal homosocial desires, the representations extravagantly draw attention to them. As we will see, the journalistic pieces are often playful, titillating the reader with sexualised accounts of all-male teams. I want to begin by turning to these representations, moving on to consider the subjective appropriation and use of these public codes by the men I interviewed. Finally, I attempt to shed further light on the testimonies given by the male creatives by considering the way partners talked about each other in competing kinds of creative partnerships, most especially within all-female teams.

husbands and wives   In October 1994, *Campaign* ran a feature article on successful working partnerships within the industry. It focused on four sets of close working relationships in particular. These were the pairings of Billy Mawhinney and Nick Welch, joint creative directors of CDP; Robin Wight and Andrew Robinson, chairman and chief executive respectively of WCRS; Graham Hinton and Tony Douglas, joint chief executives of DMB&B; and Anthony Simons-Gooding and Richard Hytner, chairman and chief executive respectively of S.P Lintas. Noting how 'unlikely double acts are the stuff of industry legend', *Campaign* journalist Tabatha Cole set out to explore what made these four successful partnerships work. Deploying the arch style much favoured by *Campaign* journalists, she suggested:

Many of advertising's duos are often likened to husbands and wives. It seems 'marriage' between workmates is a thriving institution in the industry. In addition to the happy couples featured here, a quick flick through an issue of *Campaign* reveals hundreds more littered around the ad world. There's Tim and Bruce at Leagas Delaney, who have got it together again at last; Tim and Jerry at Lowe Howard-Spink, who never go anywhere without each other; Mellors and Finky, who've just split up after the latter's departure to GGT; and a host of serial monogamists who shall remain nameless (*Campaign*, 7/10/94: 24).

Warming to her theme, Cole quoted extensively from the four sets of male pairings who formed the focus of the article. Some of the comments she chose to emphasise were extraordinary. Graham Hinton, for example, in speaking about the importance of trust in his relationship with Tony Douglas declared: 'we're very close. But we've only had sex once – Tony wasn't very good at it'. Anthony Simonds-Gooding, while less excessive in his comments, was also revealing. Describing his relationship with chief executive Richard Hyter he suggested: 'I joined because Richard seduced me . . . I think he's a delightful man.' Nick Welch and Billy Mawhinney were more restrained, but they too could not resist drawing attention to the intimacies of their relationship. They both independently spoke of their pairing as an 'arranged marriage' (ibid).

These themes were also evident in the photographs that accompanied Cole's article. The image of Billy Mawhinney and Nick Welch was the most interesting in this regard. It portrayed the men in a romantic clinch in which Mawhinney, smiling strongly at the camera, stood close to Welch with both his arms locked around his waist, while Welch held Mawhinney with one arm around his waist. The choice of the postures produced a strong sense of intimacy between the two men, with their respective positions echoing those of the couple in certain traditions of romantic heterosexual portraiture. Thus, Mawhinney was positioned in the conventionally feminine role, held in the protective arms of Welch: the clinging vine and the lofty pine, if you will.

The photographs accompanying the piece, however, did not all tell the same story. The portrait of Robin Wight and Andrew Robinson, for example, played on the generational differences between the two men. In the photograph, Wight, the older man by twenty years, was pictured standing behind his younger colleague and jokily lifting him up by his trouser braces. The act of being lifted up by his braces truncated Robertson's body and he looked like a small boy with his trousers pulled up too high. Standing behind him, Wight was positioned in an avuncular or paternal role, playing with his young charge. Elsewhere in the article, Cole drew attention to the divergent social backgrounds of a number of the pairings. This was strongest in her comments on Mawhinney and Welch where, echoing the description offered by Mawhinney, she introduced them as "toff" Nick Welch and "yob" Billy

Mawhinny'. In doing so, her comments – like the photographic image of Wight and Robinson – made much of the oddness or peculiarity of these pairings. That is, it played up the way differences in social background or age formed the unlikely basis of their partnerships. As such, then, these were 'odd couples' – as the title of her article put it – because of the apparently paradoxical combination of both social distance between the partners and the strength of their bonds. However, if the designation 'odd couple' acknowledged the class and age discrepancies between the partners it also invoked the central preoccupation of the article – namely, intimacies between men. Thus, although Cole never made it explicit that she was describing all male pairings, it was her fascination with the meaning of close male relationships that drove the article. The way in which she drew attention to these intimacies, however, was noteworthy. The tone of the article, together with the choice of composition in the images, was particularly significant in this respect. Cole's journalism and the photography were self-consciously playful, inviting the reader into a rather studied enjoyment of homoeroticism and cross-gender role-play. There was a strong element of titillation in this. The readers were invited to enjoy the thrill of seeing apparently highly conventional men occupying a number of perverse positions. Preeminently, of course, playing at being husband and wife. Cole's article assumes the familiarity of the readership with these codes and invites them to collude in the game. It is clear, however, that collusion in this transgression of gender and sexual norms is not only restricted to the readers. It is also evident in the comments of the practitioners quoted in the piece. They emerge, in fact, as willing participants in this game of transgression.

Tabatha Cole's article was not alone in deploying the metaphor of marriage and associated themes from heterosexual romance in a self-consciously playful way when commenting on all-male pairings. One of the pairs whom she invoked in her introductory comments – Tim Delaney and Bruce Haines – had been represented in the same terms a few months earlier in *Campaign*. This is how the paper elaborated upon the meeting at which Delaney invited Haines to return to the agency Leagas Delaney:

> Tim Delaney proposed at the Savoy over an intimate breakfast of eggs and crispy bacon. 'I want you back', he murmured, fixing Bruce Haines with a steely look. . . . Bruce said 'yes' immediately. 'It was a very emotional response. Love is always sweeter the second time around' (*Campaign*, 23/4/94: 24).

The article went on by quoting Delaney on his decision to approach Haines. Delaney suggested, 'There were no other natural contenders for the job.

Blind dates are difficult when you are talking to people at this level' (ibid). This use of the trope of romance was echoed by a colleague who suggested: 'Tim is a serial monogamist with account men, and Bruce is the only one who's gone round twice, so perhaps they really do have a close connection' (ibid). Charlie Parkin, the agency's new business director, on the other hand, picked up on the theme of heterosexual complementarity suggesting, 'Haines is "mum" to Delaney's "dad" – one barks orders while the other wipes away the tears' (ibid; see also, *Campaign*, 9/2/96: 21).

The article, like Cole's piece, gives an insight into the currency of the tropes of marriage and heterosexual romance in public representations of the industry. Taken together with Cole's piece it points, in particular, to the way the metaphors were applied to a wide variety of male partnerships at different levels of the industry – from chief executives and chairman to creative directors. However, it is the representation of creative pairings that particularly interests me. Trade commentaries on them were especially prone to draw upon the metaphor of marriage or the tropes of heterosexual romance. Creatives were also keener than most practitioners to collude in the forms of transgression I have already described. Two examples serve to illustrate the point. Both case are striking because, in each instance, in an excessive gesture, both pairs of young creatives went so far as to take the metaphor of marriage literally and stage a marriage. Thus, in September 1994, *Campaign* reproduced a photograph of a pair of creatives – Ben Nott and Adam Hunt of Saatch & Saatchi – dressed as bride and groom respectively. Explaining their decision the pair said: 'Everyone refers to creative teams as 'partnerships' so we thought we'd become the ultimate partnership and have a wedding photo taken' (*Campaign*, 30/9/94: 11). Significantly, this was not the first time the pair had cross-dressed in the interests of their career. Having been told by friends that they would never get work in a London agency, they had a postcard made up of the two of them dressed in suspenders and false breasts, sitting in a prostitute's window in Amsterdam. On the back they wrote: 'Ben and Adam have found work in Amsterdam' (ibid).

Six months prior to the 'marriage' of Nott and Hunt, *Campaign* reported another creative marriage. In this case it was between Pat Holden and Bil Bungay of TBWA and it was for real. Bil Bungay takes up the story:

> We were out there [Las Vegas] on a shoot and, late one night, we were having a laugh about the places we had seen that were promoting male marriages. Our producer bet us $1000 to get hitched. So next day we went ahead and did it (*Campaign*, 11/3/94: 11).

Figure 6.1 (opposite)

opular demand: Aussie double act t on their big day

like it's embarrass-an-month. Last week, the threatened to run the "wed-photo" of Saatchi and i's Ben Nott and Adam he Cannes Grand Prix-win-ntipodean duo who are just g into Charlotte Street.

and has been great — so is. It was, explains Nott, n Australia when they first e a team: "Over there, ev-refers to creative teams as rships', so we thought we'd e the ultimate partnership e a wedding photo taken."

astonishingly, the "happy " shot is not the nadir of the unt album. "This is noth-ott says, "when we left Aus-o come to Europe, every-ught we were mad and that ever get work. So when we d Amsterdam, we made a rd of the two of us, pho-ned in suspenders and false s, sitting in a prostitute's v. On the back we wrote: nd Adam have found work sterdam' and sent it to all nds."

don't bother writing in. re depths to which even the efuses to stoop.

d Nott…the happy couple

Want free places on next Canberra junket? Appar-is possible to get to the Mar-Forum conference without hrough the arduous busi-signing a cheque. But if you do it next year, you'll ha e now.

rick is to bombard the or-s with complaints about this conference — although b iously ha e to come up nething better than moans he food and whinges about k of hango er cures on

our creati e people on to this ge straight away. One little something that goes down parently, is a series of long rtfelt letters bemoaning the t the "appointment" system down and that you didn't ay of the people you paid oney to smarmo er.

definitely works. Just ask Bogle Hegarty, which felt so bout its experiences last year ot free seats to the 1994 con-— which, at some £15,000 uple of places, is quite a sa oes help, of course, if you re of agency without which no nce would be complete. But bably worth a try in any Don't e er say the Diary is seless tri ia…

Bull…'I have no idea whether there might, at some time, come an intellectual itch that I will need to scratch'

Very early retirement in south of France is a case of 'pure luck'

So farewell then, Stuart Bull. After 25 years in the business, the man who once owned nearly as much Saatchi stock as the Saatchis is calling it a day.

Bull officially leaves CME KHBB this week, 16 years after he founded the agency, then called Humphreys Bull, with his partner Richard Humphreys. Once he has fulfilled a series of long-standing speaking engagements, Bull will spend a few months in the Caribbean and then split his life between London and his other home in the south of France.

He says: "Advertising is at a fas-cinating crossroads and this is an interesting moment to call 'time'. I intend to leave the business com-pletely, but I have no idea whether there might, at some time, come a strategic or intellectual itch that I will need to scratch."

Bull, true to his name, has never been afraid to worry a few of the industry's sacred cows. In fact, he disagreed with Frank Lowe's re-cent rallying cry, believing, in-stead, that "if the business contin-ues in its current direction, it will be heading down a cul-de-sac".

Bull, by then, will be on the open road — acknowledging his for-tune, at 48, in having the choice of a very early retirement. It is a choice which, having sold out to Saatchi in 1984, he owes to one of Martin Sorrell's classic earn-out deals, which ended just weeks before the stockmarket crash of 1987.

"I would love to say it was fore-sight, but it was pure luck," Bull admits. And, heartwarmingly for the rest of us, the Bull portfolio has had a few bearish moments — most notably the leg of a reluctant racehorse and the Sutherlands restaurant in Soho which, he says, was "hugely enjoyable but not what you'd call a successful busi-ness venture".

But for a man who claims to be cashing in his *pommes frites*, Bull is worryingly well-versed about local flight times. From his home near Montpellier — he has already checked — he can leave home in the morning and be in any Euro-pean capital by 11am. Sounds like Bull's well-intentioned retire-ment plans might end up being just that, Bull.

Would-be gameshow host, Baulk, inspires latest Economist task

AMV BBDO's latest poster for the *Economist* has been drawn to the Diary's attention. It is the one which features a shortened ver-sion of the evolutionary scale — "plankton, gameshow host, *Economist* reader" — and, our in-formant says, is a subtle dig at the agency's managing director, Michael Baulk.

Apparently, a few years ago, a group of agency subversives wrote a scurrilous in-house publication in which the question was posed: What would our noble board di-rectors be doing if they were not in advertising? David Abbott, it was felt, would be a grounded Con-corde pilot, while Peter Mead would be vice-chairman of Mill-wall FC and Michael Baulk would be…wait for it…a gameshow host.

The team who created the cur-rent poster, Malcolm Duffy and Paul Briginshaw, were not at the agency when the publication was issued and claim no knowledge of it at all. So is it sheer coincidence? Or is a weird osmotic process at work? And are there any AMV di-rectors who could conceivably be described as plankton? Answers on a postcard, please.

Baulk…the next Bob Monkhouse?

Toilet humour is not central idea to King's lavatorial screenplay

You have to admire his cheek. Not only did the BMP art director, Ashley King, start dabbling with film in company time, he then went round the agency asking for money to invest in his screenplay.

Astonishingly, in just one day he raised £700 from colleagues, who felt a 30-minute film about a lava-tory attendant would be a sensible use of their hard-earned cash. Now, with help of agency staff and suppliers, *Seduction* has been shot and King is pulling more favours in order to get it screened.

Seduction is more challenging

King…on the Edgware Road set of his first 30-minute drama, Seduction

than it might first appear. Lionel, a loo attendant driven to the edge, escapes his monotonous life by creating an action film, before re-alising the damage that a cam-era…no sorry, a gun can cause.

It may sound familiar, but the au-tobiographical content is nil — King would never describe life at BMP as working in a toilet. "I've been here six years and I love it. But I'm intrigued by film."

King bought his first Super 8 five years ago and last year attended a film course which resulted in a three-minute drama about a man trying to overcome his fear of iron-ing. Yes, really.

The actor who played the creaso-phobe, Paul Andsel, so enjoyed working with King for nothing that he agreed to take the lead in *Seduction*. The fruits of his labours raised a few eyebrows in the Edg-ware Road lavatories, where large parts of the film were shot, and might well raise a few more when it is entered for various film festivals later this year.

Back at his desk, King says: "I got the post-shoot blues for a while. But I'm in the swing of agency life now and am grateful to everyone who made *Seduction* possible."

One-time advertising hopeful turns talents to comical stationery

As the industry's 1994 graduate in-take begins to appreciate the rigours of Adland, spare no pity for Oliver Christie. Having got through to — and missed out at — the final interview stages for the past two years, Christie has put his advertising aspirations on hold and set up his own business, Ac-tion Stationery, from his home in Princes Risborough.

And, with clients including Lloyds Bank and Avon Cosmet-ics, he's doing rather well. Now, he says, he is trying to sell his cartoon letterheads to ad agencies — par-ticularly those which gave him work experience during his quest for a career in the business.

Any day now, Mustoe Merri-man, Saatchi and WCRS can ex-pect a call from Christie, who ex-plains: "This is a relatively cheap way for companies to use humour effectively. Memos can be fun — but not enough of them are."

His sleeping partner is his father, a former JWT account man, Tim Christie. And, no, Dad does not get too involved. He is, you might

Christie…enjoying a stress-free life

say, the stationary partner, leaving all the action to Christie Junior.

For a young man who has sent out more agency job applications than anyone in living memory, a career in notepaper is, perhaps, an obvious choice. And with 52 dif-ferent designs from cartoonist Robert Duncan, Christie has a let-terhead for every corporate occa-sion — except, notably, a kiss-off letter to job applicants.

Even that, however, is not some-thing Christie rules out for the fu-ture. He says rejection letters are no longer a sore point: "I desper-ately wanted to get into advertis-ing, but when I look at my friends in the business and see them work-ing their nuts off, I feel quite lucky to be running my own business and enjoying a relatively stress-free life out in Buckinghamshire."

Edited by Gail Kemp

The piece camped up the implications of the marriage. It noted how Holden's girlfriend 'took a while to get used to the idea . . . in fact she threatened to leave me until she saw the size of Bil's dowry'. It also asked the happy couple about the prospect of children:

> And what about the patter of tiny feet? 'We like to consider our campaigns as babies. They have a conception, gestation period and a birth. And you don't have to change their nappies' (ibid).

The collusion between the *Campaign* journalist and the young creatives in both these instances are striking. It points again to the highly conventionalised nature of these representations, as well as alerting us to the fact that they were the product of the interplay between journalistic codes and forms of explicit self-representation pursued by the practitioners. This latter point is important because advertising is a highly image-conscious industry and the explicit cultivation of public personas among creatives is particularly strong. Indeed, it is not unknown for 'star' creatives to have PR people working to promote their image and ensure that they figure frequently – often spectacularly – in the trade press. In doing so, these practitioners are involved in a very explicit process of self-representation. The examples of Nott and Hunt and Holden and Bungay don't quite fall into this category, but they do demonstrate a self-consciousness around the presentation of themselves in public that is consistent with the protocols of an image-conscious industry.

It is the significance of both pairings' decision to take literally the metaphor of marriage, however, as much as the more general motivations behind this move, which requires further comment. Specifically, what do their respective decisions to dress as a bride and groom tell us about their masculinity? I want to suggest that the act of cross-dressing, like the use of the metaphor of marriage, I have already discussed, registers the intimacies present within these close-working relationships. In literally adopting this metaphor the two pairings are appropriating – in a particularly dramatic way – the meaning of marriage as an intimate and enduring relationship in order to acknowledge the intensity and closeness of their own partnerships. However, the fact that they choose to express these intimacies in this form, clearly points to the difficulties they experience in giving more direct public expression to these aspects of their relationships. In particular, it evidences the way anxieties about being negatively labelled homosexual require these men to route their desires through a heterosexual form.

Yet there are other dynamics at work here. The excessive and flamboyant nature of their gestures – like some of the comments made by the

Figure 6.2 (opposite)

...time story that ...horribly wrong

...n is National Bed Month,
...appropriate time for an
...which proves that even
...-regulated advertising
...leave the agency team
...bless nights.

...ssured Beds, via its Bris-
... agency, Berkeley AG,
...ed a national radio and
...npaign which included
...f a BT-arranged phone-
...ve potential customers
...rmation.

...ncy thought it was home
...once the ads had been
...and the radio commer-
...ring the heady likes of
...Lindsay and Vicki
...had been recorded - all
...the special Rest Assured
...mber.

...ast moment, BT rang to
...at it had, in fact, allocat-
...Assured's number to an-
...terprise which was al-
...ng the line.

...Rest Assured mind using
...it number? Well, yes it
...ctually. Some magazines
...dy gone to press with the
...would be awkward to get
...s back to re-record the
...mercials.

...g, it appeared, could be
...the agency re-made the
...ecorded the radio work
...ed the extremely tortu-
...ss of trying to get the ex-
...ck from BT.

...hile, Rest Assured's
...director, Fiona McLean,
...original number to find
...ad nicked it.

...und herself talking to
...from the Child Support
...— an outfit which, quite
...est Assured, has built a
...on for giving its "cus-
...nightmares of Stephen
...portions.

Elms...spent months looking for a job — and then became obsessed with receptions

KEITH MCMILLAN

Elms ensures that CIA gives its visitors the zaniest of receptions

There's nothing like a couple of
months spent job-hunting to focus
the mind on the general state of
agency reception areas.

After visiting a host of agencies
some 15 months ago, Mike Elms
decided that — wherever he ended up — he would do something
revolutionary with his new company's reception.

Now, happily ensconced at CIA
Media, he is fulfilling his promise.
By the end of this month, the CIA
reception will be decked out with
the very latest media technology.
Sophisticated computer games,
interactive information technology, full-motion video and a video
wall showing satellite and cable
channels — nothing will be too innovative for CIA.

"Reception is any company's
first chance to make an impression," Elms explains. "It should be
a statement about the business.
Every creative agency has ads on
its walls. We are a media business
and need to show that we are successful, fun, modern and right at
the vanguard of new technology."

Software will be regularly updat-
ed, thanks to dutiful monitoring of
new media by all CIA staff. The
final say about which computer
games are installed rests with Rob
Norman, resident new-tech expert
and managing director of CIA's
joint venture, WM Media.

The Diary is relieved to report
that ordinary, old-fashioned media such as magazines and newspapers will still feature prominently,
alongside radio headsets forming
what Elms describes as a "multi-
media experience".

He declines to reveal exactly
what the experience is costing
CIA, but it will doubtless prove in-
valuable. Making sure your clients
always arrive early for meetings is
quite a coup. Making them thrilled
to then discover that you are running horribly late is, let's face it,
nothing short of genius.

Ex-luvvies are back in the picture again

If your past as a member of the National Youth Theatre is going to
catch up with you, you may as well
live with the ribbing and use your
connections to best advantage.

That, at least, is the view of the
Davies Little Cowley partner, Hy-
wel Davies, whose new Gosfield
Street office features an exhibition of photos by Nobby Clark.

It was 25 years ago that Davies
was a hopeful at the NYT where he
met Clark, an aspiring theatrical
photographer, who worked behind the bar in his dad's pub — the
two are still unsure whether their
association began on the boards or
in the boozer. However, they went
their separate ways eventually,
with Clark making a business of
photography and Davies entering
the world of advertising.

Years later, at Young and Rubi-
cam, they met again. Clark was on
one of his rare forays into advertising photography with an ad for
Mencap. The account director was
none other than Davies. The two
stayed in touch, with Davies often
persuading Clark to use his skills in
the sordid world of advertising.

Last year, his exhibition at the
Battersea Arts Exhibition —
called Nobby Clark's London —
met with great acclaim and 40 edited highlights are now on show at
Davies Little Cowley. The former
frock factory is an impressive
gallery and this is the first of many
exhibitions that will entertain
clients and motivate staff — and
probably provoke more stimulating conversation than walls of ads.

Davies and Clark...old friends

What they read: David Kershaw

Saatchi's new chairman and chief
executive, David Kershaw, is Ar-
senal's biggest fan. Pandering to
this odd lapse in an otherwise
tasteful existence, he is reading
*The End: 80 Years of Life on Arse-
nal's North Bank*, by the former
Eastenders star, Tom Watt.

The North Bank terrace, recently knocked down to make way for
the North Bank stand, was where
Kershaw spent his early Arsenal-
watching life: "The book is a collection of reminiscences from
players, fans and writers. It is
beautifully put together," he says.

Also on his bedside table is *Your
One-Week Way To Mind Fitness*
by John O'Keefe, regional vice-
president with Saatchi client,
Procter and Gamble. Kershaw, on
week three, reports no change in
his mental agility. Perhaps, he
adds, his mind is beyond resuscita-
tion. Whether this is due to pressures of high office, or to a mis-
spent youth supping Bovril on the
North Bank, is anybody's guess.

...e Lintas's despatch manager, Tony West — last featured in the
...empting to transport a life-size dummy on British Rail — has
...into the public eye once again, as before, in an earnest effort to
...e interests of a Still Price client.

...ne he donned a sandwich board to become part of the agency's
...npaign promoting the new IBM OS/2 operating system. The ad-
...was a full-frontal assault on IBM's Microsoft rival, timed to
...with the recent software exhibition at Olympia.

...y before the show opened, Still Price swamped the entire area
...ser posters reading "Don't be soft. Pos/2tive thinking" in
...t's typeface. Microsoft, understandably, hit the stratosphere,
...the agency to reprint everything overnight in a different typeface.
...w posters were still being put up as crowds assembled for the
...n's first day, supported by a sandwich-boarded West
...out leaflets. Despite being asked to move off the Olympia site
...the Hammersmith Road, he still managed to give away 2,500
...n his three-day stint. Proving that, even in the 90s, truly dedicated
...personnel are happy to put themselves on the street in order to
...ir clients happy.

A bet, a wedding, two grooms and an Elvis

There is, inevitably, a close bond
between any copywriter and art
director — especially when they
have worked together for several
years. TBWA's all-male creative
duo, Pat Holden and Bil Bungay,
are closer than most. They are, in
fact, married.

According to art director Bungay, the ceremony took place last
month: "We'd talked about it for a
long time, but never did anything
about it. Then, more or less on a
whim, we flew out to Vegas where
this sort of thing is legal, nay encouraged, and tied the knot."

Really? "Well, no. We were out
there on a shoot and, late one
night, we were having a laugh
about the places we had seen that
were promoting male marriages.
Our producer, Richard Forbes-
Robertson, bet us $1,000 to get
hitched. So the next day, we went
ahead and did it."

It was, by all accounts, an extremely bizarre experience. The
minister was an Elvis imperson-
ator and the hired witness was, in
Bungay's words, "a strange old
geezer with a glass eye."

Yet, despite being $500 richer
apiece, the team had a fair bit of
explaining to do when it arrived
back in London. Holden admits
that his girlfriend took a while to
get used to the idea: "In fact, she
threatened to leave me until she
saw the size of Bil's dowry."

Whether the marriage is really
made in heaven is, however, de-
batable. The newly-weds did not
even send each other a Valentine's
Day card — although, insists Bungay, there will be a lavish celebration on their first anniversary.

And what about the patter of tiny
feet? "We like to consider our
campaigns as babies. They have a
conception, a gestation period and
a birth. And you don't have to
change their nappies..."

Holden (l) and Bungay...married

Edited by Gail Kemp

practitioners we encountered earlier – point to a certain pleasure in transgressing gender and sexual norms, as much as an anxiety about being negatively labelled. In fact, it is clear that their anxiety about homosexuality is bound up with a simultaneous fascination with it and associated forms of cross-gender role-play. This fascination can only be acknowledged, though, if it takes the form of a deliberately playful and highly circumscribed act; an act delimited as a form of licensed or legitimate excess.

By dressing as husband and wife, the men are also affirming an exclusively heterosexual model of desire. In this masquerade, then, desire between men is represented not by drawing on the tropes of homoerotic desire present within affirmative gay culture, but by routing it through the representational norms of heterosexual complementarity. The effect is to reiterate the cultural distance for these men between hetero- and homosexual masculinity.

This is not the end of the story. There are notable, if subtle, differences between the ways each pair reiterates their identification with heterosexuality. While Hunt and Nott compose a robustly exclusive form of heterosexuality, Bungay and Holden appear to occupy a more ambivalent position in relation to its norms. Central in this regard is the respective styling of each of the portraits. In Nott and Hunt's image, there is a lumpen blokishness about the way they are dressed. In particular, the way Ben Nott is dressed in bridal wear – where there is no attempt to glamourise his appearance and where the exposure of his hairy chest emphasises that he is not attempting to pass as a women but is definitely a man in a frock – plays up the ridiculousness of the 'marriage'. The image of Bungay and Holden is, on the other hand, altogether a more highly styled composition. In terms of dress – be it Bungay's sari or Holden's stylised regency fop look – there is a degree of accomplishment around the styling of appearance that is missing from Nott and Hunt's image. The postures of Holden and Bungay – while highly staged – further suggest a preparedness to enter into more sexually ambivalent roles. Both through dress and posture, then, their image hints at a greater ambivalence in their identification with these perverse positions. Thus, while in the end they too reaffirm the cultural divide between heterosexuality and homosexuality, they hint at sexual ambiguity. In this sense, an important difference exists in the inflections given to the metaphor of marriage in these representations of creative partnerships – a difference bound up with the subtle differences between the masculinities composed by these men. This, however, was not the only way in which the intimacies between men were handled and the metaphor of marriage inflected. In the accounts of the men I interviewed there were further distinct ways in which the metaphor signified. It is to these accounts that I now turn.

the ties that bind   Phil Chantler was a thirty year old art director working for the Soho-based agency Rowlands and Partners. Like many of the practitioners I interviewed, he had first met and then teamed up with his current creative partner while at college. In Chantler's case this had been Newcastle College of Art and the pair had initially been drawn to each other by a mutual recognition that each was committed to working hard on the course and were serious about succeeding in their chosen studies. When I interviewed Chantler, his partnership with Steve was in its ninth year and had clearly developed over that time into a close friendship. This closeness was evidenced by the fact that Steve had been best man at his marriage and that they were, as he put it, 'good mates'. The intensity of their bond was evidently strong enough to not go unnoticed by colleagues. Picking up on the way they related to each other – and echoing the more titillating language seen in the trade press – Geoff Rowlands, the pair's creative director suggested, 'Phil and Steve are like husband and wife. I can tell which one is which, you usually can'. Chantler put things somewhat differently. Reflecting on what made their relationship work, he suggested:

> We're both from Newcastle and the same age and come from similar backgrounds. I think some teams are alike and we're quite alike. He's more . . . I can't stand the music he likes – he likes Frank Sinatra and stuff. That's quite annoying. It's like being married almost. But I think we are quite different. [. . .] It's almost like a marriage with a purpose though. It's not just being together. We're here for a purpose. To do good work.

In searching for a way of explaining his working relationship with Steve, Chantler moves fairly quickly in this extract to describe it in marital terms and, in the end, to offer a description of their partnership based upon a qualified use of this metaphor. In doing so, he inflects the metaphor largely away from the more sexualised meanings prevalent within the trade representations and towards other, more prosaic, meanings. Central to these is his emphasis on the time they spend together. The metaphor of marriage works here to articulate the sense of familiarity and closeness based upon the enduring and long-term nature of the bond. It also captures the mundane and routine dimensions of the relationship and the petty niggles – such as putting up with someone else's taste in music – that stem from such enduring and close proximity. Chantler also uses the metaphor of marriage to capture the way their interests are tied in together, and to register both the forms of dependency upon each other and the commitment to a common project, which characterises the relationship. While he feels the need to qualify the metaphor in order to make explicit the common endeavour they are engaged in – namely, to produce good work – this is already implied in the older meaning of marriage as a contractual relationship in which the fortunes of each partner are intertwined in the pursuit of social and material, as well as emotional, gains.

An emphasis on the meaning of marriage as an enduring and supportive relationship was evident in the comments of Mike Walker and Steve Goode, the 26 year old art director and 30 year old copywriter, respectively, at Direct Arts. Like Phil Chantler and his partner Steve, Goode and Walker had teamed up while at college. And – again – as with Chantler and his partner, they had been drawn to each other by recognition that they came from similar social backgrounds and had dispositions in common. For Goode and Walker this was sharpened by a shared sense of being ordinary in a group of students from whom they felt somewhat detached. Thus, in response to my question about what was it that they had liked about each other, they suggested:

> **SG**: It was the crack out of work, wasn't it?
>
> **MW**: But a lot of the people on the course were ex-, a couple were ex-public school, weren't they, with journalists and . . .
>
> **SG**: I think we were, sort of, the same sort of level really.
>
> **MW**: I think it was a similar background, and stuff like that.
>
> **SG**: We used to have a crack in the pub . . . I'm really pleased we did it that way, because our tutor . . . probably the one bit of bad advice he gave was 'Go with who you think's going to be the hardest worker, don't worry if you don't get on with them'. We didn't do it like that at all. Obviously we thought each other was good workers and stuff, but it was more like . . . I could see myself getting on with him, I'd say more so, wouldn't you?

In reflecting further on how they teamed up, Steve Goode drew attention to the enduring character of their partnership by invoking the idea of an anniversary. He suggested:

> At Watford, he [Tony Cullingham, course director] teams you up with everybody, so you have a day working with everybody on the course. And when it got to about Christmas, he said, 'Right, now, I want you to go and pick who you're gonna work with' . . . and Mike suggested we work together. Christmas this year will be two years, won't it?

In conjuring the idea of an anniversary, Goode was clearly drawing an analogy between their working partnership and more romantic forms of attachment – most obviously, of course, marriage. The manner in which he did this was also important. By posing the reference to their anniversary as a question, he drew Mike Walker into the exchange and invited his complicity in this disclosure of intimacy. The effect is to publicly mark the closeness of their relationship.

Elsewhere in the interview Mike Walker was more explicit in drawing on the metaphor of marriage to describe their relationship with each other. Thus, in reflecting on how they supported each other through difficult times, the following exchange took place:

SN: Did you keep each other cheerful?

MW: keep each other miserable!

SG: I kept you cheerful, didn't I!

MW: You know, it's kind of like a marriage, when they've got money problems. Do you know what I mean? And when its going well, you're ok.

The exchange is noteworthy not only for the way they deploy the metaphor of marriage, but also for the way it dramatises their closeness and solidarity with each other. This most obviously emerges in the way they alternate in the telling of their story, with Walker building on and adding to Goode's comments about the way they supported each other. Within this exchange – and across the interview as a whole – they operated as a redoubtable double act. In doing so, Steve Goode recurrently played the supportive role, allowing Mike Walker to talk energetically at length while monitoring his comments and often backing him up. Often, as we've seen above, he would draw Walker into the exchanges by directing a question at him and inviting him to confirm or authorise a statement Goode himself had just made. Throughout the interview, then, Goode worked hard to oversee the interaction between the pair and myself. This arrangement revealed much about the respective dispositions of each partner, in particular the greater maturity and worldliness of Goode. It is also hard not to see it – in the light of their deployment of the metaphor of marriage – as the playing out of complementary gender roles, with Goode acting in the supportive, feminine role and Walker taking on the position of masculine pontificator (see Roper, 1994: 92).

The enduring nature of creative partnerships and the intimacy generated through spending long periods of time together emerged in the account of another of the practitioners I interviewed, a 32 year old art director at Knight & Peters called Dylan Wrathall. It was these aspects of his working relationship with his copywriting partner that Wrathall had in mind when he too invoked the metaphor of marriage. Wrathall was keener than almost all the other practitioners I interviewed to establish his authority in relation to the topics that we covered in the interview. In fact, he approached the interview by attempting to determine which issues he thought I needed to know about. There was something almost pedagogic in his manner, and he clearly saw it as his responsibility to introduce a novice outsider like me into the pertinent features of his world. All this was paradoxical because he was the least confident of all the practitioners I interviewed, and the one least secure in his own abilities as a creative. It was clear from what he let slip on occasions that he had something of a reputation of being difficult to work with and had gone through a number of partners. This lack of confidence evidently lay behind his concern to position himself to me as an authoritative insider. It also clearly informed what he had to say about creative partnerships. Thus, almost before I had finished explaining the themes I wanted to cover, he leapt in with an explanation of creative partnerships as marriages:

> **DW**: If you think of the partnerships as marriages that won't take you too far wrong.
>
> **SN**: In what way?
>
> **DW**: Because of the intensity, if you think of the amount of time you spend with a partner. I mean Mike gets into work about 10 leaves at 5.30. We're in the office together most of the time. Make each other a cup of tea. But that's more time than you spend with your spouse, really. . . . The other key thing to understand is that your fortunes are intertwined.

He underscored this sense of partnerships as marriages when he went on to describe the process of being teamed up with Mike and the early stages of their relationship. Thus, he suggested,

> I was recruited by a headhunting system that's a bit like a dating agency. There's no practical difference. The partnership itself, it's just like a girlfriend or boyfriend. It's only a few months later when you're through the honeymoon period, and you start to realise . . . there are issues that come up, and I did find myself dealing with them much better. Also I was having therapy at this stage, which sometimes you need, 'cause . . . because almost like a relationship quite a lot hinges on it. Your income. Your reputation in the industry. And managing differences of opinion about the work you do is difficult.

In this passage Wrathall moves through the different stages of the partnership in setting out an account of his working relationship with Mike. As he does so, he turns to the tropes of marriage and heterosexual romance to explain the dynamics of the partnerships: from dating through to the honeymoon period and relationship problems. Significantly, his account gives this a slightly different gloss from those we have already encountered by introducing in a rather outré way a therapy-derived description of relationship problems. More significantly, he combines the meaning of marriage as an enduring and supportive social bond made up of banal, almost domestic rituals (like making each other tea) with the tropes of romance and the inference of desire that they more clearly signal. In doing this, Wrathall brings together more explicitly than either Goode and Walker or Phil Chantler, the meaning of marriage as both an intimate and a contractual bond.

The sparking of desire within a close relationship was even more central to the account of his partnership given by Paul Cantelo. In fact, what he had to say very clearly centre-staged these aspects of desire bound up with the tropes of marriage and heterosexual romance. Cantelo was a 33 year old art director working for Serendipity. When I interviewed him he was in a particularly reflective and expansive mood. When I asked him about what it was like working in a team, he launched into an extended commentary on his partnerships and, in particular, on how he had come to meet his current partner, Jess Brown. This is what he said:

I've only ever worked with 3 different partners, and one of them was for about 7 years. [. . .] After a while, our relationship just kind of fell apart, and it is like a relationship that you'd have with any other type of partner, and what you have to do is kind of develop it, and it has to improve and . . . become better. . . . You just won't survive if you remain static. So I worked with this guy for 7 years, and then I worked with Jess, whom I'm working with now, for . . . I worked with him for a period while this bloke went away for a month on holiday. And I worked with Jess then, and it was just such a breath of fresh air, it was like having an affair in the middle of a marriage, you know it was just. . . . Christ! It was brilliant! And then . . . and then this other guy came back and it just went downhill from there on. And I, I left and then got a new partner for about 18 months, just to kind of get my head together. . . . When I did that stretch, during my first time with him [JB], when we worked together for that month, it was just kind of unbelievable. It made me also realise my relationship with my previous partner had been so bad, but . . . it was just incredible.

Cantelo's comments are striking in a number of ways. First, there is a strong ambiguity running through his comments in the way he describes his partnerships. He runs together an assessment of their effectiveness as, on the one hand, a working relationship whose success can be measured by the quality of the work produced and, on the other hand, their status as interpersonal relationships whose success might be based upon other criteria. This ambiguity is revealing because it clearly illuminates the way both dimensions of the partnerships are inextricably intertwined in his perception of them. Thus, his comments suggest that constantly working to improve the partnership is key if the team is to innovate creatively. This innovation is at the root of being a successful team and clearly lies behind one meaning of his phrase 'you just won't survive if you remain static'. However, the same phrase is also mobilised to carry another meaning that is associated with a developmental model of relationship. In this sense a successful relationship is one in which each partner is growing and changing and continuing to bring new things to the relationship. It is clear that Cantelo sees the former aspects of the partnerships – the team's ability to innovate creatively – as dependent upon its emotional dynamics. His comments suggest, then, a dovetailing of the need to develop fresh and distinctive ideas as a team with a conception of relationships and life in general as a project. Given this, we can see why Cantelo should invest so much in the successful relationship with Brown.

What is more striking is the way he describes his feelings when working with Brown. They do suggest – more so than any of the other comments made by the practitioners we have encountered to date – the active articulation of desire in relation to another man. As Cantelo begins to relive the moment of first working with Brown, this intensity of feeling is largely carried through the exclamatory mode of expression as Cantelo searches for a way of communicating the experience. This intensity is also, however, evidently articulated through the flamboyant use of the tropes from heterosexual romance. His description of this teaming up as being like 'having an affair in the middle of a marriage' foregrounds the strength of his feelings towards Brown.

Later in the interview, Cantelo elaborated on the dynamics of his relationship with Brown and was more explicit about the place of this relationship in the context of his wider life. Describing Brown, he said,

He is certainly the most competitive man I've ever met . . . which actually kind of works really well in a team. . . . I think the way it works for us is just having a massive amount of respect, and always trying to be positive about it [the process of creating]. . . . I'm not very good at other types of relationships, but I tell you what, this one has been probably the only one that's progressed, consistently, over the last 7 years.

As Cantelo talks about his partnership in this passage he reveals the depth of the investment he has in it. It is, in particular, the pathos of his comments about the lack of successful relationships in the rest of his life that is highly effecting and makes clear the importance of the partnership to him. What emerges, in fact, is a strong sense of his pride in the relationship he has managed to forge with Brown. Thus, while he views both his significant creative partnerships through the lens of heterosexual romance, it is in his comments on his successful relationship with Brown that desire is expressed most strongly. Cantelo's comments, however, do beg a big question – and it is a question that is central to the accounts of all the practitioners I have discussed and runs right to the heart of this chapter. Namely, to what extent is the deployment of the metaphors of marriage and heterosexual romance bound up with gender? And, in particular, how does the masculinity of men like Cantelo show itself in the turn to these tropes? I have already begun to suggest answers to these questions, but I want to shed further light on them by turning briefly to the accounts of practitioners working in other kinds of partnerships before coming to some conclusions.

boys, girls and feminine intimacies Perhaps the most illuminating comparison with the accounts of the male practitioners I interviewed came in the comments of women creatives who worked or were working in all-female teams. Their accounts were marked by an almost complete absence of the metaphors of marriage and heterosexual romance that figured so prominently in the testimonies of the men. These women often talked with as much intensity about their partnership and each other as the men we have encountered, but what was noteworthy was the explicit disclosure of their feelings for their partner and a relative openness about revealing these intimacies. Teresa Walsh, an experienced art director at CTRL, was exemplary in this regard. Her most striking comments were made about the first woman partner she worked with. They had been teamed up at another agency and had worked together for four and a half years. A strong friendship was forged during this time and survived the ending of the working relationship. This is how Walsh described the relationship. She begins by talking about her first job:

> TW: I took the job at French Harris Smith in the end. It was to work with another girl, Charlotte Roberts. We used to spend 90 per cent of our time chatting. I think that's what girls do when they work together.
>
> SN: Tell me about the relationship with Charlotte?
>
> TW: Oh, it was lovely. Lovely. We were together 24 hours a day virtually and I really love her. I am godmother to her son and she'll probably be my best woman at my wedding. I just love her to pieces. But we were both art directors. Two art directors

> working together. So after 2½ years, our creative director said, 'Look, I think you should split up, I'll get two writers in to work with you.' And we burst into tears. And we still speak to each other and we were on the phone the night before last. I think she's fantastic.

Walsh had clearly established a strong and enduring friendship with Roberts and so the comparison with the accounts of the men I interviewed is perhaps exaggerated. None the less, the open disclosure of love in her comments is noteworthy and stands in stark contrast to the testimonies of the men I have discussed. The qualitative difference between Walsh's comments and those of the men I talked to is also underscored by the way she encloses her feeling for Roberts within a strongly gendered account of their relationship. Thus, Walsh marks out the intensity of the relationship as tied up with femininity by drawing on ideas of girls chatting and being overemotional. Her comments suggest that a shared culture of femininity underlies the quality and intensity of the relationship; that there was something about being young women of a similar age that was integral to the strength of the bond.

The contrast between her account of this partnership and the one in which she was involved with a young male creative is also revealing. When I spoke to her she was teamed up with a junior copywriter called Christopher. This is how she described him:

> He's good because he's completely opposite [to me]. We have things in common. He likes to work within a certain time. He's quiet and not a lad. And he's very interesting and very clever . . . I think he reads *The Guardian* everyday and I don't. . . . I don't have to put the news on, I listen to him. . . . I've grown to really like him after encouraging him to . . . I do feel I'm mentoring him in a way. But then he's doing the same to me. I really quite like working with him. There are things he does that really get on my nerves – what juniors do when they go out with producers which is eat as much as they can and order the most expensive thing on the menu. People notice that. And he misbehaves like that.

Her comments about Christopher reveal a much less intense relationship. Thus, while she acknowledges that they share certain values in common, she twice marks the distance between them – most noticeably in terms of seniority and experience. Her comments suggest that this is much more clearly an exclusively working relationship and not one in which they share or disclose intimacies. Elsewhere in the interview she was also keen to downplay any possibility of sexual desire in the relationship with Christopher. Thus, when I explicitly put it to her that commentators often compared creative partnerships to marriages and wondered whether she felt this comparison got at something important in the working relationship with Christopher. She said,

Its funny because my boyfriend said he couldn't work with a girl because he'd find it daunting and anyway, he said, you'd get really jealous. And I said, would I buggery. 'Cause I know once you are working with someone that sort of thing doesn't come into it. You never think, oh what would it be like to fancy Christopher. Christopher is just someone I work with. He is without sex in a way . . . you have to respect the partner, the other, and trust them. I haven't really been working long enough with Christopher to know whether it's definitely going to work out. But it is getting better. It's going in the right direction. Whereas all the other relationships were great from the start. Me and Charlotte are like best friends.

As with Paul Cantelo's earlier reflections, there is an ambiguity in Walsh's comments in this passage between the work related and the intersubjective dimensions of the partnership. As she considers her relationship with Christopher, it is not clear at times whether she is reflecting on whether the relationship is effective in terms of the process of creating work or whether she is referring to the possibility that something more than this institutional linkage might grow out of the partnership in terms of friendship or intimacy. In doing so she, again, deploys a strongly developmental model of relationships. However, it is the contrast between the relationship with Christopher and her relationship with Charlotte that punctuates her comments and which produces a strong sense of difference between them in terms of the lack of intimacy within the former relationship and its overflowing in the latter.

It would be wrong to overplay the significance of Walsh's comments on the two partnerships and I want, below, to come to some qualifications about the gender implications of her testimony. Clearly, the differences between her two partnerships cannot be adequately explained by a reductive recourse to gender and are manifestly tied up with the way seniority and age differences overdetermine the relationship. However, another of the practitioners I interviewed, Dylan Wrathall, offered a rather different account from Walsh's of the dynamics of a mixed partnership. This was one in which, in contradistinction to Walsh, a strong sense of intimacy emerged.

Wrathall had worked with a female art director prior to teaming up with Mike. It had not turned out to be a happy experience and, as the working relationship broke down, his investment in it became clear:

I was having a lot of trouble with my then girlfriend and I was talking to friends and, actually, to a therapist about it. They stopped being able to differentiate when I was talking about the girlfriend or this art director. There was something very dysfunctional in both relationships and what had actually triggered off the problem was having some success together, ironically, and she didn't feel part of that success. . . . It was a horrible, horrible thing. She kept accusing me of blowing out all her good ideas. It was competitive in the wrong way. It had all the hallmarks of a very bad relationship. . . . It reached a tragic comic level. I sat opposite her and she put the angle poise lamp so that it was in front of my face. Why are you doing that, I said and she said 'because I don't want to look at your horrible face, cunt.

As he describes the breakdown of the partnership, Wrathall's comments reveal something of the intimacy and emotion bound up in the working relationship. This emerges, on the one hand, through the degree of hostility released as the relationship unravels, and on the other, through his confession about confusing his sexual partner and his working partner in comments to various interlocutors, which suggests that, at least at that moment of crisis, they had equivalence in his own mind. As he himself effectively suggests, being involved in a bad working relationship is like being involved in a bad sexual relationship. In both instances, desire turns into disgust.

In reflecting on this particular partnership in this way, Wrathall was, in fact, unusual in acknowledging the presence of intimacy within a mixed team. As we have seen, the trade representations focused exclusively on the place of intimacy between men within all-male partnerships. And while anecdotal evidence suggested that it was not unknown for the partners in mixed teams to get married to each other, there was little or no public acknowledgement within the discourses of the industry of intimacy and desire between these kinds of partners – including an absence of the metaphor of marriage to describe them. Given this, what does Wrathall's unusual revelation tell us about the dynamics of creative partnerships and about the accounts of the men involved in all-male partnerships that I discussed earlier?

conclusion   Given that the focus of this chapter has been on intimacies between men, it is perhaps paradoxical to have ended by reflecting on the place of intimacy and desire in relationships between men and women in mixed creative teams. Opening up the way masculinity was bound up with the structuring of intimacy, however, has necessitated considering not only all-male partnerships, but also drawing on evidence from other kinds of creative pairings. In doing so, my aim has been to work with Sedgwick's provocations about the centrality of gender to the contemporary structuring of close social bonds between persons of the same sex. As I suggested in the introduction, it was Sedgwick's central claim that the potential continuum that exists between the social and sexual aspects of these relationships was radically disrupted for men. What she termed the continuum of male homosocial desire was interrupted by, preeminently, homophobia. This contrasted strongly with close relations between women in which there was, despite crosscutting pressures, a relatively continuous relation between female homosocial and homosexual bonds (Sedgewick, 1985: 5).

The mixed creative teams that I have discussed throw a particular light on homosocial relations. Whereas the former – as an instance of relations between men and women – are typically assumed to be saturated with sexuality, the latter are conventionally imagined being devoid of it. However, the mixed teams that I discussed, reveal, first, the problems that arise in disclosing or making explicit forms of intimacy between men and women, and second, the importance of being able to differentiate between different intensities within these relationships. It is clear that one of the reasons for the difficulty in disclosing these intimacies stems from the legal rulings and moral pressures that govern relations between men and women at work in the light of the moves against sexual harassment and add significant complications to acknowledging the play of desire between men and women. Certainly these external pressures make it difficult for the advertising trade press to represent these intimacies between men and women at work. The examples of Teresa Walsh and Dylan Wrathall further suggest that the cultural assumptions about the ever present possibility of desire between men and women fails to grasp the nuanced and differentiated way these relationships might work themselves out. The Wrathall example suggests that these feelings can be expressed indirectly and take the form of aggression or competition. In this sense, there were notable parallels between the dynamics of mixed partnerships and those between men. Walsh's experience suggested something else as well: that relations between men and women could be friendly without sustaining desire or intimacy and that they might be overlaid by other dimensions of the relationship.

Teresa Walsh was illuminating, as I suggested earlier, in other ways. In particular, it was her contrasting experiences of working with a male and female partner that pointed to the place of gender in shaping the dynamics of these close-working relationships. Her comments certainly have some immediate descriptive fit with Sedgwick's formulations. When read against the commentaries of the men who worked in all-male teams, they form an even sharper contrast. In particular, it was her open disclosure of intimacy and the unabashed declaration of feelings that was so strikingly different from the displaced form in which intimacy between the men was acknowledged.

Despite its suggestiveness, there remains a danger of overburdening Walsh's account and of generating overly categorical interpretations of the way the men and women I interviewed represented their partnerships. Guarding against this has been central to the ambitions of this chapter. I have, especially, tried to draw out the different ways in which the men I talked to described their close working relationships. Thus, while I drew attention to the recurrent use of the metaphors of marriage and heterosexual romance across their accounts, I suggested that these metaphors were given different inflections within the accounts of individual men. These ranged from an emphasis on the contractual meanings of marriage as an enduring and supportive relationship to a mobilisation of the meaning of marriage as an intimate relationship that included an acknowledgment of desire. These contrasting inflections, I suggested, alert us not only to the different intensities of these men's relationships, but also point to the different ways they handled both the intimacies present within the relationships and the broader public perception of close male relationships – particularly the anxiety about homosexuality often associated with them.

Thus, while the tropes have a wide currency within the industry and offered a legitimated set of terms through which to represent their experiences, the ways in which particular men deployed the metaphors tells us something about their subjective investments in particular forms of masculinity. As we have seen, for most of the men this was a form of masculinity shaped around pleasure in the close company of another man, but rooted in an assumption of a cultural divide between heterosexual and homosexual masculinity. However, for other men – most clearly Paul Cantelo – this identification with heterosexual masculinity was more open to some of the sexual ambiguities of close male relations. For Cantelo, the cultural divide between homosexuality and heterosexuality was not so absolute and his sense of heterosexual masculinity not so exclusive.

pleasure at work: the gender ambivalences of work-based sociability

In March 1999, *Arena*, the men's lifestyle magazine, in one of its regular feature articles, set out to explore the cultures of work prevalent within the newer parts of the media and cultural industries. The article focused on a new social type, the 'flexecutive', whom its author, Richard Benson, saw as embodying the distinctive orientations to work of practitioners within this sector. To this end, he emphasised both the stylistic self-consciousness of these 'flexecutives' and the importance to them of a work-based lifestyle that put a high premium on forms of socialising lubricated by drinking, drugs and a consumption-based ethic of enjoyment. He described them – or 'him' – as follows:

I first saw him in a loft in the fashionable London area of Old Street, attending an un-fancy dress party to which everyone appeared to have come as the same person. There were about a hundred there, all aged between 27 and 38, and most affecting a slight over-confidence, toning down their accents, and dressed in high maintenance connoisseur sports and work wear. The basics were familiar – combat trousers, fleeces and all-terrain trainers – but the labels were conspicuously flash. . . . The cropped haircuts (slightly greying, slightly balding) and goatee beards (compulsory) looked as though they were tended at upwards of £25 a time, and the drugs (Absolut and Cranberry, high grade grass, cocaine) upmarket. It was a typical 1990s contradiction; clothes and accessories from youth culture that could be afforded only by people whose age and income were not 'youth' at all (*Arena*, March 1999: 88).

In codifying this social type, Benson's article drew upon a well-established genre of style-based journalism in which an attention to the phantasmagoria of contemporary metropolitan (usually, London) life loomed large. Through a detailing of both specific districts of the city and the dress codes and argot of its inhabitants, this journalism offered a particular mapping of urban life and its *dramatis personae*. His account of the 'flexecutive', however, also rehearsed an argument about the nature of work in the 'creative industries' that had a wider currency beyond the pages of the style press. This emphasised how employment in these sectors was distinguished by its blurring of established divisions between 'work' and 'leisure' in the way a job was organised and performed. Angela McRobbie has done most to draw attention to this apparently hybrid character of 'creative work' and, in particular, to the influence of the whole panoply of jargon, clothes and music derived from club culture to the organisation of these worlds of creative employment. As she polemically puts it, 'the intoxicating pleasures of leisure culture have . . . for a sector of the under-35s [working in the cultural industries] provided a template for managing an identity in the world of work' (McRobbie, 2003: 115; see also Leadbeater, 1999; Scase and Davis, 2000).

This emphasis on the hybrid nature of these kinds of creative employment identified by Benson and McRobbie – the difficulty of fitting them into some of our conventional assumptions about work and leisure – reveals an important, if ultimately, a partial truth. I want to take this observation as the starting point for exploring the place of work-based and work-related forms of sociability within the informal cultures inhabited by the men I interviewed. What interests me in this chapter is the way the kinds of understandings of creative work deployed by Benson and McRobbie surfaced within the creative cultures of advertising itself. An image of creative jobs as precisely 'enjoyable', 'fun' and allowing access to a world of glamour and style had considerable currency among creative people and would-be creatives themselves. As we will see, for the young practitioners that I interviewed, it was clear that they were often initially drawn to the job because of this perception. However, their experiences of working as creatives were more contradictory. While the job did allow them access to these forms of sociability, it was not without its costs. More than that, the very centrality of hedonism to the representation of their jobs provoked anxieties about the occupational standing of the work they performed. In exploring the feelings of ambivalence that they expressed, I centrally want to reflect on what this tells us about the gender subjectivities of these men, because their accounts suggest both an investment in particular hedonistic, consumerist forms of masculinity, while simultaneously revealing a deep-seated gender anxiety about the status and standing of their jobs.

In the first part of the chapter, I turn to the choices made by creatives in how they dressed and presented themselves at work. Their sartorial decisions are important because claims about the hybrid nature of 'creative work', as we have seen, often homed in on the informal dress codes apparently championed by creative people. Given the additional significance of dress in marking out gender identity, the way these practitioners dressed also tells us much about their masculinity. In fact, it is this interweaving of gendered and occupational meanings through their self-presentation I want to highlight. In doing so, I compare my group of practitioners with other men working in agencies and associated fields and briefly reflect on the way female creatives dress for work.

In the second part, I turn to the social rituals and forms of sociability participated in by the practitioners and set their testimonies within a wider account of the social rituals of the London-based advertising industry. In doing so, I further suggest that the participation of creative people within these forms of work-based and work-related sociability needs to be set in a longer history of metropolitan consumption by subaltern social actors. Specifically, the practitioners I interviewed shared much in common with their historical precursors – what Gareth Stedman-Jones has called 'those socially indeterminate young men' working in the service industries – who were increasingly visible in London from the mid-nineteenth century onwards (Stedman-Jones, 1989: 289–90). The participation of creative people within contemporary patterns of urban consumption and entertain-ment also brought them into contact with other participants in these metropolitan leisure cultures. How the men I interviewed rubbed up against and negotiated their relationships with these other users of London's spaces of entertainment represents a further focus of this section.

Finally, I reflect on some of the tensions associated for my practi-tioners with these social rituals and, in so doing, push at the partial nature of recent claims about the hybrid character of creative work. Looming large here was their handling of the more negative consequences that flowed from the public image of the job as 'fun' and its associations with a stylish and glamorous world. Some of the men I interviewed were certainly troubled by the perception held by other practitioners and by a wider public of the job they did. This was recurrently expressed as an anxiety over the gender status of their jobs.

dressing up or down

If you're a creative you have to look casual in your Levis or your Paul Smith, a smart shirt without a tie, a jacket and trousers. It says you're a certain type of person (Robin Wight, Esquire, Feb 1993: 66).

Robin Wight's advice to the prototypical advertising creative, cited above, was, with modifications, well taken by the majority of art directors and copywriters whom I interviewed. Combinations of casual shirts, sweatshirts, t-shirts, sportswear inspired zip-up tops, jeans and trainers confronted me throughout the interviews. Steve Goode, a copywriter at Direct Arts, for example, wore an anonymous dark sweatshirt and jeans, with short, styled hair. His creative partner, Mike Walker, loafed in a crumpled, casual olive-green checked shirt and jeans, and was unshaven with longer, less styled hair. At Knight & Stewart, Chris Bradshaw, an established art director, wore a navy blue crew necked t-shirt under a navy, pale-blue and white zip-up top, dark blue jeans and trainers. He was shaven-headed and sported a closely cropped moustache and short beard restricted to his chin. His partner, Steve Dempsey, had short hair, the beginnings of a goatee beard and wore a grey t-shirt with a surfing logo on it and white jeans. Andy Hanby, the young creative director at Paul & Rogers, wore a smartly pressed blue Nike sweatshirt over a white crew neck t-shirt and jeans, while his counterpart at Serendipity, Paul Cantelo, wore a Ben Sherman short sleeved checked shirt, jeans and Reef surf wear sandals. Cantelo was clean-shaven, having shaved off his goatee beard, and sported a severe crew cut.

These stylistic choices were far from unique. Not only were they repeated across the interviews, but evidence from the advertising trade press suggested the wide currency of these casual styles of self-presentation. Thus, the panel of young, though established, art directors and copywriters who formed the 1996 jury for the annual trade award hosted by the advertising Creative Circle and who featured in a *Campaign* supplement, displayed a similar preference for sportswear brands, plain casual shirts or t-shirts worn under either a suit jacket or leather jacket and cropped and sometimes dyed hair. Generic industry representations similarly foregrounded these same stylistic choices, with *Creative Review*'s survey of the lifestyles and tastes of creative practitioners, for example, depicting them wearing sportswear brands and funky eyewear (*Creative Review*, August 1996: 29–31).[1]

A closer look at the stylistic choices of the creatives I talked to, however, reveals some subtle differences between them. For instance, Murray Wright, a freelance copywriter at Direct Arts, cultivated a bookish, slightly academic style in casual, if slightly dowdy knitted jumper and jeans. In contrast, the studied informality of men like Cantelo, Hanby and Bradshaw evidenced a level of stylistic competence and self-consciousness at some remove from Wright and the scruffier, more avowedly down-market dress sense of Goode and Walker. While they were not quite in the same rarefied league as the 'flexecutives' described by Benson, Cantelo et al none the less combined name-label items with high street clothes in a carefully produced version of dressing down. Further glimpses of the stylistic self-consciousness that informed these men's relationship to clothes was revealed by the most senior of the group of creatives I talked to, Mark Stephenson. When I interviewed him he was wearing a crisp white shirt open at the neck and Armani jeans. Later he talked at length about the importance to him of clothes and revealed a good deal about what he liked. His preference was for the designer menswear produced by Yohji Yamamoto and Comme des Garçons. Explaining this predilection he said, 'beyond the job, its an aesthetic thing. I like my clothes to be aesthetically pleasing, just as I like my house to be aesthetically pleasing. I'm willing to pay for people like Yamamoto and Kawakubo [Comme des Garçons' designer] to improve the way I feel. You could hang some of their suits on a wall, they're so well conceived. Given the choice between looking average and looking good, I'd rather look good'.[2]

The choice of clothes made by these men was shaped in relation to the wider developments in menswear that had been consolidated through the 1990s and by the broader cultural languages associated with men's style (see, for example, GQ, May 1991: 135–7; 'Leave the office in style'). Looming large here was not only the continuing importance of the designer menswear market – particularly in suits and outerwear – but also (as Richard Benson's comments at the top of this chapter make clear) the proliferation of sportswear and work wear influenced brands.[3] The development of these latter forms of apparel was important in extending the casual or informal wardrobe available to young and youngish men. The rise to near ubiquity of these casual styles in the area of leisurewear was matched by a relaxation of certain elements of more formal styles of menswear. Men's suits – particularly under the influence of Giorgio Armani – softened in their outlines and fit and became less structured (see Esquire, May 1991: 114–121). The introduction of lightweight materials and slimmer fits also transformed the look and feel of men's suits.

These developments in the design and 'look' of menswear contributed to a partial loosening of men's dress codes in the areas of professional and white-collar work. The widespread introduction of so-called 'Dress Down Friday' within the City of London among financial services companies – in which workers are able to wear casual clothes to work – represented one extreme manifestation of this trend of informalisation (Independent on Sunday, 6/10/96: 25; Independent, 19/6/00: 8). More importantly, while formal dress codes persisted within these areas of employment outside licensed or permitted relaxation, a small space none the less emerged for individual expression. The fields of law and financial services – including banking, insurance and accountancy – serve as a good illustration of this. GQ, the men's style magazine, interviewed a group of young professionals working in these fields at the turn of the decade. Their comments gave some insight into the unwritten rules that structured dress codes in these occupations. Thus, Andy Cain, a 26 year old insurance analyst, revealed the following story: 'working in the City you are expected to maintain certain standards. The old guard tends to favour rigid, Saville-Row style suits, while the younger generation go for a softer, more Italian look. You can express yourself through shirts, ties and braces – it's the clash between the formal exterior and what's beneath that exemplifies the new City style' (*GQ*, May 1991: 135–7). Yuri Kookland, a 27 year old trader at the Swiss Bank, echoed this emphasis on individuality within the restrictions set by accepted dress codes. He noted, 'The City still has extraordinarily strict dress codes. I can get away with a formal Paul Smith suit, and it makes me feel good to know there's something subtly different about it – maybe the lapels are more curved, or the pin stripes further apart. After that it's the ties that do the work. The tie is a small item, but it can speak volumes'.

Despite the concessions to greater fashionability and individuality evidenced here and the stylistic self-consciousness associated with it, the dress codes described by these men remained markedly different from the relaxed, casual styles chosen by the young art directors and copywriters I talked to. In fact, much of the distinctiveness of their self-presentation – that of the art directors and copywriters – stemmed from its conspicuous distance from the male attire of adjacent professions. This was a differentiation reproduced within the advertising industry itself. The dress codes of the male creatives I interviewed marked them apart from male colleagues who worked in other core advertising jobs. The strongest contrast was with account handlers, the practitioners involved with overseeing particular client accounts and liaising with clients. Popularly known as 'the suits', account handlers, as the epithet suggests, typically dressed in sober suits and were closer in attire to those male workers in the legal and financial services sectors than they were to advertising creatives. Commenting on this distinction in an article in *Esquire* magazine that featured advertising people among other white-collar professionals, Peter Meed, Joint Chairman of AMV BBDO, noted that

most account executives [handlers] would wear a suit. It's very rare that you'd see a waistcoat, a pin-stripe suit or a severe double-breasted jacket. . . . It's more informal than it was before. The creatives call the account executives 'suits', but I regard that as a very affectionate remark. The creatives are the ones who lay the golden eggs, the account executives are the ones who have to go out and sell them. So they have to dress with a certain smartness. After all, why wear outlandish clothes and run the risk of distracting attention from the project you are selling (*Esquire*, February, 1993: 73).

Seniority and rank also played its part in differentiating male practitioners in terms of dress. Creative directors typically wore suits or smarter casual wear given their dealings with clients, though, as Robin Wight noted, these suits needed to be contemporary and stylish. As he suggested, 'if [a creative director] presents to a client wearing a third-rate suit then you're not really supporting what you're offering. . . . The creative [director's] suit should be original because . . . when you're selling creativity the whole presentation should reflect it' (*Esquire*, February, 1993: 67).

The adoption of relaxed and informal dress codes was not the exclusive preserve of young male creatives. Their female counterparts also presented themselves through combinations of casual clothing and some more formal attire. In fact, the small group of young women creatives I interviewed revealed two distinct ways of dressing. Samantha Jones and Miranda Harris, a creative team at Direct Arts, for example, presented themselves in a feminised version of the informal style worn by many of the men I interviewed. Thus, they were both casually stylish in jeans and a black roll-necked sweater (Miranda) or cropped jersey top (Samantha). Teresa Walsh, an older art director at CTRL, on the other hand, was dressed more smartly in a dark trouser suit. In Walsh's case this was a toned down version of how she had previously tended to dress. She confessed that she 'loved dressing up. I have got boxes and suitcases of stuff, pink feather boas, hats, bows and glass shoes. If I'm dressed in a black A-line skirt and a black top I feel miserable, so it does affect the way I work . . . I always buy things that don't go together and wear them together, I like a mish mash. I deliberately don't follow fashion. I don't want to be the same as everyone else'. This commitment to individualism, particularly in Walsh's case, linked these three women with the male creatives we have heard from. Unlike the men, however, there is a suggestion in their sartorial choices that women creatives choice of dress was partly determined by the demands of working in a male dominated workplace and by the enduring problem for 'professional' women of distancing themselves from secretarial staff (Entwistle, 1997). Certainly, the boyish style of Jones and Harris represented a way of fitting into the established young male culture of their department, while Walsh clearly used the formality of a suit to establish her authority in a similarly male dominated setting.

It was notable that the sartorial choices made by the men I interviewed, and the occupational and gender distinctions with which they worked, had, for them, a deeply taken for granted quality. A number of them, however, spoke more explicitly about the importance of being able to wear casual clothes to work. Certainly, a large part of the allure of the job seemed to stem from the freedom it offered from the tyranny of sober suits. Andy Hanby, the 28 year old creative director at Paul & Rogers, for example, described how he had been attracted to advertising by the experience of meeting a friend from home who was working in the industry. Hanby was impressed by the fact that his mate was – as he put it – 'lagered up and wearing posh kit'. Wesley King, a copywriter at RHIP, on the other hand, remembered how his interest in working in advertising had been stirred by watching a television programme. He recalled,

> In this programme they showed this room with these creative guys sitting around having mad ideas and I thought, 'Oh, that sounds like fun'. . . . That's a job that seems a bit unusual. You know its not your typical 9–5 . . . I quite liked the idea of enjoying work. And I remember in this programme all these people seemed to be quite well paid, but they could dress in whatever way they liked. I thought it seemed a bit more like me, not having to wear a suit everyday.

What was almost certainly the same programme (BBC2's Def II's Rough Guide to Careers) also had a big impact on Marcus Lawson at Smith & Mighty and for almost identical reasons. As he said, 'I'd always liked writing but I'd never seen it as anything other than a hobby, something I did to kill time. And here was a very lively working environment, and there were people who weren't wearing suits, feet on the desks, they were earning vast amounts of money and they were being creative'.

While these testimonies point to other reasons for the appeal of creative jobs – notably the perceived financial awards – it is striking how their antipathy towards workaday suits figures so strongly. Behind this aversion, and the actual stylistic choices made by these men, was a larger issue to do with the gendered meanings carried by men's dress. The desire of these men not to wear a suit to work was closely bound up with how they positioned themselves in relation to competing versions of masculinity. As a number of authors have noted, the iconography of the business suit carries powerful meanings about gender, status and authority (Roper, 1991: 195; Breward, 1999: 54–96). It is typically seen to downplay the individual identity of its wearer and to promote corporate loyalty. It emphasises sobriety and a general lack of display. And it establishes the authority and status of its wearer as business-like and efficient. Not least, the business suit helps to demarcate the domains of work and leisure. For the creatives I interviewed, these meanings and the style of conventional masculinity typically produced through them was what they precisely wanted to refuse. Setting themselves against what WCRS chairman Robin Wight called 'all those poor sods who have to wear boring suits all day' (*Esquire*, February 1993: 66), the creatives emphasised their youthfulness, their lack of responsibility and a greater openness to display and individuality in the way they dressed. More than that, they signified the fluid boundaries between work and leisure in their sartorial choices. Being a creative was for them, then, strongly bound up, with the exceptions that I have already noted, with these styles of self-representation and the relaxed and highly contemporary codes of masculinity associated with them.

a world of glamour and excess   If dressing in a certain way was important to how the creatives I interviewed lived out particular versions of masculinity in the work they did, then other aspects of their accounts of both the initial allure of the job and their experience of it revealed more about the kind of men they were. Looming large here was their investment in the forms of socialising that constituted a large part of the daily life of agencies and of the wider social calendar of the industry. Opening up this aspect of their testimonies requires a reflection on the social spaces and rituals of the London-based advertising industry. Unlike the not dissimilar world of financial services concentrated in the City of London, the London-based advertising industry lacked the kind of large-scale, corporate pro-vision of leisure and recreational facilities for its key workers (McDowell, 1997). The leisure and entertainment culture associated with the industry had a far more informal character and was generally serviced by a plethora of commercial restaurants, bars and clubs. At the heart of this recreational culture was the liberal consumption of alcohol. Many of the larger agencies supported this activity by running their own bars (see, for example, *Campaign*, 21/4/00: 30–1). Others put agency money into subsidising drinking, as well as underwriting day and sometimes weekend excursions for staff in which alcohol figured prominently. One of the creative directors whom I interviewed, for example, described the following activities that he fostered:

Last year and the year before that, I took the entire Department [40 people] to the Kinsale Advertising Festival which is, basically, just 48 hours on the piss, with a few ads thrown in. It is just a stunningly good crack . . . I'm probably organising a department go-kart evening. I organise piss ups from time to time. Whenever there is reason for a party, I'll always put a couple of hundred quid behind the bar.

The industry's main social events, including the prestigious annual creative awards ceremonies hosted by D&AD, the Advertising Creative Circle and the international advertising festival in Cannes, were celebrated for the drinking that took place. Drinking with colleagues after work in the local pub on Friday nights, as well as frequently in the week, formed a more regular social ritual. For more senior agency staff – notably creative direc-tors and other agency managers – dining out at restaurants or enjoying the benefits of socialising at one of a number of private clubs was also an important part of their professional lives. Access to these clubs was determined by rank and seniority and they were generally well beyond the means of my group of practitioners.

Perhaps the most striking feature of much of this industry related social activity – and one that was most readily noted upon by a range of commentators – was its strong concentration within one particular quarter of London – Soho (*Campaign*, 29/4/89: 55–6; 13/12/91: 22–3; Mort, 1996: 170–82; *Creative Review*, August 1997: 29–31). Certainly those establishments that were heavily used by advertising people and most associated with the industry were geographically concentrated in this area of London's West End. The Ivy (West Street, WC2, off Long Acre), Coast (Albermerle Street, W1), Soho House (Greek Street, W1), The Groucho Club (Dean Street, W1) and The Union (W1) were all within shouting distance of each other in and around Soho. There were notable exceptions to this picture. The prestigious advertising clubs were found in the more rarified atmosphere of Claridges (The 30 Club of London), The Dorchester (The Solus Club) and The Savoy (WACL) (On these clubs see *Campaign*, 27/5/94: 26–8). This spatial differentiation was not without its significance. These clubs formed part of the industry's inner court and were a place where the social elite of British advertising mixed with other business leaders and politicians. Modelled on gentlemen's clubs, they were within or adjacent to the networks of established business and political culture, and were notably distanced from the more polymorphous space of Soho. It was this feature of Soho that was important in shaping the character of the industry's more informal social rituals. As Frank Mort has argued, Soho has a long history as the recipient of avant-garde and bohemian culture. It is this history, laid down in the fabric of the district, which has helped to shape its continuing association with transgressive and bohemian social scripts. The more recent influx of social actors, including advertising and media people, while transforming the area through their economic and social presence, continued to draw on and be formed in relation to this sedimented history (see Mort, 1996: 170–182). For advertising practitioners – including those central to my project – these associations were often expressed through a valorisation of Soho as a centre of cultural provision and innovation, a place of stimulating energy. Paul Davenport, a creative at Klein & Hart, for example, was enthusiastic about the industry life centred upon the district. Reflecting on the nature of his working life at Klein & Hart, which was based in London Docklands, at the eastern edges of the city, he suggested,

> Soho is where the industry is really based. We miss it big time . . . massively. Mind you, the distractions are immense in Soho. You do get a lot more work done here, because there's bugger all else to do. There's an energy in Soho . . . because you've got everything there. You've got cinemas, you've got libraries, you've got restaurants, you've got odd little things, you've got Foyles.

Ben Langdon, Managing Director of CDP, was also reverential towards Soho. In an interview in *Campaign* he gushed about the pleasure of returning to work in the district. CDP had long been exiled on the Euston

Road and for Langdon returning to Soho produced in him a state of near reverie. As he put it, 'we did miss the stimulation of Soho and are delighted to be back. It has made us feel vibrant again' (*Campaign*/8/95: 26–7). Even those agencies that had taken the positive decision to relocate from Soho in the mid-late 1990s – in large part because of the limited availability of suitable office accommodation – acknowledged its symbolic power. Thus, Steve Gatfield, Chief Executive of Leo Burnett, an agency that had moved to Kensington, spoke of the wrench of moving from Soho and the pull of its 'buzz', while Lance Smith, Director of UK operations of DMB&B, which had moved to Victoria, confessed to the 'strong emotional' appeal of the district (ibid). These comments hint at a strong sense of ownership of the district and of feeling centred through an assertion that the advertising industry was now a part of the heritage of Soho. As another of the young creatives I talked to earnestly put it, 'Soho is the spiritual centre of the industry'.

The location of so much of the informal work-based and work-related entertainment and recreation participated in by advertising people in and around Soho gave these forms of sociability a strongly metropolitan character. Precisely what this meant for these practitioners and how the group of men I interviewed, in particular, inhabited these social relations is very difficult to gauge. At issue here is the complex cultural heritage of Soho that I noted earlier and the contemporary diversity of social actors that populated its social spaces. As Frank Mort has argued, the expansion of legitimate commercial developments in Soho through the 1980s and 1990s (including the increasing presence of media companies and advertising agencies) interacted in complex ways with the bohemian and avant-garde culture formed in Soho over the preceding century. One form this took was the updating of older forms of bohemianism into contemporary style culture by some of the newer commercial *arrivistes*. For example, the free magazine for office workers, *Midweek*, celebrated this new vision of Soho bohemianism:

Cosmopolitan, bohemian and wildly trendy . . . the land of the brasserie lunch and the after-hours watering hole, the land of accessories and attitude, where fashion relentlessly struggles to become style and image is simply everything; the glittering heart of medialand where the worlds of art, journalism, film, advertising and theatre blend into one glamorous heady cocktail (*Midweek*, 20/2/92, quoted in Mort, 1996: 157–8).

The relations between old and new *habitués* of Soho were not always smooth, however. The journalist Jeffrey Barnard, himself a member of a post-war circle of artists, actors and literary types (including the artist Francis Bacon) who frequented the famous Colony Room in Dean Street, was scathing about the new media interlopers. Clearly feeling his version of Soho bohemianism was under threat, he railed against the new inhabitants of Soho. Writing in the early 1980s, he melodramatically claimed that, 'Soho is dead. Massive injections of advertising executives with pocket bleepers and a taste for cheap wine . . . have finally killed off what was just about the best part of London for anyone who never saw virtue in work for its own sake' (Taki and Bernard, quoted in Mort, 1996: 162). Elsewhere he castigated these new players as 'tight assessed nancy boys' and offered a withering parody of the dispositions of advertising creatives in his diatribe against these interlopers: 'The TV commercial boys sat there plucking their croissants and saying "Yes, I know love, but if we cut it then – bang, bang – like that, we wouldn't have to hold the long shot coming down those stairs. . . . Let's face it, loves, we're basically trying to sell wretched stuff". . . . By this time my coffee was cold and my mouth locked in open-jawed disbelief' (Taki and Bernard, 1981: 23).

Soho's history had also been shaped by a long tradition of tolerance to sexual dissidence and transgression, including both a long tradition of male homosexual culture (itself increasingly visible and expanded through the 1980s and 90s) but also the licensed sex industry of cinemas, bars and clubs (Mort, 1996: 157-182). The relationship between advertising people and these other Soho constituents is hard to unpack. Certainly – Barnard's insinuations notwithstanding – the relations with gay male culture were particularly difficult to read and the accounts generated by the advertising trade press and by my interviewees were notable for occluding these relationships in their valorisation of Soho life. It is possible, however, to get some clues as to the character of the informal cultures participated in by advertising people. *Campaign*, in its limited coverage of the industry's social life, certainly gave tantalising glimpses of the place, most notably, of an entrenched masculine culture of excess within the industry's social rituals. For example, in December 1991, the paper reported the drama of that year's D&AD award ceremony held not in Soho, but in the more rarified setting of the Grovesnor House hotel in Park Lane, Mayfair. The event had been marred by what *Campaign* described as an 'outbreak of drunken vandalism' in which thousands of pounds of damage was done to the hotel (*Campaign*, 20/12/91: 7) Detailing the event, the paper claimed that 'a bunch of cretinous creatives high on booze and drugs left a trail of destruction' (ibid). *Campaign* also reported how in August 1996, staff from the agency APL had caused considerable damage to a hotel by squashing food and drink into the venues' carpet and indulged in playing games such as pouring water over each other (*Campaign*, 16/8/96: 11). In March of the preceding year, the paper's regular diary page further documented the emergence of a new game practiced in nightclubs by a group of enterprising young admen. Known as 'hotlegging', it involved urinating down the leg of a colleague if you caught them 'chatting up a girl' (*Campaign*, 24/3/95: backpage).[4]

The gendered character of these social rituals was also a feature of the more routine forms of sociability engaged in by advertising creatives. This much was certainly evident in the testimonies of the women creatives I interviewed. For the older and more established women, in particular, there was no doubting the conventionally masculine character of much of the informal industry socialising. Their accounts revealed a familiar story of negotiating what felt to them like a 'man's world' of drinking and the dilemmas this generated. Reflecting on this, Liz Sheldon, executive creative director at Petersons recalled:

> It's [the classic problem] do you join the blokes in the pub. I've never had any truck with that, can't stand pubs, not in London anyway, I can't see after 5 minutes because of the smoke and I don't like drinking that filthy wine they have. And that can be difficult if you don't join in.

In Sheldon's case it was evident that her early career success and subsequent seniority and standing allowed her to avoid what she clearly, if rather haughtily, depicts as the blokish cultures of drinking. Katy Smith, creative director at Henry Brown, confirmed this sense of the social character of these forms of sociability. In doing so, she echoed Sheldon's experience that industry recognition and rank allowed her to step outside these cultures. She recalled,

> I'm not into drinking, I don't go to pubs. I did try when I started out, but I haven't for many, many years now. And I don't play pool and I don't watch football and all those things everyone else is interested in. I just don't join in. It was like that at other agencies. Some women get by either having a relationship with someone in the department or by being one of the lads if you're a young creative. Which is what I did. I got very good at darts. And did go to the pub in the early days and become one of the lads. But since I've been a bit truer to myself, I've simply been an outsider.

Other women I talked to negotiated these cultures in different ways. Samantha Jones and Miranda Harris, for instance, were more comfortable inside these forms of sociability. As Samantha Jones revealed, 'It used to be [that we went drinking] every single Friday at the Crown, and it got to a point where there were actually quite a few nights during the week to the extent that we had to knock it on the head because we were drinking too much'. Miranda Harris continued: 'if you're not careful, when your agency's going through a period of having a good social life, you find you're having several [drinks] every night, maybe more'.[5]

Teresa Walsh also confessed to youthful excesses. She recalled:

> I used to drink a lot. I remember one year I went to an industry event – and I used to wear the most ridiculous clothes like a tutu and things like that to work. And I remember once going to the creative ball and dancing on the table in my tutu and the table collapsing. And next morning I was so embarrassed. The following year, they ran an ad for the event and there I am stood on the table going 'agaaah'. I was a bit of a wild one in those days.

Walsh's former antics belonged within a distinct tradition of feminine excess associated with what Mort has described as the 'unattached female hedonist' (Mort, 1996: 173) and formed part of a flamboyant public persona in which, as we have seen, she dressed in spectacular ways. A large part of this was wilful exhibitionism and helped her to gain a high profile within the industry. She was certainly adept at using these displays of wild behaviour to promote herself aggressively in the trade press. Her self-presentation, however, also stemmed from, again, a fundamental problem for women creatives concerning how they should behave in the strongly masculine worlds they were forced to inhabit. In Walsh's case, being as wild as the men represented one way of holding her own in this context. Jones and Harris took a rather different route and, just as Katy Smith had done before them, they became 'one of the lads'. They were, in fact, explicit about appropriating these codes of masculinity. Reflecting on their departure from a previous agency they suggested, 'we were the wrong type of women. . . . The creative director liked young, quiet, very pretty, tall women, and we didn't fit into that category. We were a bit loud and brash and rude, a bit laddish'. When I quizzed them on what they meant by that they confessed, 'Well, we swear, and burp and fart and muck about and we have a good sense of humour',[6]

For the men I interviewed, their accounts of the industry social life in which they participated pointed to a smoother, less self-conscious passage into work related cultures of drinking. In fact, for some of the men, gaining access to this world was a central part of the declared appeal of the job. Both Steve Dempsey and his partner Chris Bradshaw, creatives at Knight & Stewart, for example, became very animated when recalling the levels of social drinking that opened up to them during summer placements in an advertising agency when they were students. For Steve Dempsey in particular, access to subsidised drinking stood as a defining feature of his experience of the placement and set it apart from his experience in the adjacent field of graphic design:

I spent a couple of weeks at Michael Peters and Partners, and they had tea and cakes in the afternoon, which was very 'nice'. There was one girl there who was very 'nice', and she spent three weeks drawing a little sheaf of corn, and she drew it about fifty times, in different ways. And for me, it was a sheaf of corn when I arrived, and it was a sheaf of corn when I left . . . On the last day, we went down the pub. And I had a pint and everyone else had halves. And as soon as the drinks were drunk, people went. And then we went to the ad agency, and I think pretty much the first day we were there, they won a new piece of business and at 4 o'clock in the afternoon, it was 'right, everyone downstairs', to this big room, and there was basically beer and champagne and we got hammered.

Dempsey's commentary is noteworthy in terms of the way he dramatises the appeal of agency life next to a denigration of graphic design work. Thus, he conjures an image of graphic design as a quaint and genteel world, with its rituals of afternoon tea and quiet civility and a careful, almost studious approach to work. Against this he sets up his identification with the more exuberant culture of the ad agency, with heavy drinking spilling over into the hours of the working day and extending beyond it. The association with memories of youthful hedonism undoubtedly heightened the drama of Dempsey's account and, as we'll see, he was keen elsewhere in his comments to demarcate the excesses of life as a junior from the more serious and sober character of his contemporary working life. None the less, as he relives the excitement of the placement, he reveals his investment in conventionally gendered forms of socialising and definitions of enjoyment.

A similar identification with these masculine scripts was also evident in the comments of other practitioners I interviewed when they too reflected on the initial appeal of the job. For Dave Cantelo and Jack Chantler, however, it was not so much the possibility of heavy drinking that they emphasised, but rather the access to a world of glamour and style. Dave Cantelo recalled,

My Dad used to have a restaurant, and a lot of advertising people used to go and eat there. . . . And I remember, I was probably 14, I remember seeing all these really good looking blokes coming in, surrounded by good looking, beautiful women, driving these amazing cars, and they'd park them on the pavement, and then just chuck the waiter the keys, and say 'when the warden comes round, just move it'. And I thought, fucking hell, that looks good.

Cantelo's testimony is shot through with desire for the kind of social confidence and glamour embodied by the ad people who were customers in his Dad's restaurant. It conjures an evocative image of a lower-middle-class boy dreaming of access to a world of privilege beyond his current social horizon; a world of glamour that gave you access to style and beautiful women.

Jack Chantler's comments revealed the same subaltern aspirations. Recalling the placements he went on as an aspiring creative, he said,

> I just loved sitting in the foyer at BBH and JWT and just thinking 'Wow!'All the receptionists are really beautiful and glamorous and everyone was so confident. We sat out here [at Serendipity] and a stream of gorgeous girls came in and out and we were like 'Ah' [breathless]. And we were just as scruffy as this really.

There is a strong line of self-deprication in Chantler's comments, together, perhaps, with an overplaying of his ordinariness. None the less, like the comments of Dempsey and Cantelo, they suggest a similar formation of heterosexual masculinity, one shaped through specific forms of heterosociability and ideas of what constitutes the good life. We might profitably suggest, in fact, that these men – particularly Chantler and Cantelo – exhibited an investment in what Peter Bailey has described as 'parasexuality', the form of 'framed liminality' that he associates with 'glamour' and the development of modern sexualised consumerism in the mid-nineteenth century. Parasexuality for Bailey, which he explores through the venerable figure of the Victorian barmaid, represented a distinctive kind of display marked by the incitement but careful containment of sexuality. Moreover, it is also a regime characterised by gendered divisions between the feminine object of glamour and its desiring masculine subject (Bailey, 1999).

One might provocatively suggest that we should understand the 'framed liminality' associated with these desires for a world of glamour as itself the product of a form of banal social fantasy; a social fantasy that in turn tells us much about the subaltern status of those individuals – like the men I interviewed – who identified with it. In fact, there is good reason for attempting to socially place the forms of heterosociability with which these men identified. The relationship that they had to the metropolitan leisure culture that so attracted them placed them squarely within a tradition of social longing pursued by subaltern migrants to the metropolis. Their historical precursors have been well documented by both Gareth Stedman-Jones and Peter Bailey. These were the 'socially indeterminate single young men', the 'linen drapers assistants', 'counter-jumpers', 'city clerks' or 'penniless swells' who became the principle audience for the London music halls of the late nineteenth century and who found their own 'sham genteel patterns of conspicuous consumption' celebrated by music hall figures like Champaign Charlie (Stedman-Jones, 1989: 289–90; Bailey, 1999). The overwhelming majority of the men I interviewed were from provincial backgrounds, and often from lower-middle-class provincial or suburban backgrounds to boot.[6] As such they shared similar social fantasies about the delights of metropolitan culture as their historical precursors, those earlier provincial *parvenus*. Their provincial and subaltern origins were certainly evident to practitioners from more securely middle-class and established metropolitan backgrounds. Ian Harding, for example, a creative director at XYZ, who came from what he described as an 'intellectual bohemian background' in London – he had grown up in Earls Court and Putney before being dispatched to a minor public school – suggested that he was constantly surprised by the frenetic embrace of the delights of metropolitan life by the young creatives he worked with and by their desire to be part of a more established metropolitan culture. He suggested,

I'm a Londoner. Not many of us are. Born and bred Londoner, so this is my patch. Simon, my ex-creative partner, came from Belfast and his life, because he'd upped sticks, centred much more around the creative business. My life was up and running and in fine shape before I came anywhere near advertising. So I have a separate social life. Agencies have always been much more a place to work for me.

Testimonies of this sort suggest important differences between the social aspirations expressed by the men I interviewed and that of differently con-stituted practitioners.

ambivalent pleasures

To people outside advertising (and even within other departments within the agency), it seems that creative staff start work at 10.30am, spend all day messing about or reading magazines, knock-off early and are allowed to look as scruffy as they like. To us, the job is obsessive, taking up 23-hours a day (We're allowed an hour's sleep). The thing is ideas can hit you at anytime, so you always have to be ready for them. And what looks like messing around is actually an attempt to relax and free the mind after you've assimilated the available facts (Anonymous copywriter, Association of Graduate Information, 1992, AA 4/2a)

We were toiling away and they were having a frigging good time (Account handler reflecting on the creatives he worked with).

155

The gender and class-specific pattern of social longing evidenced in the testimonies of the practitioners that I interviewed coexisted with other kinds of subjective investment in the world of work they inhabited. These revolved around a more negative sense of the status and standing of their jobs that sprung from its 'fun' and hedonistic public image. Certainly for the more senior of the men I talked to, reliving the appeal of the industry in the early stages of their career sat alongside an attempt to mark their distance from their youthful investment in the glamorous image of creative jobs. It emerged strongly in their accounts through what we might call a coming of age story and was based upon the limitations and contradictions of the world of glamour and excess that had appeared so seductive to their younger selves. Steve Dempsey and Chris Bradshaw were perhaps most keen to signal their distance as senior creatives from the superficial glamour of the industry. When I pressed them about the social life in the agency, they responded as follows:

> **CB**: Because we're getting on now, you know, mid-30s, and we used to go down the bar, down the pub, and we do it less and less. I think we don't like bars, we really don't like that kind of advertising scene, go to Groucho's, you know, take a load of cocaine . . .
>
> **SD**: And say what a great time you had in the morning, when you didn't really.
>
> **CB**: And probably not be very talented either, because a lot of those people, they like the lifestyle and wearing the Gaultier jacket, but we're the opposite of that, we actually like doing the work, and trying to do something good. And if we go anywhere, we like go down the pub with some close friends, but we're both quite intimidated by this kind of Groucho's . . . it's nice once in a while to go to these places and maybe see Kylie Minogue or someone like that and it can be quite exciting.

As they consolidate a common position in this exchange, we can see them distancing themselves from precisely those forms of sociability that were so appealing to their younger selves and emphasising their seniority and integrity in relation to both the job they did and the relationships they forged around work.

Taking up a critical distance from the 'glamour' of the industry also surfaced in Mark Stephenson's comments. When I asked him about the industry social life, he said,

> My wife works for the Holborn Art Gallery. She has a lot of social stuff around that, and I'm quite involved in that, I enjoy it . . . there's no-one in advertising there. The last thing I wanna do, is go to Grouchos and talk about advertising. So I do that, or I stay up and watch football, or I go out and have a drink.

Stephenson's distance from the social relations of 'adland' was also bound up with an anxiety about the standing of his chosen career. More so even than Dempsey and Bradshaw, he was at pains to foreground his commitment to the work of being a creative and to distance himself from perceptions that the work was easy and involved large amounts of socialising. Against this he emphasised the hardness and strenuous nature of the work he did. Thus, describing how he got his first job as a copywriter in the late 1980s, he recalled,

I got in at quite an interesting time, the real sort of money/glamour time for advertising, and I found this really curious thing that we were just working our butts off. I mean we didn't go out to lunch for two years. And all this stuff you hear from the outside like 'oh, let's do lunch', and its all very glamorous and no-one works very hard, you only work in the morning and then you're out for three hours, and no-one gives a shit. And we were just going, 'this is bloody like being in a coal mine!' And it was . . . you'd get there, work like shit, you'd have 10 minutes for lunch, you'd work like shit, you'd go home at 10 o'clock, you'd get up, you'd be in at 8.30 [am].

What is so interesting in Stephenson's comments is the lengths he goes to in order to emphasise how tough and demanding the job was; lengths designed to counter perceptions of the job as glamorous and dominated by high levels of socialising. First is the hyperbole of being effectively chained to the office desk for two years and unable to take a proper lunch break and then the use of the metaphor of working in a coal mine and the repetition of the length of the working day that function to present the job as incredibly tough and hard. A similar emphasis was clear in other comments he made:

I still get . . . not angry, but slightly miffed at people's perception of what advertising is. People still perceive it as being a slightly airy-fairy industry where, really, people don't work hard do they. It's all about getting on with people . . . and having long lunches. Believe me, it ain't! It's about, you know, 14 hours work a day.

Both these passages tell us something about Stephenson's masculinity. They reveal his subscription to an established gendered hierarchy of work in which manual labour stands as the most manly of forms of endeavour. In attempting to align his job with hard, assertively manly work, his aim is clearly to resist the connotations of creative jobs in advertising as complacent and effete, as 'airy-fairy'.

Mike Walker also made a similar move. Like Stephenson, he too expressed ambivalence about the public image of creative jobs and was anxious not to be swept up by the fantasy of 'adland'. Cautioning against the tendency of young creatives to attempt to live out the stereotypical hedonistic advertising life, he piously suggested, 'we still need to remember that we are labourers, you know, we do a trade'. Steve Message, a young creative director at CTP, was another practitioner who attempted to distance himself from those he saw as being seduced by the public image of advertising. Again, like Hastings, he emphasised the demanding nature of creative work and was concerned to contest the perception of advertising as an industry in which people were over-paid for doing very little. In doing so, he conjured a conflictual scenario in which bright young men like him had to take on and displace an older generation that had grown too comfortable. As he put it,

> I think that there are a lot of lunchy old gits out there who are drawing salaries and doing nothing. And they are essentially keeping bright, young enthusiastic people out of the business. I don't think anybody deserves to draw a big salary and have an easy life if they're not contributing much.

Later in the interview, in underlying his distaste for these representatives of complacency in advertising, he sought to distance himself from them by suggesting that he and his partner had never turned into 'Soho luvvies'. Behind Message's comments lay not only hostility to what he elsewhere called 'dandies at the court of advertising', but clearly an anxiety that he too would be drawn into this effete world. His aggression was as much self-directed as it was aimed at the 'luvvies' and 'dandies'.

conclusion   Message's comments, like those of some of the other men I interviewed, suggested a strongly gendered anxiety about the nature of creative jobs. His comments reveal, as we've seen, a desire to challenge, in particular, perceptions of the work as easy and relaxed and devoid of any hard graft. Like Stephenson and Walker, he revealed an investment in a hierarchy of masculine jobs that placed manual labour at the top of a scale of value as embodying the most manly form of work. The perception that creative jobs blurred the established distinctions between work and leisure was especially troubling for all three men and they needed to refute these associations by asserting the hardness of the job and its overall demanding character.

Taken together, their responses bear some comparison with the way other groups of white-collar and professional men have also tended to emphasise the strenuous nature of their work and its parallels with manual labour when faced with perceptions that 'desk jobs' were easy and even feminised. Certainly, in Mike Roper's study of a group of senior managers in the postwar UK manufacturing industry, there is a recurrent emphasis among these men of the tough and demanding nature of their managerial work (Roper, 1994: 105–131). The men I interviewed were a very different group of men in terms of social background and age from those discussed by Roper, and they lacked the daily confrontation with the culture of the shop floor and its proletarian forms of masculinity that prompted Roper's managers to emphasise that they were not the 'soft' men manual workers often castigated them for being. None the less, their embrace of a gender hierarchy of labour was equally strong, though more clearly related to their handling of the cultural associations of creative work and advertising's standing as a sector. It was also undoubtedly the case that their perceptions of me as an academic researcher with a potentially critical view of the pernicious and superficial commercial world in which they worked acted as an important stimulus for these responses. The irony, of course, is that the anecdotal evidence would suggest that academic men are also plagued by similar gender anxieties about the life of ease they live. Like Thomas Carlyle, we might suggest that scholars are haunted by the 'strenuous idleness' of their jobs (Clarke, 1991).

The social standing and character of their jobs, however, did not only play out in negative ways for the advertising creatives. We have also seen how some of the men revealed a simultaneous investment in the forms of work-based leisure associated with the job. In doing so, their testimonies tell us more about the kind of men they were. At the heart of this was their identification with hedonism and a consumption-based ethic of enjoyment that shaped both the appeal and performance of the job. These forms of enjoyment were generally bound up with conventional forms of hetero-sexual masculinity, though they also indicated the importance of display and an embrace of the most contemporary signs of maleness through their choice of dress among these men. These sartorial choices signalled a highly self-conscious sense of masculinity that was ordered through the ongoing processes of self-fashioning and self-reflection that consumerist models of identity recurrently rely upon. The tensions between these competing ways of relating to their job suggested that their sense of themselves as men at work was organised around these competing identifications and the ambi-valent feelings that flowed from this.

conclusion

Organisations in the media and creative industries represent 'critical cases' for the management of creativity. It is our belief that trends occurring in these industries are indicative of wider organisational patterns relating to the management of creativity (Scase and Davis, 2000: ix).

Imagine a company staffed from top to bottom by individuals whose creative energy is being directed into exercising their power of choice in the opportunities they have been given, taking responsibility, participating at every level and creating the kind of career dialogue . . . with the company he or she works for. A dynamic is being created that is palpable, it is a pleasure to be there, and that is what makes it work (Jackie Townsend, management consultant, *Independent on Sunday*, 19/10/97: 3)

The respective comments of Scase and Davis and Townsend, above, were indicative of the expanded currency that the idea of creativity has acquired within academic, journalistic and management writing on business and economic life over the last decade or so. For Scase and Davis, as we have already seen, the new salience of creativity was associated with the increasingly central role played by the creative industries in the transformation of Western economies. Not only were these industries important to the economic fortunes of these societies, but ways of working within these sectors were also paradigmatic of broader shifts in the organisation and performance of work in other areas of employment. In this latter sense, Scase and Davis's analysis shared much with the prescriptions of a management consultant like Townsend, and all three authors, despite the different audiences they were addressing, held a common understanding that ways of working within the creative industries and the subjective dispositions of creative people in particular could be taken as the model for the conduct of work in other sectors. Thus, as Townsend's guidance suggests, successful companies were the ones that facilitated the transformation of their key workers into autonomous, resourceful and creative individuals along the lines laid down by the modes of conduct associated with artists and other creative types,[1]

These claims about the new salience of creative people within what used to be called the media and cultural industries to economic life more broadly have provided an important impetus for the arguments developed in this book. But, as I argued from the outset, it has been as much the under-developed nature of the accounts of 'creative employment' and trends occurring within the 'creative industries' that typically informed these claims, reproduced across a swathe of critical commentaries, that has shaped my account. One of the central arguments that I have developed has concerned an interrogation of the very idea of creativity itself that is seen as integral to these jobs and to the wider restructuring of economic life. Clarifying what we might mean by this most over-exposed term and understanding its specific currency and meaning in relation to advertising practices has been an important preoccupation of the book. We have seen that the idea of creativity had a vigorous currency at both the level of institutional and organisational life within the London-based advertising industry and surfaced with subjective force in the testimonies of creative people themselves. The idea was deployed as an umbrella term by agencies and their corporate representatives to capture the particular kinds of expertise and know-how that they deployed in servicing client's marketing needs. It was this expertise and skill – evident in the problem solving capacities of agencies and the representational strategies mobilised in the advertising that they produced – that was central to agencies' more elaborated sense of themselves as 'creative businesses'. Moreover, it was their privileged capacity to deliver this kind of expertise (so they claimed) that set them apart from the more prosaic guidance of other groups of cultural intermediaries, like management consultants, who were increasingly competing with them in the field of marketing and associated business services.

What was striking about the valorising of creativity at the upper echelons of the advertising industry and its inscription within their business and corporate strategies was its totemic character and the way it informed a whole system of belief about the commercial practices they performed. The vaunting of creativity had profound consequences for the way agencies viewed those practitioners principally charged with bringing this elusive attribute to bear upon the advertising process. While, as we saw, one of the distinctive features of agency life in the 1990s was the attempt by agency bosses to 'free-up' the capacity for creativity residing in all their core employees, the way agencies recruited and managed their staff continued to broadly differentiate between the more business minded and more creative practitioners. Underlying these ongoing distinctions was an assumption not only about the special qualities of creative people, but, furthermore, a deeply held conviction that creativity was something that resisted the organisational moves to contain it within bureaucratic or professional structures. These assumptions about creativity did much to shape the way creative jobs were organised, working to establish their privileged and exceptional position within the social relations of agency life. At the same time this valorising of creativity tended to obscure much of what went on in the development and execution of advertising ideas by art directors and copywriters. It has been a central contention of the book, in line with other contemporary critical thinking, that creativity is not best thought of in the quasi-mystical terms often favoured by advertising people or, for that matter, as a general human capacity for invention and novelty that they also made recourse to. Rather, I have deployed the term to refer to the rather more modest – but none the less hard to achieve – innovations within the cultural practices of advertising.

This insistence carried particular weight in relation to the rubric of creativity deployed by creative people themselves. While they may have celebrated their own quest for newness and originality in the cultural practices they performed, advertising creatives worked within tightly defined genre worlds and what was typically at stake in their strenuous claims to newness were quite small degrees of 'different-ness' – to coin Keith Negus's formulation. The preoccupation of these practitioners with creativity, however, required some explanation and I argued that their obsession with creativity derived less from some internal existential drama and more from a strategy of distinction as they sought to establish themselves in an intensely competitive world of work. Striving to produce work that broke new ground, that overturned the approach characteristic of an older generation of practitioners, that shifted the vocabularies of promotion, was bound up with making the team stand out and of winning peer recognition and the career success that could follow from that.

The cult of creativity pursued by these practitioners was, in this sense, intimately connected with the particular structure of the labour market in creative jobs and its combination of both the promise of high material rewards and the downsides of job insecurity and the possibility of failure that lay close to the surface. It was also profoundly connected with a concern to elevate the standing of the forms of commercial practice that they undertook. This rested on attempts to emphasise their role as auto-nomous cultural intermediaries and was marked by a simultaneous desire to resist the very different constitution of their identities as hacks or mere commercial artists.

Reflecting on the rubric of creativity within advertising also prompted me to insist on the way it connected with broader cultural formations. Central to my arguments in this regard was an attention to the way creat-ivity was often understood within the industry in highly gendered terms, particularly through recourse to gendered images of the creative person. In fact, it has been a central contention of the book that it is not possible to understand the organisation of creativity and creative jobs in advertising without grasping how these jobs were rooted in gendered workplace cultures. It was this linkage, occluded within the celebration of the creative industries in accounts like Scase and Davis', that I explored in Part 3 of the book. We saw how agency creative departments were the resting place for ideas of romantic individualism and the whole baggage of gendered attributes that have historically accumulated to this model of the creative person. We also saw how these were further glossed with more contemporary conceptions of masculine juvenility and the childlike qualities of creative people. Chapter 5 further argued that it was the intense bonds between young male creatives and the older men who managed creative departments that helped to fix the culture that developed around these jobs as intensely masculine and to mark out art directing and copywriting as fundamentally masculine forms of endeavour. We saw how the promotion of aggressive self-advancement and competition and the sanctioning of excessive behaviour among young male creatives formed a recurrent element in the life of these departments. Behind this linkage lay the assumption that sanctioning these forms of masculinity was essential to the generation of effective, creative advertising.

Opening up the subjectivities of creative people has formed a further central ambition of this book. I detailed the way the group of advertising men whom I interviewed displayed a strong investment in some of the most contemporary signs of masculinity, particularly through dress and self-presentation. There were subtle differences in their various sartorial choices, but all shared a commitment to a casual, and often stylised, form of masculine dress. Their take-up of these casual styles was bound up with a broader investment in hedonistic and consumerist forms of identity. As we saw in Chapter 7, much of the appeal of the job to these young men appeared to be grounded in the relaxed style of dress they could wear to work and the access to the delights of metropolitan life and its circuits of drinking and sociability that working for London-based agencies afforded them. In this regard, I argued that these contemporary advertising men shared much with a set of historical precursors within the service sector and locating the fantasies of the good life of the contemporary practitioners within well established patterns of social longing, characteristic of subaltern migrants to the city, was an important dimension of the argument that I develop in Part 3.

I suggested that there were some notable limit positions to the forms of gendered sociability in which they participated. This was evident in the way these practitioners negotiated the spaces of London life that they shared with competing versions of metropolitan masculinity. The sharpest distinctions here were with more transgressive social actors, especially the diverse forms of urban gay male culture. The men I interviewed were silent on their relationship to these competing forms of urban masculinity and their silence revealed much about the robustly heterosexual nature of both their own identifications and the occupational culture they inhabited. The cultural division between homo- and heterosexual masculinities that these practitioners tended to reproduce was paradoxical given both the wider associations of creativity and the creative arts with myths about the creative sensibilities of homosexual men and, more importantly, the close homosocial bonds between young men that were integral to the organisation of creative partnerships at the heart of creative departments. However, while these intense bonds did throw up some ambivalent attachments, I suggested that their structuring within agency life worked to generally regulate and circumscribe the kinds of masculinity that could be openly composed within this creative world.

Other competing identifications also jostled in the inner life of these men. If, in one sense, they aligned themselves with a version of metropolitan modernity and its post-permissive styles of masculinity, their experience of the job they performed revealed a simultaneous commitment to a hierarchy of masculine labour that seemed to run counter to these consumerist forms of masculinity. Grasping this competing component of their subjectivities was germane to my arguments. Despite the cultural rise of advertising over the last two decades, the men I interviewed remained troubled by negative perceptions of their chosen career's social standing. Part of the problem stemmed from the strong reputation of creative jobs as precisely 'fun' and enjoyable. Playing up the hardness of their jobs and aligning them with a hierarchy of labour in which manual work stood as the manliest form of endeavour, the young advertising men I interviewed revealed a deep-rooted gender anxiety about the work they performed. Their identification with the values of an older order of work told us much about the kind of men they were. But it also had wider significance in prompting a revision of the more celebratory visions of creative work that we have encountered. Here were a group of practitioners performing a job that was officially seen in government circles and beyond as close to the beating heart of Britain's new creative economy drawing on a set of values from a hierarchy of labour formed in industrial society. Their identifications suggested, then, that in a sector that was often taken as exemplary of the 'new economy' there persisted some rather old productivist ideas of work and gender.

Foregrounding the gender identities of creative people and the informal cultures with which they were associated connected with the central conceptual contention of the book. I argued at the outset that detailing these aspects of the world of creative employment was indispensable to an adequate account of the forms of commercial practice in which advertising agencies were engaged. As I insisted, while not wanting to reduce advertising practices to the subjectivity of its key practitioners or the cultures of agencies, it was none the less crucial to recognise the role played by the informal knowledge and dispositions of art directors and copywriters in shaping the way agencies reached out to connect with consumers. I highlighted the significance of these determinants upon agency practices in relation to a specific set of consumer markets in which advertising practitioners have played an increasingly important role over the last decade or so. These were style and lifestyle commodities aimed at young men. It was the links between the gender cultures and identities of creative people and these forms of gendered commerce that I have been particularly concerned with exploring. In the course of the book I have not pursued these connections through close analysis of the role played by the interviewees in relation to specific campaigns. Ethical considerations prevented me from drawing out how these informal cultural influences bore upon particular adverts.

None the less, in setting out the detailed arguments of the book some clear connections have emerged. It is appropriate in concluding this book, to draw out some of the general ways in which the social make-up of creative jobs, the values and motivations of creative people and the wider workplace cultures they inhabited, can be seen to have shaped the cultural practices performed by the men I interviewed in relation to these markets. The first theme that has emerged strongly concerns the way these creative cultures were marked by a high degree of self-consciousness concerning public codes of masculinity. This was particularly evident in the subjective investments made by the men I interviewed in highly contemporary styles of masculinity. As I have already noted in this conclusion, as a group these practitioners identified strongly with consumerist forms of masculinity and the social rituals of urban life through which these cultural scripts were constituted. In their own sense of self, then, these practitioners were strongly addressed by and sensitive to the nuances of these commercial forms of gender. This was most apparent in their relationship to the robust, 'laddish' forms of masculinity that have increasingly dominated these circuits of consumption. Their identification with these particular styles of youthful masculinity was evident not only in their self-presentation through the codes of dress at work and in the consumption rituals in which they participated in and around work, but was also reinforced by the fit between these gendered codes and the performance of their jobs. We saw how the social relations of creative departments and the close, but typically competitive bonds between creative staff and between creatives and their creative directors worked to privilege these kinds of robust masculinity. The importance of tension releasing rituals in how they handled the pressure of these jobs provided the conditions in which scripts of laddish excess were useful cultural resources. Part of the reason for the rapid take-up and dissemination of the idioms of the 'new lad' within advertising representation in this sense derived from this close identification that these practitioners had with these cultural scripts. It was the cultural proximity of these practitioners to and the investment in the codes of laddishness that drove the appropriation and deployment of the idioms of the 'new lad' in marketing to young men. Other factors, of course, were also crucial in shaping the extensive currency within commercial cultures of these gender codes – most notably, the resonance that they had in the lives of groups of consumers – but it was the influence of the styles of masculinity within the creative cultures of advertising that partly accounts for their prodigious currency.[2]

The rubric of creativity central to the working lives of creative people was also important in shaping their approach to these men's markets. We have seen how the practitioners were motivated by a distinctive set of values concerning the commercial practices they performed. One version of this concerned their ambition to be close to innovative currents within the wider culture and to connect quickly with new cultural trends and styles of communicating. Style and lifestyle advertising aimed at young men afforded the practitioners considerable scope in pursuing these ambitions. Campaigns of this sort were seen to offer the possibility of producing innovative, challenging work and enabled practitioners the chance of pushing back the conventions of advertising. Again, there was a certain fit between their pursuit of newness and creativity and the targeting of young male consumers through style and lifestyle products. The furore surrounding the 'yobbishness' debate that I touched on in Chapter 4 was precisely indicative of the way conflicts between different groups of practitioners around the limits of innovation in advertising – particularly regarding the codes of taste and decency – were played out with particular intensity in relation to the targeting of young men.

In opening up these determinants upon the commercial practices of advertising, *Advertising Cultures* has sought to develop a distinctive cultural analysis of this field of economic and cultural endeavour; one that has attempted, as I have suggested repeatedly, to break with the dominant approaches to the consumer economy within both sociology and cultural studies. Attending to the 'cultures of commerce' that have loomed large in this book has, in this sense, formed part of a broader intellectual project to which this book belongs to extend the analytical focus of cultural studies into the domain of economic life broadly conceived. In doing so, the arguments that I have set out have attempted to push at the boundaries of economic life, particularly those of the domain of work. Although I explicitly limited the scope of this process in the book, it has been integral to my arguments that grasping the place of practices of consumption in and around the workplace is essential to understanding the cultures of work within advertising. I have argued that, most notably, the work-based identities of creative people were forged through social rituals and cultural practices that were not narrowly work based, but spread into the domain of leisure and personal life.

One of the challenges for future work in this area is to extend further analysis of the constitutive relations between economic life narrowly conceived and the fields of consumption that adjoin it. This might include a more enlarged account of the cultural and intellectual formation of these practitioners than I have developed in this book. In particular, we need to know more about the lifestyles of these commercial players, like the advertising people I have focused upon, their broader patterns of consumption and residence, as well as the intellectual ideas and political principles that galvanise their relationship to the world of commercial practice in which they operate. Given what we know about the salience of these practitioners to contemporary economic and cultural formations, future cultural studies of this kind will undoubtedly pay rich dividends.

endnotes

introduction

1 The book is based upon interviews with 26 male and 6 female art directors and copywriters working for London-based advertising agencies. The interviews were conducted in the summer and autumn of 1997.

2 The most celebrated ennoblements were those of the three former Saatchi & Saatchi people, Maurice Saatchi, Tim Bell and Martin Sorrell, all of who were knighted by the Conservative government 1992–7. The *Guardian* media page, the *Financial Times* 'Creative Business' section and the *Independent*'s 'Let's do Lunch' feature have provided space for advertising practitioners views. Advertising people have also appeared on BBC Radio 4's 'Start the Week' programme.

3 There are some strong historical precursors to the contemporary moves to celebrate the 'creativity' of British advertising. See, for example, Saxon-Mills' comments on the 'aesthetic achievements' of British advertising and the raising of its 'creative standards' in his biography of Sir William Crawford (Mills, 1954).

4 Some of these adverts are discussed in Nixon, 1996 and Mort, 1996. The most high profile was BBH's press and television work for Levi's 501 jeans that began in 1985.

5 There is an extensive sociological, social historical and cultural studies literature on interview methods and forms of qualitative research upon which I have drawn. See, in particular, Bourdieu, 1996; Clifford, 1988; Hollands, 1985; Atkinson, 1990 and Roper, 1994.

chapter 1: advertising and commercial culture

1 Lash and Urry also draw attention to the importance of information and communication structures in providing resources for reflexivity, see Lash and Urry 1994, Chapter 3.

2 Lash and Urry cite three ideal type forms of 'reflexive accumulation' (1994: 63).

chapter 2: 'purveyors of creativity: advertising agencies, commercial expertise and creative jobs

1 See Appendix 1 for typical structure of a full-service agency. The jobs of art director and copywriter made up 8.9 per cent and 5.7 per cent of agency staff in

IPA member agencies (IPA Census, 2000:7). This compared with 23.7 per cent in account handling, 14.5 per cent in media buying/planning, 4.8 per cent in account planning and research, 9.2 per cent in finance, 7.8 per cent secretarial (ibid).

2   Advertising expenditure recovered through the late 1990s and stood at 1.94 per cent of GDP in 1999 (IPA, 2000).

3   In the IPA census of 1998 there were 20 large agencies, 44 medium agencies and 142 small agencies. The IPA includes 206 of the 1872 or so advertising agencies in Britain. All the top thirty agencies are members and 75 per cent of the top 100. IPA members account for over 80 per cent of advertising placed in the UK (IPA, 2000). 75 per cent of agency staff are employed in London, smaller concentrations in Manchester, Leeds, Birmingham, Glasgow, Edinburgh, Newcastle and Belfast (ibid: 11).

4   Terrestrial television hours grew from 471 in 1983 to 671 in 1995 in a typical week (Scase and Davis, 2000: 50).

5   The Media Partnership bought media for WPP's two UK agencies, O&M and J. Walter Thompson, as well as for the top ten agencies AMVBBDO and BMP DDB.

6   BBH employed 425 people and had billings of £238M in 1999. It was ranked at 18 in the top 100 agencies by billing. While it remained a private company, BBH sold a 49 per cent share of the business to the American giant Leo Burnett in 1997 in order to gain access to their global media buying resources.

7   While anecdotal evidence suggested that in the late 1980s commission payments accounted for 86 per cent of most agencies gross income, this had fallen to 46 per cent by 1996 (*Campaign*, 13/8/93: 22–3).

8   HHCL had 202 staff and £180M billings in 1999. It was ranked number 19 in the top 100 agencies based on billings. It was bought by Chime Communications, a group linked to WPP Group in 1997.

9   'Romping' was an acronym for 'radical office mobility piloting!'

chapter 3: *déclassé* and *parvenus*? the social and educational make-up of creative jobs

1   Mike Featherstone has done most to take up Bourdieu's arguments on the 'new occupations'. However, Featherstone's work has explored the social make-up of these intermediary occupations in rather abstract, general terms and not generated any new evidence about their social make-up. Empirical sociologists have shown little specific interest in these occupations and most of the debate concerning changing occupational divisions of labour and class recomposition has focused on the so-called 'service class'. See Goldthorpe, 1980; Marshall et al, 1988; Savage et al, 1992. There is a richer, more nuanced historical literature on the lower-middle classes. See especially, Crossick & Haupt, 1995 and Bailey, 1999.

2   See, for example, Marshall et al, 1988 and Abercrombie and Warde, 1992.

3   With the assistance of the IPA, I collected data on the social backgrounds of practitioners working for IPA agencies through a self-completion questionnaire. Data was drawn from a total of 102 practitioners. This included the 32

practitioners whom I interviewed. The class categories used here are derived from and broadly follow the schema of The National Statistics Socio-economic Classification (NS-SEC) Interim version. I use the term middle class to include those higher managerial and professional occupations that fall within category 1; lower middle class to include those occupations within categories 2–4; and working class those occupations within categories 5–7 (Martin and Deacon, 1997: 33).

4   Savage et al also cite figures for the manual working class that suggest that 72 per cent of unskilled manual workers had fathers who were manual workers (Savage et al, 1992: 134). The most well known sociological study of social mobility and class divisions in Britain is the Oxford mobility study led by John Goldthorpe (1980). Goldthorpe's work privileges the analysis of what he calls the 'service class' – by which he means professional, administrative and managerial positions. Marshall et al, drawing on Goldthorpe's work, suggest that there has been considerable upward mobility into these positions and that the 'service class' has been recruited from throughout the social structure (Marshall et al, 1988: 101).

5   Fielding argues that the petit bourgeoisie have always been a highly diverse group in terms of their social mix with regard to origins (Fielding, 1995). One would perhaps expect this of intermediary social groupings. See also Crossick and Haupt, 1995.

6   The reputation persists today. As Caroline Marshall noted, 'Once upon a time, a certain type of man got the top job at JWT, London. Requirements included an education at public school followed by the Guards, a long, long career exclusively at JWT and at least two surnames' (*Campaign*, 2/2/01: 12).

7   These figures are based on a sample of 55 profiles taken from the trade press between 1993–8.

8   These figures are derived from a sample of 40 media planners/buyers collected by the IPA. I am grateful to Ann Murray Chatterton for sharing this information with me.

9   The top four universities from which account handlers currently come are Oxford, Bristol, Edinburgh, and York (Ann Murray Chatterton, per comm.).

10 On the place of qualifying associations in the formation of professions see Millerson, 1964. On professionalism see Johnstone, 1982 and 1989.

11 The D&AD's remit was as follows: 'setting and maintaining standards of creative excellence; communicating the value of creative excellence to the business community; educating and inspiring the next creative generation' (*D&AD Annual*, 1996: 1).

chapter 4: the cult of creativity: advertising creatives and the pursuit of newness

1   For a discussion of the adverts see *Campaign*, 24/3/95: 11 and *Independent on Sunday*, 3/9/95: 10.

2   For a very different approach to questions of creativity developed within art theory and theories of the avant-garde, see, Krauss, 1985; Crow, 1996.

3   On the relationship between art and advertising see Bogart, 1995; Tozer, 1997.

4   One of the creative directors I interviewed, Steve Buckland, confessed to a similar reverence for CDP's press advertising. He recalled, 'They [CDP] started

to produce broadsheet page advertising for the Army which wanted to have an intelligent conversation with me. They were really very well written. The intelligence that was expressed in that advert really impressed me.'

chapter 5: a homosocial world? masculinity, creativity and creative jobs

1 Advertising is clearly not unique among media industries in being unrepresentative of the wider population in terms of its ethnic and 'racial' mix. McRobbie (2002a: 112) quotes the BFI Television Industry Tracking Study that showed that 94 per cent of new entrants to television were white.

2 The IPA published two long reports on the position of women in advertising in 1990 and 2000 (Baxter, 1990; Klein, 2000). The issue remains a high priority for the Institute, per comm. Ann Murray Chatterton, IPA Director of Training and Development. D&AD had long been attacked for the lack of women jurors for the D&AD awards (see, inter alia, *Campaign*, 15/12/95: 28; 31/5/96: 24). The D&AD not only collaborated with the IPA on its 2000 report, but Larry Barker, the D&AD's President in 2000 also signalled the lack of women in creatives jobs as a major issue for his presidency (*Campaign*, 4/2/00: 14).

3 Baxter makes this point explicitly in Baxter, 1990: 11.

4 It was not entirely clear that this fear was well founded. It appeared that what clients often wanted from agencies was access to 'creativity' in its untamed form. See *Campaign* 14/11/97: 38–9.

5 Mort makes a similar point in discussing the debate about gender bias in the early 1990s in advertising (Mort, 1996: 114).

6 On Kaye see, *Campaign*, 3/2/95: 5; 14/4/95: 12; 30/6/95: 24; 26/5/95: 24–6. This cultural script has a long pedigree. Lears quotes US admen in the 1940s that liked, as he puts it, to be seen as free spirits, 'a little bit crazy' (Lears, 1994:320).

7 For profiles of Hegart and Abbott see, inter alia, *Independent*, 29/9/97: 5; 8/9/97: 10.

8 Perhaps the most striking public persona was that of Kiki Kendrick, a successful art director. She was well known for her flamboyment dress sense, which included wearing an eye patch for a period for purely stylistic effect and for her hedonistic lifestyle. She also appeared on the television programme 'Blind Date' wearing a wedding dress (see *Campaign*, 18/8/95: 11; 27/10/95: 10; 3/11/95: 13).

9 This was the mean figure from 1995–9 derived from the UCAS website.

10 The key source here was John Gray's bestseller *Women are from Venus and Men are from Mars*.

11 The key text was Fletcher's 1990 study.

chapter 7: pleasure at work: the ambivalences of work-based sociability

1 In the mid-1990s, the sporting of goatee beards became widespread among young advertising creatives. *Campaign* devoted its back page to this phenomenon in April 1996. (See *Campaign*, 12/4/96.)

2   Trevor Robinson, the freelance commercials director, and a contemporary of the group of men I interviewed, also revealed a strong interest in the way he looked. As he put it, 'I enjoy dressing up. I can afford it now and I don't see why I shouldn't enjoy it. Its not vain or sad – that's a really English attitude, to be slightly embarrassed about looking good and to think it is cool to walk around in smelly old jeans (*Creative Review*, August 1996: 30).

3   On sportswear see 'Natural high, winter sportswear goes up in the world', *Arena* Oct 1997: 198; 'Das Boot', on Napajiri's polar inspired performance clothes', *Arena* Oct 1997: 204; 'Fleeced', May 1997: 170–1, on the way polar fleeces have revolutionised sportswear.

4   Such behaviour is clearly not new. For a fascinating exchange of correspondence from 1982 between the Creative Circle and The Light Fantastic Gallery see History of Advertising Trust Creative Circle Box. The circle's meeting left the gallery's carpet with extensive cigarette burns and heavy staining. As one of the members of the creative circle, David Holmes, was forced to admit, 'I've seen the damage and it is a bloody mess'.

5   It was not only alcohol that was heavily consumed. Two of the practitioners I interviewed revealed that illegal drugs were readily available within the agency.

6   The practitioners I interviewed hailed from a wide range of provincial towns and cities, such as Norwich, Warrington, Loughton, Ware and Manchester. Only one of them came from metropolitan London (Hampstead).

appendix 1

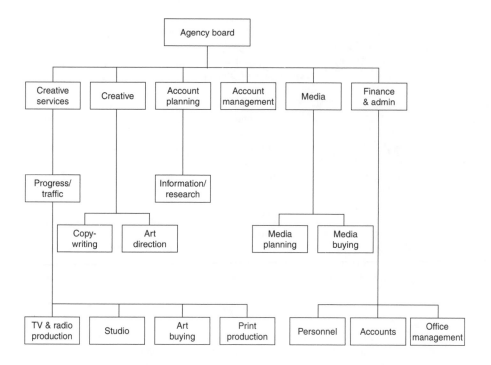

Job functions in a typical full-service advertising agency

bibliography

Abercrombie, N. and Warde, A. (1992) *Social Change in Contemporary Britain*, Polity, Cambridge.

Advertising Association Archives, London.

Alexander, S. (1994) *Becoming a Woman and Other Essays*, Virago, London.

Arena (1996–9) Wagodon, London.

Atkinson, P. (1990) *The Ethnographic Imagination*, Sage, London.

Bailey, P. (1998) *Popular Culture and Performance in the Victorian City*, Polity, Cambridge.

Bailey, P. (1999) 'White collar, gray lives?' in *Journal of British Studies*, 38: 273–290.

Bartle Bogle Hegarty (1996) *Business Practice*.

Baudrillard, J. (1988) 'Consumer society', in *Selected Writings*, Poster, M. (ed.), Polity, Cambridge.

Baumann, Z. (2000) *Liquid Modernity*, Polity, Cambridge.

Baxendale, J. and Pawling, C. (1996) *Narrating the Thirties: A Decade in the Making, 1930 to the Present*, Macmillan, Basingstoke.

Baxter, M. (1990) *Women in Advertising*, IPA, London.

BBC Television 'Def II', broadcast 1988–1993.

Beck, U., Giddens, A. and Lash, S. (1994) *Reflexive Modernization, Politics, Tradition and Aesthetics in Modern Social Theory*, Polity, Cambridge.

Bennett, T. (1992) 'Useful culture', in *Cultural Studies*, vol 6, number 3, 12–25.

Bennett, T. (1998) *Culture, a Reformers Science*, Sage, London.

Blair, H. (2001) 'You're only as good as your last job: the labour process and labour markets in the British film industry', in *Work, Employment & Society*, 15(1): 149–169.

Blair, H. and Raimie, P. (2000) 'Flexible firms?', in *Media, Culture & Society*, 22(2): 15–27.

Bogart, M. (1995) *Artists, Advertising and the Borders of Art*, Chicago, University of Chicago Press.

Bourdieu, P. (1984) *Distinction, a Critique of the Judgement of Taste*, Routledge, London.

Bourdieu, P. (1996) 'Understanding', in *Theory, Culture & Society*, 13(2): 17–37.

Breward, C. (1999) *The Hidden Consumer, Masculinities, Fashion and City Life 1860–1914*, Manchester, Manchester University Press.

Brewer, J. and Porter, R. (1993) *Consumption and the World of Goods*, Routledge, London.

Burns, T. (1977) *The BBC, Public Institution and Private World*, Macmillan, London.

Campaign (1990–2001) Haymarket Publications, London.

Christopherson, S. and Storper, M. (1989) 'The effects of flexible specialisation on industrial politics and the labour market', *Industrial and Labor Relations Review*, 42, 331–470.

Clarke, N. (1991) 'Strenuous idleness, Thomas Carlyle and the man of letters as hero', in Roper, M. and Tosh, J. (eds) *Manful Assertions, Masculinities in Britain since 1800*, Routledge, London.

Clifford, J. (1998) *The Predicament of Culture*, Harvard University Press: MA.

Creative Review (1983–2000) London.

Crossick, G. and Haupt, H.G. (1995) *The Petite Bourgeoisie in Europe, 1870–1914, Enterprise, Family, Independence*, Routledge, London.

Crow, T. (1999) *Modern Art in the Common Culture*, New Haven, CT, Yale University Press.

Daniels, P. (1995) 'The internationalization of advertising services in a changing regulatory environment', in *The Service Industries Journal*, 15(3): 276–294.

D&AD Annual (1994–8) Design and Art Directors Association, London.

Design and Art Directors Association (1997) *D&AD Advertising Workshop*, London.

Donzelot, J. (1977) *The Policing of Families*, Johns Hopkins University Press Paperback, Baltimore.

Dougary, G. (1994) *The Executive Tart and other Myths, Media Women Talk Back*, London, Virago.

du Gay, P. (1996) *Consumption and Identity at Work*, Sage, London.

du Gay, P. (2000) *In Praise of Bureaucracy, Weber, Organization, Ethics*, Sage, London.

Entwistle, J. (1997) 'Power dressing and the construction of the career women', in Nava, M. et al. (eds) *Buy this Book, Studies in Advertising and Consumption*, London, Routledge, pp. 311–23.

Esquire (1991–9).

Featherstone, M. (1991) *Postmodernism and Consumer Culture*, Sage, London.

Fielding, T. (1995) 'Migration and middle class formation in England and Wales 1981–91', in Savage, M. and Butler, T. (eds) *Social Change and the Middle Class*, UCL Press, London.

Fink, G. (1996) 'President's Award', in *D&AD Annual*, London.

Fletcher, W. (1990) *Creative People, How to Manage them and Maximize their Creativity*, Hutchinson, London.

Forrester, M. (1987) *Everything you Always Suspected was True about Advertising, but were too Legal, Decent and Honest to Ask*, Roger Houghton, London.

Fox, S. (1997) *The Mirror Makers*, University of Illinois, Illinois.

Frith, S. (1996) *Performing Rites, On the Value of Popular Music*, Oxford, Oxford University Press.

Frith, S. and Horne, H. (1987) *Art into Pop*, Routledge, London.

Glennie, P. (1995) 'Consumption in historical studies', in Miller, D. (ed) *Acknowledging Consumption*, Routledge, London, pp. 164–203.

Goldthorpe, J. (1980) *Social Mobility and Class Structure in Modern Britain*, Oxford University Press, Oxford.

GQ (1990–2000) Condé Nast, London.

Green, N. (1990) *The Spectacle of Nature, Landscape and Bourgeois Culture in Nineteenth Century France*, Manchester University Press, Manchester.

Guardian (1993–2002).

Hall, S. (1980) 'Reformism and the legislation of consent', in National Deviancy

Conference (eds) *Permissiveness and Control, the fate of the Sixties legislation*, London, Macmillan, pp. 1–43.

Hall, S. (1984) 'The culture gap', *Marxism Today*, May, pp. 5–7.

Hall, S. and Jefferson, T. (1976) *Resistance Through Rituals*, Hutchinson, Birmingham.

Hall, S., Critcher, C., Jefferson, T., Clarke, J. and Roberts, B. (1978) *Policing the Crisis*, Macmillan, London.

Harvey, D. (1989) *The Condition of Postmodernity*, Polity, Cambridge.

Hearn, J. and Parkin, P.W. (1987) *Sex at Work: Power and the Paradox of Organization Sexuality*, Harvester, Brighton.

Hebdige, D. (1979) *Subculture, the Meaning of Style*, Methuen, London.

Hebdige, D. (1988) *Hiding in the Light, On Images and Things*, London, Comedia.

Hirst, P. and Zeitlin, J. (1991) 'Flexible specialization versus post-fordism: theory, evidence and policy implications', in *Economy & Society*, 20(1): 1–56.

History of Advertising Trust (HAT) Archives, Raveningham, Norfolk.

Hollands, B. (1985) *Working for the Best Ethnography Centre for Contemporary Cultural Studies*, University of Birmingham Press: Birmingham.

Howell Henry Chaldecott Lury (1994) *Marketing at a Point of Change*.

Hull, J. (1993) *Redundancy in Advertising*, NABS, London.

Ignatieff, M. (1994) *Blood and Belonging, Journeys into the New Nationalism*, Vintage, London.

Independent (1993–2002)

Independent on Sunday (1993–2002)

Institute Information (1953–62) London, IIPA/IPA.

Institute of Practitioners in Advertising (1965) *The Artist in Advertising*, London.

Institute of Practitioners in Advertising (1995) *Graduate Careers in Advertising*, London.

Institute of Practitioners in Advertising, *IPA Census 1998*, London.

Institute of Practitioners in Advertising (1998) *Information Pack*, London.

Institute of Practitioners in Advertising, *IPA Census 2000*, Sage, London.

Institute of Practitioners in Advertising (2000) *Portfolio People*, London.

IPA Newsfile (1993).

Jackson, P., Lowe, M., Miller, D. and Mort, F. (eds) (2000) *Commercial Cultures, Economies, Practices, Spaces*, London, Berg.

Jameson, F. (1984) 'Postmodernism or the cultural logic of late capitalism', in *New Left Review*, 146: 53–93.

Johnstone, T. (1982) 'The State and the professions, the peculiarities of the British', in Giddens, A. and MacKenzie, G. (eds) *Social Class and Divisions of Labour*, Polity, Cambridge, pp. 35–52.

Johnstone, T. (1989) 'Review of A. Abbott *The System of Professions*' in *Work, employment & Society*, 3(3): 413.

Kendall, N. (1996) Unpublished interview with author.

Klein, D. (2000) *Women in Advertising, Ten Years On*, IPA, London.

Krauss, R.T. (1985) *The Originality of the Avant-garde and other Modernist Myths*, Cambridge, Mass, MIT Press.

Laclau, E. (1990) *New Thoughts on the Revolution of Our Time*, Verso, London.

Lash, S. and Urry, J. (1994) *Economies of Signs and Space*, Sage, London.

Leadbeater, C. (1999) *Living on Thin Air, the New Economy*, Viking, London.

Lears, J. (1994) *Fables of Abundance, a Cultural History of American Advertising*, New York, Basic Books.

Lockwood, D. (1995) 'Introduction', in Savage, M. and Butler, T. (eds) *Social Change and the Middle Class*, UCL Press, London, pp. 1–12.

McDowell, L. (1997) *Capital Culture, Gender at Work in the City*, Blackwell, Oxford.

McFall, E.R. (2002) 'Advertising, persuasion and the culture/economy dualism', in du Gay, P. and Pryke, M. (eds), *Cultural Economy*, London, Sage, pp. 148–66.

McGuigan, J. (1992) *Cultural Populism*, Routledge, London.

McKendrick, N., Brewer, J. and Plumb, J.H. (1982) *The Birth of a Consumer Society, the Commercialization of Eighteenth Century England*, Indiana University Press, Bloomington, IN.

McRobbie, A. (1993) 'Clubs to companies: notes on the decline of political culture in a speeded up creative world', *Cultural Studies*, 16(4): 516–31.

McRobbie, A. (1989) 'Second-hand dresses and the role of the ragmarket', in McRobbie, A. (ed) *Zoot Suits and Second-Hand Dresses*, Macmillan, Basingstoke, pp. 23–49.

McRobbie, A. (1998) *British Fashion Design, Rag Trade or Image Industry*, Routledge, London.

McRobbie, A. (2002a) 'Club to company: the decline of political culture in the speeded up world of the cultural economy' in *Cultural Studies*, 16(4): 15–22.

McRobbie, A. (2002b) 'From Holloway to Hollywood: happiness at work in the new cultural economy' in du Gay, P. and Pryke, M. (eds) *Cultural Economy*, Sage, London, pp. 97–114.

Marshall, G., Rose, D., Newby, H. and Volger, C. (1988) *Social Class in Modern Britain*, Routledge, London.

Martin, K. and Deacon, J. (1997) 'Development of a self-coded version of the new national statistics socio-economic classification (NS-SEC) preliminary results', in D. Rose and K. O'Reilly (eds) *Constructing Classes: Towards a New Social Class Sytem for the UK*, Swindon, ESRC/ONS.

Mattelart, A. (1991) *Advertising International, the Privatization of Public Space*, Routledge, London.

Millerson, G. (1964) *The Qualifying Associations, a Study of Professionalisation*, Routledge and Kegan Paul, London.

Mills, G.H.S. (1954) *There is a Tide . . . the life and works of Sir William Crawford*, William Heinemann Ltd., London.

Millum, T. (1975) *Images of Woman, Advertising in Women's Magazines*, Chatto and Windus, London.

Moeran, B. (1996) *A Japanese Advertising Agency: an anthropology of media and markets*, Richmond, Surrey, Curzon Press.

Mort, F. (1989) 'The politics of consumption', in S. Hall and M. Jacques (eds) *New Times*, Lawrence and Wishart, London, pp. 160–72.

Mort, F. (1996) *Cultures of Consumption, Masculinities and Social Space in Late Twentieth Century Britain*, Routledge, London.

Mort, F. (2000) 'Introduction: paths to mass consumption, historical perspectives', in Jackson, P., Lowe, M., Miller, D. and Mort, F. (eds) *Commercial Cultures, Economies, Practices, Spaces*, Berg, Oxford and New York.

Nava, M. (1992) *Changing Cultures, Feminism, Youth and Consumerism*, Sage, London.

Nava, M., Blake, A., MacRury, I. and Richards, B. (1997) *Buy this Book, Studies in Advertising and Consumption*, Routledge, London.

Negus, K. (1992) *Producing Pop, Culture and Conflict in the Popular Music Industry*, Edward Arnold, London.

Negus, K. (1995) 'Where the mystical meets the market, creativity and commerce in the production of pop music', *Sociological Review*, 43(2): 316–41.

Negus, K. (1998) 'Cultural production and the corporation: musical genres and the strategic management of creativity in the US recording industry', in *Media, Culture & Society*, 20: 359–79.

Negus, K. (1999) *Music Genres and Corporate Cultures*, Routledge, London.

Negus, K. and Pickering, M. (2000) 'Creativity and cultural production', in *Cultural Policy*, 6(2): 259–82.

Nixon, S. (1996) *Hard Looks, Masculinities, Spectatorship and Contemporary Consumption*, UCL Press, London.

Nixon, S. (1997) 'Circulating culture', in du Gay, P. (ed) *Production of Culture/ Cultures of Production*, Sage, London, pp. 177–234.

Nixon, S. (2000) 'In pursuit of the professional ideal: advertising and commercial expertise in Britain 1953–64', in Jackson, P., Lowe, M., Miller, D. and Mort, F. (eds) *Commercial Cultures, Economies, Practices, Spaces*, Berg, Oxford and New York.

Nixon, S. (2001) 'Intervening in popular culture: cultural politics and the art of translation', in Gilroy, P., Grossberg, L. and McRobbie, A. (eds) *Without Guarantees, in Honour of Stuart Hall*, Verso, London, pp. 254–65.

Ogilvy, D. (1983) *Confessions of an Advertising Man*, London, Pan.

Orton, F. and Pollock, G. (1996) *Avant Gardes and Partisans Revisited*, Manchester University Press, Manchester.

Osborne, T. (1998) *Aspects of Enlightenment, Social Theory and the Ethics of Truth*, UCL Press, London.

Parker, R. and Pollock, G. (1981) *Old Mistresses, Woman, Art and Ideology*, RKP, London and Henley.

Pearson, J. and Turner, G. (1965) *The Persuasion Industry*, Eyre & Spottiswoode, London.

Pratt, A.C. (1997) 'The cultural industries production system: a case study of employment change in Britain, 1984–91', in *Environment and Planning A*, vol 29: 1953–74.

Rappaport, E. (2000) *Shopping for Pleasure, Women in the Making of London's West End*, Princeton University Press, Princeton.

Robins, K. (1996) *Into the Image, Culture and Politics in the Field of Vision*, London, Routledge.

Roper, M. (1991) 'Yesterday's model, product fetishism and the British company man 1945–85', in Rober, M. and Tosh, J. (eds) *Manful Assertions, Masculinities in Britain Since 1800*, London, Routledge, pp. 190–211.

Roper, M. (1994) *Masculinity and the British Organization Man since 1945*, Oxford University Press, Oxford.

Roper, M. (1996) 'Seduction and Succession: circuits of homosocial desire in management', in Collinson, D.L. and Hearn, J. (eds) *Men as Managers, Managers as Men*, London, Sage, pp. 115–35.

Rose, N. (1991) *Governing the Soul*, Routledge, London.

Savage, M., Barlow, J., Dickens, P. and Fielding, T. (1992) *Property, Bureaucracy and Culture, Middle Class Formation in Contemporary Britain*, Routledge, London.

Scase, R. and Brown, P. (1994) *Higher Education and Corporate Realities, Class Culture and the Decline of Graduate Careers*, UCL Press, London.

Scase, R. and Goffee, R. (1995) *Corporate Realities, the Dynamics of Large and Small Organizations*, Routledge, London.

Scase, R. and Davis, H. (2000) *Managing Creativity, the Dynamics of Work and Organization*, Open University Press, Milton Keynes.

Schama, S. (1987) *The Embarrassment of Riches, an Interpretation of Dutch Culture in the Golden Age*, University of California Press, Berkeley.

Schudson, M. (1993) *Advertising, the Uneasy Persuasion, its Dubious Effect on American Society*, London, Routledge.

Scott, A.J. (1997) 'The cultural economy of cities', in *International Journal of Urban and Regional Research*, 21: 323–39.

Scott, A.J. (1999) 'The cultural economy: geography and the creative field', in *Media, Culture & Society*, vol 21: 807–17.

Sedgwick, E.K. (1985) *Between Men, English Literature and Male Homosocial Desire*, Columbia University Press, New York.

Slater, D. (1997) *Consumer Culture and Modernity*, Polity, Cambridge.

Smith, C. (1998) *Creative Britain*, Faber & Faber, London.

Smith, M. (1996) unpublished interview with author.

Stedman-Jones, G. (1989) 'The "Cockney" and the nation, 1780–1988', in Stedman-Jones, G. and Feldman, D. (eds) *Metropolis-London, Histories and Representations since 1800*, Routledge, London, pp. 1–55.

Steedman, C. (1986) *Landscape for a Good Woman*, Virago, London.

Sunday Times Magazine (2000).

Taki, ?. and Bernard, J. (1981) *High Life, Low Life*, Unwin, London.

The Department of Culture, Media and Sport website, www.culture.gov.uk.

Thrift, N. and Glennie, P. (1993) 'Consumers, identities, and consumption spaces in early-modern England', in *Environment and Planning A*, vol 28: 25–45.

Tozer, J. (1997) 'High "culture" – Low "art": advertising and the avant garde', in *Transcript*, 3(1): 92–100.

Universities UK (2002) *Higher Education in Facts and Figures*, Universities UK, London.

Wernick, A. (1991) *Promotional Culture, Advertising, Ideology and Symbolic Expression*, Sage, London.

Whiteley, N. (1994) 'Design in enterprise culture: design for whose profit?, in Keat, R. and Abercrombie, N. (eds) *Enterprise Culture*, Routledge, London, pp. 151–72.

Williams, R. (1976) *Keywords*, Fontana Press, London.

Willis, P. (1990) *Common Culture*, Open University Press, Milton Keynes.

Winship, J. (2000) 'Culture of restraint: the British chain store 1920–39', in Jackson, P., Lowe, M., Miller, D. and Mort, F. (eds) *Commercial Cultures, Economies, Practices, Spaces*, Berg, Oxford and New York, pp. 15–34.

WPP (1997) *Annual Report*, WPP Group, London.

Wynne, D. (1998) *Leisure, Lifestyle and the new Middle Class: A Case Study*, Routledge, London.

Wynne, D. and O'Connor, J. (1995) *City Cultures and the new Cultural Intermediaries*, www.mmu.ac.uk.

York, P. (1995) *The Eighties*, BBC books, London.

Index